THE SOCCER ENCYCLOPEDIA

Brazil and England contest their 2002 World Cup quarter-final in Japan's Shizuoka Stadium Ecopa. The 50,600-capacity arena hosts the bigger matches of two Japanese J-League sides, Jubilo Iwata and Shimizu S-Pulse.

THE
SOCCER
ENCYCLOPEDIA

CLIVE GIFFORD

KINGFISHER
LONDON & NEW YORK

KINGFISHER
LONDON & NEW YORK

Published 2020 by Kingfisher
Published in the United States by Kingfisher,
120 Broadway, New York, NY 10271
Kingfisher is an imprint of Macmillan Children's Books, London
All rights reserved

Copyright © Macmillan Publishers International Ltd 2006, 2010, 2014,
2016, 2018, 2020

Consultant: Anthony Hobbs
Cover design: Matthew Kelly

ISBN 978-0-7534-7546-1

First published in 2006 by Kingfisher
This fully revised and updated edition published
2020 by Kingfisher

Library of Congress Cataloguing-in-Publication data has been
applied for.

Kingfisher books are available for special promotions and
premiums. For details contact: Special Markets Department,
Macmillan, 120 Broadway, New York, NY 10271

Printed in China
9 8 7 6 5 4 3 2 1
1TR/1219/WKT/UG/128MA

CONTENTS

CHAPTER 1
INTRODUCTION

The beautiful game	6
Then and now	8
Soccer's origins	10
The global game	12

SNAPSHOT

Madrid's magnificent seven	14

CHAPTER 2
PLAYING THE GAME

Basic skills	16
Movement and space	18
Officials	20
Defending	22
Goalkeeping	24
Attacking	26
Goalscoring	28
Free kicks and penalties	30

SNAPSHOT

Baggio's penalty miss	32

CHAPTER 3
SOCCER LEGENDS

Goalkeepers	34
Defenders	37
Midfielders and wingers	41
Strikers	47

SNAPSHOT

Maradona's World Cup	56

CHAPTER 4
THE BRAIN GAME

The brain game	58
Formations	60
Tactics	62
The coach's role	64
Great coaches	66

SNAPSHOT

A hat trick of wins	68

CHAPTER 5
GREAT TEAMS

National teams	70
Club sides	78

SNAPSHOT

Les Bleus triumph again	92

CHAPTER 6
SOCCER FORTUNES

Soccer dreams	94
A pro's life	96
The players' stage	98
Fans and teams	100
The soccer industry	102
Soccer nightmares	104

SNAPSHOT

Spain win at last	106

CHAPTER 7
COMPETITIONS

The World Cup	108
The European Championships	118
The Olympics	120
The Copa America	122
The Africa Cup of Nations	123
The Asian Games and Asian Cup	124
The CONCACAF Championship	125
Soccer leagues	126
Club cup competitions	130
European Champions	132

SNAPSHOT

Brazil 2014	134

REFERENCE

U.S. soccer	136
Facts and figures	137
Glossary	140
Index	142
Acknowledgments	144

THE BEAUTIFUL GAME

Pelé described football as the "beautiful game," and the emotion and loyalty football inspires in its fans means that this simple sport has much to live up to. But soccer delivers it all—cramming dynamic action, breathtaking skills, and heart-stopping tension into 90 minutes of play. It is dramatic, making heroes and villains out of its players, coaches, and referees. From its recognized beginnings in the 1800s to its global dominance today, soccer has provided great moments of excitement, celebration, and despair; no other game has the same power to unite and divide.

▲ Soccer is a sport that generates intensely strong bonds between supporters and their teams. This fan, facepainted in the national colors of Portugal, awaits an international match against the Netherlands.

RAPID GROWTH

In a little more than 100 years soccer has boomed from a casual game played by a small group of amateur gentlemen to a highly sophisticated, money-focused sport that is played and watched by millions of people. As soccer has grown, dozens of changes have occurred. Some have involved the rules of the game—from the two-handed throw-in, introduced in 1883, to the back-pass rule for goalkeepers that was adopted 99 years later. Other changes—such as the arrival of promotion and relegation up and down a league—have shaped the competitions of which matches are a part.

Soccer's adaptability has been one of its strengths. Another great part of its appeal is that people of all ages and skill levels can play the game. At its most basic, soccer is a simple sport that can be enjoyed without expensive equipment and played almost anywhere—from a sandy beach to an office or hallway with a crumpled ball of paper.

The simplicity of soccer is a big selling point with new fans. The finer details of rules and tactics may not be understood at first, but the basics of the game and the skills of star players—their pace, ball control, passing, shooting, and tackling—can be admired by almost anyone.

▼ Soccer arouses the emotions of players as well as fans. Here, Bayern Munich's Carsten Jancker (left) and Thomas Helmer are inconsolable after their team was beaten by Manchester United in the last minute of the 1999 Champions League final.

▼ *Argentina and Barcelona star Lionel Messi (front) battles for the ball with Manchester United's Michael Carrick during a Champions League game. Outrageously skilful, Messi was voted the world's best player for four years in a row (2009–12) and again in 2015.*

▲ *Soccer can be played practically anywhere, in almost any conditions. These South African schoolchildren are enjoying a casual but competitive game just days before their country hosted the 2010 World Cup.*

THE NUMBERS GAME

In its full version, soccer is a game in which two teams of 11 people play two halves of 45 minutes. Today more than 50 million soccer players around the world play in official competitions. Many millions more play the game on a regular basis—a survey by world soccer's governing association, the *Fédération Internationale de Football Association* (FIFA), estimates that figure to be more than 265 million. Top leagues, such as Serie A in Italy, Spain's La Liga, and Germany's Bundesliga, attract millions of viewers globally. In 2017, English Premier League games or highlights were broadcast to more than 190 countries. The final of the 2018 FIFA World Cup between France and Croatia was watched by 1.12 billion people—a seventh of the entire human population.

▲ *A Brazilian goalkeeper holds a commemorative soccer ball celebrating Brazil's successful bid to host the FIFA World Cup for the first time since 1950. Major tournaments generate huge interest and millions are spent on stadiums and facilities for the huge numbers of visiting fans.*

THEN AND NOW

Going back in time 140 years, a modern soccer fan would be surprised to find no referees, corners, or field markings at a game. Players wore coats and even top hats; they handled the ball in the air and wrestled with each other on the ground. Over time, soccer has evolved into the game that we know today.

▶ The referee's whistle was first blown at a soccer match in 1878. British company Acme Whistles, astonishingly, has sold over 200 million Acme Thunderer whistles, which have been heard at World Cups and in top leagues around the globe.

THE FIELD

Unlike in most sports, the field in soccer can vary in size. Most are around 328 ft. (100m) long and 213–230 ft. (65–70m) wide. Back in the 1860s, a field could be as long as 590 ft. (180m). The first markings arrived in 1891, including a center circle and a line running the width of the field, 36 ft. (10.98m) in front of the goal line. A penalty could be taken from any point along that line. It was another 11 years before the field markings we know today were introduced. Since then only two additions have been made—the penalty arc at the front of the penalty area (in 1937) and the corner quadrants (in 1938).

▶ Referee Ken Aston came up with the idea of red and yellow cards after a stormy World Cup game in 1966. Here, he sends off Italy's Georgio Ferrini in 1962.

▲ At the 2002 World Cup, held in Japan and South Korea, the grass at the Sapporo Dome was grown away from the stadium and then moved as an entire pitch into the arena on a "cushion" of air.

GOALS

To score a goal, a team has to propel the entire ball over the goal line, between two posts that are set 24 ft. (7.32m) apart. On many occasions, controversy has occurred over whether the ball crossed the line—from the 1966 World Cup final between England and West Germany to the DFB-Pokal Cup final in 2014 between Borussia Dortmund and Bayern Munich.

Early goals consisted of just two posts. Following arguments over the height of a shot, a white tape was attached to the posts, 8 ft. (2.44m) above the ground. Wooden crossbars began to replace tape in the 1870s. Goal nets came later, invented by an engineer from Liverpool, England,

THE MEN (AND WOMEN) IN BLACK

Referees did not feature in early games of soccer because the sport's founders believed that gentlemen would never intentionally foul or cheat. Instead, each side had an umpire to whom they could appeal. By 1891, games were controlled by a referee in order to cut down on controversial decisions and long stoppages for debate, and the two umpires became linesmen. (Since 1996, linesmen have been known as assistants.) Despite often being described as the "men in black," referees have played in all sorts of colors. Early referees tried to keep up with play dressed in the popular fashions of the time—pants, a blazer, and even a bow tie.

John Alexander Brodie. They were first given a trial in January 1891, when Everton's Fred Geary became the first player to put the ball in the back of the net. Incidentally, that game was refereed by Sam Widdowson, who had invented shin pads 17 years earlier.

FACT FILE

he Belgian referee at the 1930 World Cup final, Jean Langenus, wore a dinner jacket, golfing plus fours, and a red striped tie.

CLEATS AND BALLS

No game is complete without the soccer ball, 40 million of which are sold every year. It is the referee's job to check the game ball and spare balls for size (26.5–27 in./68–70cm), weight (14–16 oz./410–450g), and correct air pressure. Modern balls are made from leather or synthetic materials, with a waterproof outer coating. Brazilian team Santos pioneered the use of a white ball (instead of the traditional brown leather ball) for greater visibility during evening games. Early soccer balls were made from the inflated bladder of a pig or sheep, covered in a leather shell that was secured with a set of laces. Contrary to popular myths, soccer balls of the past were not heavier than today's, at least when they were dry. Without a waterproof covering, however, early balls soaked up moisture and gained weight.

Soccer cleats were certainly heavier in the past. Originally, players used their heavy work boots, tying them up over the ankles. The boots often had reinforced toe caps, and players sometimes nailed metal or leather studs into the soles. Modern cleats are lightweight and flexible, allowing a player to "feel" the ball on his or her foot. Their soles come in a range of stud, dimple, and blade patterns. Each design gives the right level of grip for a particular field condition.

FACT FILE

India withdrew from the 1950 World Cup when FIFA refused to allow their players to be barefoot.

▲ Some modern cleats have molded dimples for playing on hard or artificial fields; others have screw-in studs to increase the grip on wet or soft fields.

▲ Alex James, a star for Arsenal in the 1930s, tries out a muscle-enhancing machine. Today's players undergo carefully planned exercise regimes and eat a diet that is scientifically monitored by their teams.

ALL DRESSED UP

Today's lightweight soccer uniforms are the result of years of research and development. During the first international game ever in 1872, the Scotland and England teams wore knickerbockers (long shorts), long shirts, and "bobble hats" or caps. Gradually, soccer uniforms developed to give players more freedom of movement, although shorts remained almost knee length until the 1960s. Numbers appeared on shirts regularly for the first time in the 1930s, but player names did not arrive until the late 1980s. In 1924 the English Soccer Association (FA) began to insist that teams have a second shirt (known as an away shirt) that could be worn in the event of a color clash. Today, uniform manufacturing is a highly profitable business. Teams often have two or even three away strips; they update their uniform design every season and sell many thousands of replica shirts to supporters.

▼ Samuel Eto'o wears Cameroon's radical all-in-one uniform at the 2004 African Nations Cup. The figure-hugging design gave opponents little material to tug or pull, but broke FIFA's rule that shirts and shorts have to be separate. An earlier Cameroon uniform with sleeveless shirts—worn for the 2002 World Cup qualifying games—was also declared illegal.

SOCCER'S ORIGINS

A tavern in Victorian England seems an unlikely place to launch a sport that would become the world's biggest and most popular. Yet that is precisely what occurred in 1863 at the Freemason's Tavern in London, England. There, representatives of 12 clubs met to form the Football Association (FA) and draw up a single set of rules for the game.

HISTORY MYSTERY

No one knows where the first forerunner of soccer was played. The Ancient Greeks took part in a team ball game known as *episkyros* or *pheninda*, while the Romans played *harpastum*. Paintings dating back more than 2,000 years show men and women enjoying the Ancient Chinese game of *tsu chu*, in which players tried to propel a ball made of stuffed animal skin through bamboo goal posts up to 33 ft. (10m) tall. During the Ch'in dynasty (255–206BCE), a form of *tsu chu* was used to help train soldiers.

In medieval Europe, games of mob soccer were so unruly and violent that the leaders of several countries, including Charles V in France and Oliver Cromwell in England, attempted to ban the sport. In contrast to mob soccer, the Italian game of *calcio* was first played in the 1500s by aristocrats and religious leaders, including three popes. Each team was made up of 27 players, and goals were scored by kicking or throwing the ball over a certain spot on the edge of the field.

GETTING ORGANIZED

By the late 1700s and early 1800s, a kicking-and-rushing ball game was played in schools and universities across Great Britain, but rules varied from place to place. In 1848, players at Cambridge University drew up soccer's first set of rules. This attempt to bring order into the game had only limited success, and so in 1863 representatives of 12 clubs (including the Crusaders, No Names of Kilburn, and Crystal Palace) met in London. They formed the FA, developed the laws of the game, and, eight years later, set up the world's oldest surviving cup competition, the FA Cup. The first international game, between England and Scotland, was played in 1872, and in 1888 the first soccer league was founded in England.

▼ This illustration shows a friendly international game between England and Scotland in 1878. Between 1873 and 1888, Scotland lost just one out of 31 international matches.

▼ The Japanese game of kemari *is at least 1,500 years old. Players had to stop the ball from touching the ground by juggling and passing it with their feet. This re-enactment was held to celebrate Japan's co-hosting of the 2002 World Cup.*

HIT THE NET

www.11v11.com
The website of the Association of Football Statisticians has historic photos and features on soccer's early history.

http://uk.women.soccerway.com
This website contains results of all leading women's soccer clubs and national competitions.

www.soccerballworld.com/History.htm
A thorough guide to the history and evolution of the soccer ball, from its ancient origins to the latest versions.

▼ Mana Iwabuchi of Japan pursued by Lauren Holiday in the 2015 Women's World Cup final between USA and Japan.

WHAT'S IN A NAME?

Around the world, many teams have taken their names from European clubs. Here are just a few:

ARSENAL LESOTHO
Lesotho Cup winners 1989, 1991, 1998

LIVERPOOL
Namibia, league champions 2002

BARCELONA
Ecuador, league champions 1995, 19'97, 2012, 2016

BENFICA DE MACAU
Macau, league champions, 2018

JUVENTUS
Belize, league champions 1999, 2005

BEREKUM CHELSEA FC
Ghana, league champions 2011

AJAX CAPE TOWN
S. Africa, league runners-up 2008, 2011

QPR SC
Grenada, league champions 2002

THE WOMEN'S GAME

Women's soccer struggled from the beginning against male prejudice that it was "'unladylike" for females to play the game. Interest in women's soccer reached its first peak after World War I thanks to the exploits of the Dick, Kerr Ladies side (see page 81). The women's game was then stifled for almost 50 years following the introduction of a ban on women playing at the grounds of FA member clubs. Between 1969 and 1972, bans were lifted in a number of countries and women's soccer slowly began to expand. The first European Championships for women were held in 1984, while an Olympic competition was launched in 1996. More than 60 nations entered the qualifying competition for the first Women's World Cup in 1991.

SOCCER EXPORTS

Soccer spread rapidly around the globe in the late 1800s. The game was exported first by British players and then by players from other European nations, especially to their colonies. Soccer was introduced to Russia in 1887 by two English mill owners, the Charnock brothers, while resident Englishmen founded Italy's oldest league club, Genoa, six years later.

In 1885, Canada defeated the United States 1-0 in the first international match to be played in the Americas. In Argentina, British and Italian residents encouraged the formation of South America's first team, Buenos Aires, in 1865. The first league in South America was set up 28 years later.

In 1904, FIFA was founded in Paris, with seven members: Belgium, Denmark, France, Holland, Spain (represented by Madrid FC), Sweden, and Switzerland. Over time, FIFA became the dominant organization in world soccer. In 1930, it had 45 member nations; in 1960, that figure stood at 95. In 2016, FIFA welcomed Gibraltar and Kosovo as its 210th and 211th members.

▶ W. R. Moon of the Corinthians, an English team, poses for a photograph in his uniform. The Corinthians helped spread soccer's popularity by touring the world. Their 1910 trip to South America inspired the formation of the famous Brazilian side Corinthians Paulista.

THE GLOBAL GAME

FIFA is in control of world soccer. At continental or regional level, the game is organized by six confederations. The traditional powerhouses of international soccer have been Europe and South America, home to the world's richest teams and to the winners of every World Cup. But as other regions begin to exert more influence, the global game is changing.

BALANCE OF POWER

Huge advances have been made by the federations and national teams of regions outside Europe and South America. More and more national soccer teams have become truly competitive on the world stage, thanks to the emergence of dozens of high-quality footballers in Africa, Asia, Oceania, and North and Central America. Australia's 2018 World Cup appearance was their fourth in a row. Before 2006, they had last qualified in 1974. New Zealand was the only team at the 2010 World Cup not to lose a game. African teams have featured in three of the last four Olympic soccer finals, winning two golds and one silver. By April 2017, the continent had ten teams ranked in FIFA's top 50. There have also been strong showings by Japan, Costa Rica, and the United States at recent international tournaments. As a reflection of this, African and Asian nations have been chosen to host many tournaments, including the World Cups of 2002 (South Korea and Japan), 2010 (South Africa), 2022 (Qatar), and the Women's World Cup of 2007 (China). Additionally, Africa and Asia now enjoy more automatic places at the World Cup than ever before.

▲ Steve Mokone was the first black South African to play professionally in Europe. From the 1950s, he played for England's Coventry City, Dutch team Heracles, Spain's Valencia, Marseille in France, and Italy's Torino. Mokone later played in Australia and Canada.

> **FACT FILE** All four of the 2018 FIFA World Cup semi-finalists were from Europe.

◀ Argentina line up to play Germany in the 2006 World Cup. At the time, only keeper Roberto Abbondanzieri played club soccer in Argentina. After the tournament, he signed for Spanish club Getafe.

CONCACAF

Confederation of North, Central American, and Caribbean Association Football
www.concacaf.com
Founded: 1961
Members: 41

Mexico and the U.S.—traditionally the strongest CONCACAF nations—have hosted three World Cups, while smaller nations, such as Costa Rica, have reached the tournament. CONCACAF teams have often been invited to play in South America's Copa America competition, and the federation actually includes two South American nations, Guyana and Suriname.

UEFA

Union of European Football Associations
www.uefa.com
Founded: 1954
Members: 55

As the most powerful confederation, UEFA was awarded 14 of the 32 places at the 2018 World Cup. It runs the two largest competitions after the World Cup—the European Championships and the UEFA Champions League. Thousands of foreign footballers play in Europe, but UEFA clubs may soon be forced to include a minimum number of homegrown players in their teams.

CONMEBOL

Confederación Sudamericana de Fútbol
www.conmebol.com
Founded: 1916
Members: 10

CONMEBOL teams have won nine men's World Cup finals, whilst the Brazilian women's national team was World Cup runner-up in 2007. Argentina won the 2004 and 2008 Olympic men's finals and are rarely out of the top five of FIFA's world rankings. Domestic leagues, however, are suffering with clubs in debt and most of the continent's top players heading for Europe and elsewhere to play.

CAF
Confédération Africaine de Football
www.cafonline.com
Founded: 1957
Members: 56

Africa was not awarded an automatic World Cup place until 1970, but the CAF sent six teams to the 2010 World Cup including the host nation, South Africa. While national teams continue to improve, the domestic game struggles because of a lack of money and the movement of its best players out of Africa. In 2010, for example, more than 570 African footballers were playing in the top leagues of Europe.

AFC
Asian Football Confederation
www.the-afc.com
intro.asp
Founded: 1954
Members: 47

Asian soccer is booming. The highly successful Asian Champions League was set up in 2002, and national leagues are now well supported. Many foreign players play in Asia—more than 29 Brazilians played in Japan's J-League in 2013, for example. Australia joined the AFC in 2006, but all eyes are now turning to China, which has the world's largest pool of potential players and supporters.

OFC
Oceania Football Confederation
www.oceaniafootball.com
Founded: 1966
Members: 11

Football has struggled for support in Oceania. In the larger countries, it has to compete with more popular sports, while smaller nations suffer from a lack of money, facilities, and players. Australia, the OFC's biggest and most successful nation, became frustrated by the lack of an automatic World Cup place for the confederation. In January 2006 it left the OFC to join the Asian Football Confederation.

FACT FILE
Austalia was the first OFC side to reach a World Cup, in 1974.

HAVE CLEATS, WILL TRAVEL

Soccer is flourishing all over the world, but Europe remains the most attractive destination for the world's top players. The globe's 20 richest clubs are all European, and this situation is unlikely to change for some time as a result of the huge sums of money that teams receive from television rights, advertising, and qualifying for the

◄ *Givanildo Vieira de Souza, known as Hulk, stars for Brazil in a 2013 exhibition game against Italy. By the age of 25, the powerful striker had played all over the world for clubs in Brazil, Japan, and Portugal before being signed by Russian side Zenit Saint Petersburg in 2012.*

Champions League. The revenue enables European clubs to pluck the best talents from around the globe. At the 2018 World Cup, only one of Belgium, Nigeria, and Iceland's 23-man squads played club soccer in their home country. In contrast, all of England's, 21 of Russia's and 19 of Spain's team members played at home.

In the past, South American soccer teams held on to many of the continent's stars. Every member of Brazil's 1970 World Cup-winning team played for a team in his home country. This has changed, with hundreds of players moving to Europe in search of higher salaries and the chance to play in the most prestigious competitions, from Serie A and La Liga to the Champions League.

HIT THE NET

www.worldsoccer.com
World Soccer magazine's website focuses on global soccer and its best players, teams, and competitions.

http://uk.soccerway.com
A comprehensive match website, searchable by continent, to give you the fixtures and results of all leading soccer competitions.

www.soccerstats.com
Get the latest soccer news and competition standings from around the world.

Alfredo di Stefano (in white) lashes Real Madrid's second goal past Eintracht Frankfurt goalie Egon Loy. Despite making a number of fantastic saves, Loy conceded seven goals.

MADRID'S MAGNIFICENT SEVEN

Soccer's capacity to surprise, excite, and, above all, entertain has rarely been better showcased than in the final of the fifth European Cup in 1960. Real Madrid, winners of the first four competitions, met Eintracht Frankfurt in front of a record crowd of more than 130,000 at Scotland's Hampden Park. Eintracht took an early lead. Was Real's reign as the unrivaled master of Europe about to end? The answer was an emphatic no. Led by Hungarian genius Ferenc Puskas and Argentinian all-rounder Alfredo di Stefano, the Spanish side put on a dazzling display of attacking soccer. In an electrifying 45 minutes, Real went from 1–0 down to 6–1 up, courtesy of goals by both Puskas and di Stefano. But the enterprising German team was just as committed to attacking. They fought back, scoring two goals and hitting the woodwork twice, while Real countered with its seventh and di Stefano's third goal to eventually triumph 7–3. No one who witnessed the game would ever forget the spectacle of Europe's best team playing at the peak of its skills.

BASIC SKILLS

In the words of former Liverpool coach Bill Shankly, soccer "is a simple game based on the giving and taking of passes, on controlling the ball, and on making yourself available to receive a pass." Shankly's words highlight the most important skills in soccer.

BALL CONTROL

The world's top players, such as Cristiano Ronaldo and Lionel Messi, appear to control the ball effortlessly. Their easy command and movement of the ball hides thousands of hours of practice and training, often from a very early age. As children, many great players spent long hours playing games with a tennis ball, a crumpled ball of paper, or a battered piece of fruit.

Players can control the ball with any part of their body except their hands and arms. Cushioning is a technique in which a player uses a part of the body to slow down a moving ball and then bring it under control with his or her feet. High balls can be cushioned using the chest, thigh, or a gentle header to kill the ball's speed and bring it down. For a low, incoming ball, the foot is preferred—either the inside of the boot or its instep (where the laces are). A ball that is rolling across the field can be stopped with the sole of the foot—a technique known as trapping.

▲ French female players practice their close control skills by keeping the ball up using their heads and feet. Good ball control only comes with hundreds of hours of practice.

▶ David Beckham leans back to perform a chest cushion during a Real Madrid training session. A good chest cushion sees the ball drop at the feet of the player, who can then pass, run, or shoot.

▲ French legend Zinedine Zidane uses the side of his foot to control the ball during a Champions League match against Bayer Leverkusen.

◀ An instep cushion is used to control a ball that is arriving from the front. Here, the player meets the ball with his shoelaces and instantly pulls back his foot, stopping the speed of the ball.

SHIELDING AND OBSTRUCTION

When players have the ball at their feet, they are said to be in possession and have a number of options. These include running with the ball, dribbling with the ball close to the feet, passing, shooting, and shielding the ball. Shielding or screening involves a player putting his or her body between the ball and an opponent in order to prevent the other player from gaining possession. This gives the shielding player crucial time to decide on the next move, which may be a pass backward to a teammate or a sharp turn and an attempt to play the ball around the opponent. Shielding players have to be careful not to hold, push, or back into the other player. They must also keep the ball close by and under control, otherwise the referee may award an indirect free kick for obstruction (in which a player unfairly blocks an opponent's path to the ball). An obstruction usually occurs when a player steps into the path of an opponent when the ball is several feet away.

◄ Sergiy Nazarenko of Ukrainian side Dnipro Dnipropetrovsk shields the ball from FC Utrecht's Etienne Shew-Atjon during a 2004-05 UEFA Cup game.

▼ Australia's Nick Carle challenges Japan's Uchida Atsuto for the ball.

▶ Voted 2018 world soccer player of the year, Luka Modric of Croatia hits a long instep drive pass.

PASS MASTERS

Passes can be made with a thrust of the chest or with a carefully directed header. Usually, however, they are made with one of three parts of the shoe—the outside, the instep, or the inside. The inside or side-foot pass is the most common and accurate pass, allowing players to pass the ball with a high level of precision. Some players attempt as many as 60 or 70 passes in a game, most of which are side-foot passes. At the 2018 World Cup, Spain's Sergio Ramos made an average 127 passes per game.

For longer passes, players tend to use the instep. This allows them to propel the ball with force. The instep can also be used for lofted drives that send the ball into the air as a cross or a clearance, as well as to stab down on the back of the ball. This makes the ball rise up at a steep angle, known as a chip. A pass's weight—the strength with which it is hit—is as important as accuracy in order for the pass to be successfully completed. At Euro 2016, strong passers such as Germans Toni Kroos and Mesut Özil and Spain's Andrés Iniesta made hundreds of passes with over 90 percent success.

▶ Brek Shea plays an accurate side-foot pass for his MLS side, FC Dallas, with his foot striking through the middle of the ball. Shea moved on to Stoke City and Orlando before moving to Atlanta United in 2019.

MOVEMENT AND SPACE

Soccer is a dynamic, fast-moving sport. Throughout a game, pockets of space open and close all over the field. A player who has an awareness of where space exists or where it will shortly open up is a great asset to a team. Just as valuable is the ability to move into that space to receive a pass. The more space a player has, the more time he or she usually has to receive the ball, control it, and attack with it.

SPOTTING AND CREATING SPACE

The ball can zip around a field far more quickly than even the quickest player. Good fplayers make the ball do the work, moving it around with quick, accurate passes. Vision is the priceless ability to spot a pass, space, or goal-scoring opportunity that other players do not see—or before they do. Players with good vision look to move into space, timing their run to give a teammate who has the ball a chance of making a pass that cannot be intercepted by an opponent. Once the ball has left the passer's control, he or she often moves into a position to receive a return pass. All players, not just midfielders and attackers, must be capable of passing well and moving into space to receive passes in return.

Players can create space for themselves or for teammates through quick, agile movement and the use of feints or dummies, with which

▶ Mesut Özil picks a pass to play to a Real Madrid teammate. Top players such as Özil play with their head up, scouring the field for teammates' moves and runs. Özil moved to Arsenal in 2013.

they attempt to fool a nearby opponent into thinking they are moving one way, before sprinting off in another direction. World-class players such as Mesut Özil, Lionel Messi, and Andrés Iniesta are especially skilled at outwitting an opponent in this way in order to find space.

◀ A wall pass (also known as a one-two pass) is a classic way to cut out an opposition player. It involves two passes that must be hit quickly and accurately, with the first passer running on to collect the return ball.

FACT FILE
At the 2018 World Cup, England completed 3,336 passes—more than any other team.

▲ Dutch winger Arjen Robben (right) attempts to move around the outside of Portugal's Miguel in the semifinal of Euro 2004.

▲ Making space can be crucial to winning the ball at a throw-in. Here, one player makes a decoy run toward the thrower, dragging a defender with him and creating space in which a teammate can collect the ball.

OFFSIDE

Teams have to stay aware of Law 11, the offside law, throughout a match. In 1847, under the rules of Eton College in England, being offside was known as "sneaking." A player was caught sneaking when there were three or fewer opposition players between him and the goal at the moment a teammate passed the ball forward. The rule has been altered over the years. The most notable change came in 1925, when the number of players between the attacker and the goal was reduced from three to two. The result was a goal avalanche, as defenses struggled to cope with the rule change and attackers took advantage. In the English leagues, for example, 1,673 more goals were scored in the 1925–1926 season than under the old law in the previous year.

Today, a player is offside if, at the moment the ball is played, he or she is in the opposition half and is nearer the opponent's goal line than both the ball and the second-from-last opponent. That opponent can be an outfield player or the goalkeeper. Players cannot be offside in their own half or if they receive the ball directly from a goal kick, throw-in, or corner.

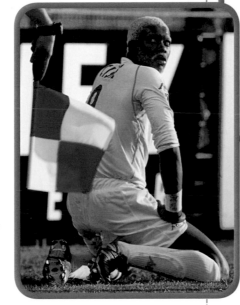

▲ French striker Djibril Cissé looks ruefully at the referee's assistant after being signalled offside in a French league match.

Being in an offside position is not always an offence. Referees must judge whether the player in an offside position is involved in active play, or moves toward the ball, or does anything to make it harder for an opponent to play the ball. This tests an official's judgement to the limit. Is a player offside but a long way from the ball involved in "active play"? Perhaps he or she is drawing defenders out as markers. If a referee does stop the game, an indirect free kick is awarded to the opposing team where the player was judged offside.

▲ Here, the player at the top left of the picture is in an offside position when the ball is struck. The referee decides that he is not interfering with play, however, and awards the goal.

▲ You cannot be offside if you are behind the ball when it is played. This scorer receives the ball from a teammate who is ahead of him, so he is onside and the goal is given.

HIT THE NET

www.dynamic-thought.com/OffsideClickette.html
Diagrams and animations that fully explain the offside law.

www.fifa.com/development/education-and-technical/referees/laws-of-the-game.html
View the latest laws of the game as approved by FIFA or download them in PDF format.

www.asktheref.com
A site for budding referees—learn more about the laws of the game and the jobs of soccer officials.

www.futsalplanet.com
A website dedicated to futsal, with tournament news and results as well as links to the laws of the game.

SMALL-SIDED GAMES

In many countries, children under the age of 11 play matches that feature six, seven, or eight players per team. These small-sided games give young players an invaluable chance to see more of the ball and improve their control, passing, and movement. Futsal is FIFA's official five-a-side game. A match lasts for 40 minutes (two halves of 20 minutes) and is played on a field the size of a basketball court, without surrounding boards or walls. Futsal was devised by a Uruguayan, Juan Carlos Ceriani, in 1930. The game flourished and developed throughout South America, with the first international competition—the South American Cup—taking place in 1965. The first futsal World Championship took place in the Netherlands in 1989. Held in Colombia, the 2016 Futsal World Cup was won by Argentina, who defeated Russia 5–4 in the final.

▲ Spain and Brazil battle it out in the final of the 2004 Futsal World Championship, held in Taipei, Taiwan. Spain won the 40-match tournament, beating the Brazilians 5–4 in a penalty shoot-out after a 2–2 draw.

OFFICIALS

Frequently abused by players, coaches, and fans, referees are soccer's guardians and the enforcers of its laws. Their job is to impose order throughout a game and prevent intimidation, injury, and cheating.

THE REFEREE'S ROLE

Referees perform a surprisingly large number of tasks before and after a game. These include checking the goals, nets, and balls and deciding whether the field and weather conditions are suitable for the game to go ahead. Afterward, they write a report containing details of disciplinary actions and other important incidents. On the field, the referee runs the game. His or her duties range from adding on time because of injuries, other stoppages, and time wasting, to deciding whether the ball is in or out of play or has crossed the goal line. If a player commits a foul or breaks a law, referees must stop play and order a restart, such as a drop ball or a free kick. They can caution players and team officials and even abandon a game if weather, crowd trouble, or another factor makes the game unplayable. Referees have to follow the laws of the game, but they have a certain amount of freedom to interpret aspects of the rules as they wish. For example, if a player is fouled when his or her side is in a promising position, a referee may let the game continue, playing the advantage rule to keep the game flowing.

ASSISTANTS AND THE FOURTH OFFICIAL

A referee relies on his or her assistants as extra pairs of eyes. Referee's assistants indicate when the ball goes out of play and whether a goal kick, corner, or throw-in should be awarded. They also use flag signals to point out that a substitution has been requested, a player is offside, or whether an offence has taken place out of the view of the referee. A referee can consult with an assistant if he or she was closer to the action, but it is up to the referee to make the final decision. In some competitions, a fourth official carries out duties before and after a match and also performs touchline tasks. These include helping with substitutions and displaying the amount of time added on at the end of a game for stoppages.

▲ The fourth official checks the shoe studs of Paraguayan substitute Nelson Vera in a World Youth Championship match against Uruguay.

> **FACT FILE**
> In 1998, English referee Martin Sylvester sent himself off after punching a player during a game in the Andover and District Sunday League.

▲ Referee Stephane Lannoy shows Mario Balotelli a yellow card after the Italian striker took his shirt off to celebrate a goal he scored at Euro 2012.

▼ Coaches and team officials can be cautioned or sent off if they use abusive language or do not behave responsibly. Here, Martin O'Neill argues with UEFA Cup officials as he is sent off during a game.

◄ Early in a game, a good referee talks to players to calm them down or issues verbal warnings rather than yellow and red cards. Here, Nicole Petignat tries to soothe AIK Solna's Krister Nordin in the first UEFA Cup game to be refereed by a woman, in 2003.

TOP-FLIGHT PRESSURES

Thousands of amateur referees give up their weekends and evenings for free, purely to give something back to the game they adore. Top referees have their performances assessed, attend training seminars, undergo regular medical checks, and are tested for fitness. A referee may run 5.6–7 mi. (9.5–11.5km) during a game (even further if extra time occurs) and often has to sprint to keep up with play. Referees work in a harsh, unforgiving environment in which footage from multiple cameras and slow-motion television replays are broadcast over and over again, highlighting each poor decision. However, the very technology that has put referees under the spotlight is now coming to their aid. Goal-line technology removes doubt about whether a goal has been scored by sensing if the whole of the ball has crossed the goal line. Some competitions, including the 2018 Men's and 2019 Women's World Cups, used a video assistant referee (VAR). Officials watch contentious penalty, goal, and discipline decisions on TV screens and can communicate via radio with the referee on the pitch.

▲ Referee Horacio Elizondo shows the red card to France's Zinedine Zidane during the 2006 World Cup final. The midfielder was sent off for headbutting Italian defender Marco Materazzi in the chest during extra time.

CAUTION

A player is shown a yellow card if he or she:

• is guilty of unsporting behavior, such as simulation;
• shows dissent by word or action;
• persistently breaks the rules, by making repeated foul tackles for example;
• delays the restart of play;
• fails to stand at the required distance at a corner kick or free kick;
• enters or leaves the field of play without the referee's permission.

A player is sent off if he or she receives two yellow cards or one red card. Red-card offenses include a very dangerous tackle, spitting, and stopping a goal with a deliberate handball.

SIMULATION

Watching for contact in the penalty area during a fast-moving attack is especially difficult for an official. In the modern game, attackers appear to fall to the ground under the slightest pressure from an opponent. Referees have to judge if a foul was committed or whether the attacker was guilty of "simulation." Many people think that simulation is only about diving without contact in order to win a free kick or a penalty. It is actually defined as pretending to be fouled in any way to gain an advantage. In a game at the 2002 World Cup, Rivaldo was guilty of a simulation led to Turkey's Hakan Ünsal being sent off. In a 2018 English Premier League game, Leicester City's James Maddison performed a simulation when diving in the opposing penalty area. The referee showed him a second yellow card that meant he had to leave the field. Fines and game bans are operated in some leagues but the issue still remains.

▲ AC Milan midfielder Andrea Pirlo battles for the ball with Deportivo La Coruña's Juan Carlos Valerón. The referee has to decide in a split second if a foul was committed and, if so, whether it is serious enough to book or send off a player.

RED-CARD RECORDS

FASTEST IN A TOP LEAGUE
Ten seconds—Giuseppe Lorenzo, Bologna v. Parma, 1990, Serie A

FASTEST IN THE WORLD CUP
55 seconds—José Batista, Uruguay v. Scotland, 1986

MOST IN ONE MATCH
36—Claypole v. Victoriano Arenas (Argentina), 2011

DEFENDING

Compared to strikers or creative midfielders, defenders are rarely praised as game winners. Yet the foundation of every successful team is a composed, secure defense. Defending consists of a range of individual skills allied to good teamwork and understanding between players so that they defend as a unit. Defenders require strength and excellent heading and tackling skills, along with intense concentration, quick reactions, and bravery. But, in truth, all players must defend if their side is to remain competitive in a match.

▼ *After tracking Bayern Munich's Arjen Robben (right), Real Madrid's Adriano times his tackle to rob his opponent of the ball. In situations like this, teammates look to pounce on the ball to gain possession.*

▲ *Portugal's Nuno Gomes (left) and Russia's Alexei Bugaev challenge for the ball. Forceful tackles that target the ball, not the player, are a key part of defending.*

TRACKING AND TACKLING

The two keys to defending well are denying the opposition the chance to score and winning the ball back. As soon as an opponent gets the ball, defenders try to get between the ball and their goal and eliminate space. Defenders spend much of a game tracking opponents as they make runs and closing down the player with the ball in order to delay his or her progress. This is called jockeying. The aim is to slow down an attack until the defending team is in a stronger position. The defender tries to guide the attacker into a weaker position, such as near the sideline where there is little support. When a defender has cover from nearby teammates, he or she may make a tackle. The defender should stay on his or her feet in order to gain possession.

► *This attacker has spotted a weak pass by an opponent and reacts quickly to make an interception. Sometimes, attackers drop back to help their team defend.*

FALLING FOUL OF THE LAW

Many of soccer's laws, such as obstruction, apply to defenders. A defender who is jockeying must be careful not to commit a foul such as pushing, holding, or shirt pulling. A poorly timed tackle may result in a foul being awarded for kicking or tripping. Tackles from behind are especially risky, often leading to a yellow or red card if the defender makes contact with the attacker. A professional foul is a deliberate foul made to deny an attacking side a clear goal-scoring chance. Two of the most common types are using the hands or arms to stop a goal-bound ball and bringing down an attacker with the ball when he or she has a clear path to goal. Both should result in a sending off.

DEFENSIVE FORTRESS

During periods of open play, defending teams "mark" opponents man to man or with a zonal system (see page 62). At corners and free kicks from a wide position, they tend to mark man to man. A team may also try to catch out attackers by playing an offside trap (see page 62). Communication between defenders is crucial to prevent attackers getting free and into space to score. Certain teams equipped with highly skilled defenders who work well together have been able to squeeze the life out of opposition attacks. The AC Milan side of 1992–1993, for example, scored 26 goals and conceded only two during its entire nine-game Champions League campaign. In England, Chelsea hold the record for conceding the fewest goals in a season (2004–2005)—only 15 goals in 38 games.

▲ A supporting defender can step in to help if his team-mate is beaten. Here, Pablo Zabaleta (right) challenges Chelsea's Fernando Torres for the ball after his Manchester City team-mate, Vincent Kompany, has been brushed aside.

SHUTOUTS

Goalkeepers and defenders are especially proud of a shutout— a game in which their side does not concede a goal. Shutouts are usually credited to goalkeepers, but, in truth, they depend on a solid defense as well as midfielders and strikers who are willing to chase, track, and tackle. Italy has a reputation for producing some of the world's finest defenders. Between 1972 and the 1974 World Cup, the Italian defense helped keeper Dino Zoff to play 1,142 minutes—more than 12 games— without conceding a goal. The run was finally ended by Haiti. In 2009 Edwin van der Sar set an English record of 1,311 minutes unbeaten in goal for Manchester United. The world record in professional soccer is held by Brazil's Geraldo Pereira de Matos Filho, better known as Mazaropi. Playing for Vasco da Gama in 1977–1978, he did not concede a goal for more than 20 games—total of 1,816 minutes.

▲ Real Madrid's Ivan Helguera and David Beckham hurl themselves bravely into the path of the ball to block a fierce shot from Asier del Horno of Athletic Bilbao.

FACT FILE
Celtic went unbeaten throughout the 38-game 2016-2017 Scottish Premiership season.

▶ Tamas Priskin of Hungarian club, Gyor, makes a defensive header above Ferencvaros' Zolta Gera.

LONGEST UNBEATEN LEAGUE RUNS (IN GAMES)

108	ASEC Abidjan (Ivory Coast), 1989–1994
104	Steaua Bucharest (Romania), 1986–1989
88	Lincoln FC (Gibraltar), 2009–2014
85	Esperance (Tunisia), 1997–2001
71	Al-Ahly (Egypt), 2004–2007
63	Sheriff Tiraspol (Moldova), 2006–2008
62	Celtic (Scotland), 1915–1917
61	Levadia Tallinn (Estonia), 2008–2009
60	Al-Hilal (Sudan), 2016–2018
	Union Saint-Gilloise (Belgium), 1933–1935
59	Boca Juniors (Argentina), 1924–1927
	Pyunik Yerevan (Armenia), 2002–2004
58	AC Milan (Italy), 1991–1993
	Olympiakos (Greece), 1972–1974
	Skonto Riga (Latvia), 1993–1996

GOALKEEPING

Goalkeepers are a breed apart. They have a different role to their teammates and even look a little different since they must wear a shirt that distinguishes them from other players and officials. The crucial last line of defense, goalies can be forgotten when things are going well but singled out for abuse when they make a mistake that leads to a goal. Goalkeepers can also be game winners thanks to their saves and decisions and their agility and bravery.

▲ *Goalkeeper Shay Given stretches to make a diving save. The veteran made 125 international appearances for the Republic of Ireland.*

◄ *At the 2003 Women's World Cup, Norway's Bente Nordby clears a dangerous ball by punching it firmly away from the goal.*

KEEPING CONTROL

Goalkeepers are allowed to control the ball with their hands and arms, but otherwise they must obey most of the same rules as outfield players. Until 1912, goalies could handle the ball anywhere in their own half, but now handling is restricted to their penalty area, with several key exceptions. Goalkeepers cannot handle the ball:

• after releasing it and without it touching another player;
• after receiving it directly from a throw-in;
• if it has been deliberately kicked to them by a teammate.

If a goalkeeper handles the ball in any of these situations or if the referee judges that the keeper is wasting time with the ball in hand (known as the six-second rule), an indirect free kick is awarded. This can be dangerously close to the goal. In the 1990s a law was passed to reduce time wasting and speed up play. It banned goalies from controlling a ball from a throw-in or a back pass with their arms or hands.

▲ *Czech goalkeeper Petr Cech gathers the ball cleanly at the feet of Manchester City defender Aleksandar Kolarov.*

In the past, goalkeepers could be tackled, but today they are well protected by referees. Even so, they have to be brave to dive at an opponent's feet, risking injury. If goalies foul or bring down an attacker, they may give away a penalty and even be sent off if the referee decides that a professional foul has been committed.

A GOALIE'S SKILLS

To achieve a shutout, goalkeepers need more than supreme agility and the ability to make diving saves. Top goalies train hard to improve their handling skills, learning to take the ball at different heights and from different angles. They must be able to stay alert for the entire game. Many minutes can go by before, suddenly, they are called into action. Goalies need good decision-making skills, too, since a cross or shot may call for them to choose whether to try to hold the ball in a save, punch it away, or tip it over the bar or around a post. Goalkeepers are in a unique position to see opposition attacks developing, and they must communicate instructions to their teammates. They line up walls at free kicks and command their goal area, urging defenders to pick up unmarked opponents. A defense and goalie that communicate well can be a formidable unit.

► *Italian goalkeeper Gianluigi Buffon instructs his defenders. Clear, decisive communication between a goalkeeper and his or her outfield teammates can stop many opposition attacks.*

DEFENSE INTO ATTACK

With the ball in hand, goalies have several ways in which they can move the ball to a teammate or upfield (known as distribution). They can roll it out on the ground, looking for options to kick the ball; they can kick it straight from their hand; or they can throw the ball. Goalies launch the ball from their hand into the opposition half by using their shoe instep to strike it on the volley or half volley. Sometimes, goalies aim their kick for a tall winger or wide midfielder who is close to the sideline. This move is often rehearsed on the practice field. Goalies can bowl the ball out underarm, usually to a nearby teammate, or they can use a more powerful sidearm or overarm motion for maximum distance. A third option, the javelin throw, is often the quickest way to get the ball moving. Fast, accurate distribution from the goalie can be vital in turning defense into a rapid breakaway attack.

HIT THE NET

www.goalkeepersaredifferent.com
A fantastic website that is dedicated solely to goalies and is packed with quirky facts.

www.fourfourtwo.com/performance/goalkeepers
A great collection of videos showing tips and training from top professional goalkeepers.

www.jbgoalkeeping.com
An impressive coaching website, with short online videos, covering all aspects of the goalkeeper's game.

▶ Spain's Iker Casillas dives for the ball during a training session. Goalies work hard in training to improve their handling, flexibility, and reactions.

▲ France's Sarah Bouhaddi makes a save against Germany during the FIFA Women's World Cup 2015 quarter final. Bouhaddi was voted the IFFHS World's Best Woman Goalkeeper in 2016, 2017, and 2018.

FACT FILE
The world's first black professional soccer player was a goalkeeper. Born in the Gold Coast (now Ghana), Arthur Wharton played in 1889 for Rotherham United in the English league.

▶ In a one-on-one situation, many goalies come off their line to narrow the angle—reducing how much of the goal the attacker can see. They stay upright for as long as possible to increase the chance of the shot striking them.

GOALSCORING KEEPERS

In 1882 goalkeeper James McAulay was pressed into service as a center-forward and scored in Scotland's 5-0 defeat of Wales. Since then many goalies have scored goals for their team or country. Some goals have been scored from long goal kicks that have surprised a defense or by goalkeepers running into the opposition's penalty area in the dying seconds of a game. Others have come from spot kicks in a penalty shoot-out (see page 31). A well-taken penalty by Portuguese goalie Ricardo knocked England out of Euro 2004, for example. A few goalies, mostly in South America, have become legends for their goal-scoring feats from regular penalties and free kicks. The German Hans-Jörg Butt scored 28 goals, while Paraguay's José Luis Chilavert struck 62 times. This staggering tally was more than doubled during the remarkable career of Rogério Ceni, who scored 131 goals during his career for Brazilian club, São Paulo. His 100th came in 2011 with a free kick struck from outside the penalty area.

ATTACKING

As soon as a team gains possession of the ball, with time and in space, its players' thoughts turn to attacking. There are many ways in which a team can launch an attack, from a fast drive into space by a player who is sprinting forward and pushing the ball ahead, to a slow, probing attack in which many players keep the ball securely in possession and look for an opening.

BEATING OFFSIDE TRAPS

Some teams play an offside trap (see page 62), in which defenders move up in a straight line to catch opponents offside. Beating an offside trap takes cunning, skill, and awareness. A perfectly weighted through pass can unlock the trap if the ball is collected by a player who stays onside until the moment the ball moves ahead of him or her. A long diagonal pass that switches play forward and across the field may also work. The receiver makes a run from a deep position, staying onside until the ball moves ahead, then collects the ball behind the defense. Individual brilliance—such as dribbling or playing a short "push and go" pass—can also beat some offside traps.

▲ Ludovic Giuly of Barcelona threads an accurate through pass between Shakhtar Donetsk defenders Anatoliy Tymoschuk and Mariusz Lewandowski in a UEFA Champions League game.

◀ France's Franck Ribéry dribbles between Dutch defender Khalid Boulahrouz and forward Robin van Persie during a Euro 2008 group match. Great teamwork and fast, accurate counterattacking saw the Dutch side win 4–1.

▲ A "push and go" pass can beat a lone defender or an offside trap. The attacker pushes the ball past the defender and then sprints to collect it.

TEAM ATTACKS

Many attacks rely on two or more teammates working together to create a promising position. The wall pass (see page 18), for example, is a good way of propelling the ball past a defender with two quick movements. Attacking players also make decoy runs that pull defenders in one direction, creating space for another attacker to run into. Using the full width of the field can be vital to the success of an attack. Fullbacks, wingbacks, or wingers who are in space near the sideline may join an attack and make an overlapping run down the line. Receiving the ball, they may be able to head further forward to put in a cross or cut infield and move toward the goal. An overload is a situation in which the attacking side has more players in the attacking third of the field than the defending team. Classic ways of creating an overload are through a counterattack—in which one team's attack breaks down, and the opposition launches a rapid, direct attack—and an accurate long pass that is received by an attacker who is supported by teammates, with only an isolated defender to beat.

SET PIECES

Set pieces are often planned in training. They are attacking moves made from a restart such as a free kick, corner, or throw-in. If a team has a player who can throw the ball a long way, it may treat a throw-in that is level with the penalty area as if it were a corner. Often, a target player just inside the penalty area will attempt to flick the throw into the goal area. Mostly, set pieces are planned from corners and attacking free kicks (see page 30). At a corner, a team's tallest players or its best headers of the ball move up, usually from defense, to join strikers and attacking midfielders in the penalty area. Corners are sometimes played short in order to catch the defending team off guard, but usually they are whipped into the goal area. The attacking side looks for a header, or shot on goal, or a flick on to a teammate.

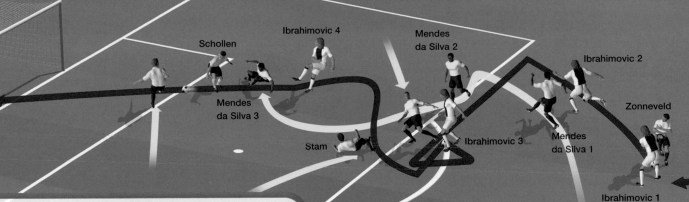

Schollen
Ibrahimovic 4
Mendes da Silva 2
Ibrahimovic 2
Zonneveld
Mendes da Silva 3
Stam
Ibrahimovic 3
Mendes da Silva 1
Ibrahimovic 1

GAME ACTION

Swedish international Zlatan Ibrahimovic moved from Ajax to Juventus for $19.5 million in late August 2004, but a week earlier he had given the Ajax fans a solo goal to savor. In a Dutch league game against NAC Breda, Ibrahimovic received a pass with his back to goal, defender David Mendes da Silva on his back and another Breda player, Mike Zonneveld, close by. Winning a tackle with Zonneveld, Ibrahimovic twisted past da Silva and headed toward the goal. Weaving his way to the edge of the penalty area, Ibrahimovic's options looked limited with four defenders around him. Yet with supreme balance and a series of feints and turns, he avoided the lunging tackle of Ronnie Stam. At the very last moment, when a shot with his right foot looked likely, Ibrahimovic switched the ball to his left foot to slide a shot past goalkeeper Davy Schollen. Ajax won the game 6–2.

▼ Ghana's Stephen Appiah (left) attempts to twist and turn sharply past Zimbabwean defender Cephas Chimedza in the African Cup of Nations. Dummy movements, stepovers, and sharp turns are all ways of disrupting a defender.

GAME MAGICIANS

Some attacks are inspired by a piece of individual skill, trickery, and brilliance. A player may be able to break free from a defense with a sudden change of speed and direction or a trick move such as the Cruyff turn or a drag back. Some players can simply outrun a defense, bursting through to score. Dribbling—kicking and moving with the ball under close control in order to beat defenders—is one of the most exciting sights on a soccer field. Stanley Matthews, Maradona, and Garrincha were all electrifying dribblers, while today's dribbling superstars include Gareth Bale, Cristiano Ronaldo, Lionel Messi, and Ousmane Dembélé. Weaving, high-speed dribblers can sometimes open up a game by themselves. They strike fear into defenders who know that one false move or a poorly timed challenge will allow the dribbler to go past or perhaps give away a free kick or penalty.

▲ An unexpected piece of brilliance can open up a defense or result in a goal. Here, whilst playing for Sevilla, Jesus Navas unleashes an overhead kick against Barcelona. After four years at Manchester City, he returned to Sevilla in 2017.

GOALSCORING

Players who score goals regularly are the most valuable of all. But scoring is not just reserved for the strikers. A successful team needs its midfielders to contribute a number of goals each season, while tall defenders who are experts at heading often score five or six goals per season from set pieces. For true strikers, goals are what they play for and are judged on. As Argentinian striker Gabriel Batistuta once said, "Goals are like bread. I need them to live."

THE GOAL SCORER'S ART

Pace, power, accuracy, confidence, and a deadly eye for a chance are just some of the qualities required to be a top goalscorer. Some skills can be honed in training—close ball control or swerving a shot, for example. Other qualities, such as confidence and vision, are harder to master. Soccer has gotten quicker at the highest level, and most strikers need a lot of speed in order to break past increasingly mobile defenders or into space to receive the ball before anyone else. Strength to hold off a challenge can be an asset too. Some strikers, however, rely more on their intuition, fast reactions, and ball skills to dribble through a crowded penalty area. Others are taller, stronger players who can score with towering headers or blasted shots. Most crucially of all, strikers have to be able to spot a chance for a goal and go for it. They need to react instinctively, using their vision to time runs into a scoring position. Once on the ball, they rarely have long to shoot. In an instant, strikers have to weigh their options, know where the goal, defenders, and goalie are, and hit a shot with enough speed, bend, or accuracy to beat the goalkeeper.

FACT FILE In 1998 Atlético Mineiro's Edmilson Ferreira celebrated a goal by eating a carrot in front of the fans of rival Brazilian team America MG. His actions caused crowd trouble and incensed America's players, one of whom was later sent off for a foul on Ferreira.

OWN GOALS

An own goal is technically any goal in which the last person to touch the ball before it crossed the line was a player on the defending team. In practice, however, an own goal is awarded not only when the ball has been deflected but also when a defending player has made a genuine error or caused a major change in the course of the ball. The history of professional football is littered with outrageous own goals. Among the most common are goalkeeping errors, skewed defensive clearances that are sliced into the net, and misdirected headers. A handful of players have scored two own goals in the same game, such as Georgia's Kakhaber "Kakha" Kaladze in a 2010 World Cup match versus Italy, and Stoke City's Jon Walters in a 2013 Premier League game against Chelsea.

◀ Brazil's Marta Vieira da Silva (known as Marta) is one the best female players of all time. The striker has won FIFA World Player of the Year six times and was the top scorer in the 2007 Women's World Cup.

FACT FILE
The world record for own goals in one game is a staggering 149! In the last match of the 2002 Madagascan league season, against champions AS Adema, Stade Olympique l'Emryne repeatedly scored own goals from the kickoff in protest at a refereeing decision in their previous game.

▶ Germany's Miroslav Klose scored five goals in the 2006 World Cup and is the competition's all-time record holder with 16 goals in four tournaments.

▲ When a scoring chance presents itself, strikers need poise and accuracy. Here, Fernando Torres scores the winning goal of the Euro 2008 final, getting the ball past the German goalkeeper, Jens Lehmann.

▶ Fabian Espindola (left) roars with joy after scoring for Real Salt Lake against LA Galaxy in 2011. The Argentinian scored more than 30 goals for Real Salt Lake before moving in 2013 to New York Red Bulls.

FACT FILE During a Group G game at the 2018 World Cup versus England, Belgian striker Michy Batshuayi celebrated his team's goal by thumping the ball, aiming for the net. The ball struck the post and rebounded to hit him painfully in the face.

GOALSCORING RECORDS

ALL-TIME LEADING GOALSCORERS
Artur Friedenreich (Brazil) 1,329 goals (1909-1939)

Pelé (Brazil) 1,281 goals (1956-1977)

MOST INTERNATIONAL GOALS (MEN)
109—Ali Daei (Iran), 1993-2006

MOST INTERNATIONAL GOALS (WOMEN)
184—Abby Wambach (USA), 2001-2015

MOST GOALS IN ONE INTERNATIONAL MATCH
13—Archie Thompson (Australia), 2001

FASTEST INTERNATIONAL GOAL
8.1 seconds—Christian Benteke (Belgium) versus Gibraltar, 2016

FASTEST INTERNATIONAL HAT TRICK
Inside 3.5 minutes—Willie Hall (England), 1938

MOST HAT TRICKS IN CONSECUTIVE MATCHES
4—Masashi Nakayama (Japan) for Jubilo Iwata, 1998

FASTEST GOAL
2 seconds—Vuk Bakic (Serbia) for GSP Polet, 2012

FASTEST OWN GOAL
8 seconds—Pat Kruse (England), playing for Torquay United, 1977

▲ Brazil's Mauro Silva (left), Leonardo (center) and Bebeto pretend to rock babies at the 1994 World Cup. The celebration—during a 3–0 victory against Cameroon—was in honor of striker Bebeto's newborn son.

GOAL CELEBRATIONS

As fans celebrate a goal, so do players. For many years celebrations were no more flamboyant than a simple punch of the air and a hug from a nearby teammate. That all changed in the 1980s and 1990s, partly thanks to the acrobatic backflips of Mexican striker Hugo Sanchez. Since then players have rocked imaginary babies, danced the conga, and pulled off spectacular gymnastic moves. Icelandic team Stjarnan FC have gained fame for their elaborate team celebrations, which include all of the team members pretending to row a boat and reel in a player acting as a fish. This performance clocked up over a million views on YouTube in 2011. Referees can penalize teams for wasting time or removing shirts during celebrations.

FREE KICKS AND PENALTIES

Referees award a free kick when a player breaks one of the laws of the game. Common free-kick offences are mistimed tackles, shirt-pulling, obstruction and offside. There are two types of free kick—indirect, which cannot be scored from without a second player touching the ball, and direct, which can be scored from directly and is awarded for more serious fouls. If a direct free-kick offense is committed by the defending team inside its penalty area, the referee may award a penalty.

FREE KICKS

Both types of free kick are taken from where the foul or offense was committed, although a rule change means that in some competitions the referee can move a kick around 30 ft. (9m) closer to goal if the other team wastes time or shows dissent. Opposition players must move around 30 ft. (9m) away from the ball, giving the team taking the kick valuable possession in space and with time. Some free kicks are taken quickly to get the ball moving in the middle of the field. Wide free kicks are often crossed with pace toward the goal.

Attacking free kicks engage the two teams in a battle of wits. Players on the defending side mark attackers in the penalty area and form a defensive wall to block a direct shot. The kick taker may pass to a teammate in space or try to hit a cross or shot past the wall. Some free kick specialists rely on powerful and direct strikes, while others—such as Paulo Dybala, Hakan Calhanoglu, and Cristiano Ronaldo—are famous for the extreme bend they put on the ball.

▲ Lionel Messi takes a free kick during a 2013 Champions League match between Barcelona and AC Milan. He strikes across the back of the ball to make it swerve around the defensive wall and into the corner of the goal.

◄ Manchester United's Wayne Rooney curls a free kick toward the penalty area.

THE KICK OF DEATH

Originally nicknamed the "kick of death," the penalty kick was introduced in 1891. It has created more controversy than any other aspect of the game. The reason is simple. A penalty is an outstanding opportunity to score, as the taker is one-on-one with the goalkeeper and all the other players are outside the penalty area. In certain situations, the referee can order the kick to be retaken—if the taker misses but a defender entered the area before the kick, for example. Penalty takers must hit the ball forward and cannot make contact with the ball again until it has touched another player. Some penalty takers favor accuracy over power, aiming the ball low into the corner of the goal; others blast the ball. For the goalie, trying to figure out where the ball will go is a guessing game.

PENALTY SHOOT-OUTS

Tense and nailbiting, a penalty shoot-out is guaranteed to bring fans to the edge of their seats. Professional soccer's first shoot-out took place in England in 1970. In the semifinal of the Watney Mann Invitational Cup, lowly Hull City held a full-strength Manchester United team to a 1–1 draw. In the shoot-out that followed, Manchester United's Denis Law became the first player to miss a shoot-out spot kick, but his team ended up 4–3 winners. The first shoot-out in a major tournament was in the 1972 Asian Nations Cup, when South Korea beat Thailand in the semifinal. Germany lost the first European Championships shoot-out to Czechoslovakia in 1976, but defeated France in the first World Cup shoot-out six years later.

In a shoot-out, five players per team are chosen to take one penalty each, all at one end of the field. A shoot-out is not considered to be part of the actual game, meaning that a goal is not added to a player's season or career tally. Neither penalty takers nor teammates are allowed to score from a rebound—each player has just one shot at glory. The goalie knows this and often does his or her best to intimidate a penalty taker. If the scores are tied after each team has taken five penalties, the competition goes into "sudden death." Teams take one penalty each until one side misses and the other scores. On the rare occasion that all the players on the field, including the goalkeeper, have taken a penalty and the scores are level, the cycle begins again in the same order. Does this ever happen? Occasionally and spectacularly. In 2007, England and the Netherlands played in the semifinal of the European Under-21 championships. It took 32 penalties before the Dutch won.

▲ *AC Milan's Giampaolo Pazzini scores on a penalty kick during the Serie A match between AC Milan and Cesena, February 2015.*

▼ *Juventus keeper Gianluigi Buffon shows excellent reactions to save a penalty from AC Milan's Christian Brocchi during an Italian Super Cup game.*

MOST PENALTIES IN A SHOOT-OUT

PENS	SHOOT-OUT SCORE	COMPETITION
48	KK Palace 17 Civics 16	Namibian Cup, 2005
44	Argentinos Juniors 20 Racing Club 19	Argentinian league, 1988
40	Obernai 15 ASCA Wittelsheim 15	French Cup, 1996
40	Tunbridge Wells 16 Littlehampton Town 15	English FA Cup, 2005

▲ *Oliver Neuville of Germany keeps his nerve to place a penalty past Argentina's Leonardo Franco. Germany won the shootout 4–2 to book a place in the last four of the 2006 World Cup.*

SNAPSHOT
BAGGIO'S PENALTY MISS

"The difference between heaven and hell is one minute," said Spanish internatiional Josep Guardiola after an epic 4-3 win over Yugoslavia at Euro 2000. For Italy's Roberto Baggio, six years earlier, it took mere seconds. In the final of the 1994 World Cup, Italy and Brazil were locked in a 0–0 stalemate. Extra time ended, and a nerve-shredding penalty shoot-out began. With Italy 3–2 down, Baggio stepped up to take his side's pressure-laden fifth penalty. He decided to drive the ball down the middle, as he knew that Taffarel, the Brazilian goalie, tended to dive to one side.

Taffarel did dive, but Baggio sent the ball sailing high over the bar to hand the World Cup to Brazil. Baggio later wrote, "It was the worst moment of my career. I still dream about it. If I could erase a moment from my career, it would be that one." What is often forgotten is that two Italians before Baggio, Daniele Massaro and the highly experienced Franco Baresi, missed their penalties. Even if Baggio had scored, Brazil would have had the chance to win with their fifth spot kick. That said, the photograph of a crushed Baggio remains the iconic image of the 1994 World Cup.

Roberto Baggio hangs his head in disbelief as Brazilian players celebrate victory in the final of the 1994 World Cup.

SOCCER LEGENDS

From France's Zinedine Zidane to Argentina's Lionel Messi, soccer has been lit up by the talents of thousands of highly committed and skilled players, all of whom have enthralled spectators and inspired their teams to great achievements. Packed into this section are profiles of more than 75 of the finest players to have graced the game.

> **KEY**
> Country = international side
> Caps = international games
> Goals = international goals
> (to August 2019)

GAO HONG
China, born 1967
Caps: over 100 Goals: 0

An instinctive shot-stopper, Gao Hong began playing soccer for her factory team before moving to the Guangdong club in southeast China. She became a member of the Chinese national side in 1989 and played in both the 1995 and 1999 World Cups. Gao was in goal for China's two Asian Games successes, in 1994 and 1998, and she also won a silver medal at the 1996 Olympics. At the end of her international career, she appeared in the WUSA league for the New York Power.

GOALKEEPERS

PETER SCHMEICHEL
Denmark, born 1963
Caps: 129 Goals: 1

After playing for Hvidøvre and then Brøndby, Schmeichel became one of the best keepers of the 1990s after Alex Ferguson took him to Manchester United in 1991 for the modest fee of $900,00. The high point of his international career came with winning the 1992 European Championships, while the silverware poured in at team level. The hugely committed Dane redefined one-on-one goalkeeping, standing menacingly tall and large or bravely sprawling at an attacker's feet. After winning a treble (English Premiership, FA Cup, and Champions League) with Manchester United in 1999, he moved to Sporting Lisbon and helped the Portuguese side win its first league title in 17 years.

He made a surprise return to the English Premiership in 2001, with Aston Villa and then Manchester City, before injury forced him to retire.

▶ *Iker Casillas focuses up the field during a 2013 La Liga match between Real Madrid and Valencia.*

◀ *Peter Schmeichel makes a typically brave save for Manchester City in 2002.*

> **FACT FILE** As an amateur, Peter Schmeichel played as a striker. He showed those skills in the 1995-1996 UEFA Cup when he came up for an attack and scored with a header against Russian team Rotor Volgograd.

IKER CASILLAS
Spain, born 1981
Caps: 167 Goals: 0

Spain's number one goalie for more than a decade, Casillas played over 700 times for Real Madrid, with whom he won five La Liga titles, before moving to Porto in 2015. In 2000 he became the youngest goalkeeper to play in a Champions League final, which Real won 3–0. With his razor-sharp reflexes and superb positioning, Casillas has been voted goalie of the year five times and has captained Spain to two European Championship titles and the 2010 World Cup.

BEST GOALKEEPER AT THE WORLD CUP

Since 1994, FIFA has given an award to the best goalie of the tournament.

YEAR	WINNER
1998	Fabien Barthez (France)
2002	Oliver Kahn (Germany)
2006	Gianluigi Buffon (Italy)
2010	Iker Casillas (Spain)
2014	Manuel Neuer (Germany)
2018	Thibault Courtois (Belgium)

LEV YASHIN
Soviet Union, 1929–90
Caps: 75 Goals: 0

In South America, Yashin was called the "Black Spider." In Europe he was the "Black Panther"; but everywhere he was regarded as the finest goalkeeper of his era and, possibly, of all time. Blessed with extraordinary anticipation and agility, Yashin made countless, seemingly impossible saves and stopped as many as 150 penalties during his career, which was spent entirely at Moscow Dynamo. In 1954 he made his debut for the national team. Yashin's bravery, vision, and shot-stopping skills helped the Soviets to an Olympic title in 1956, the European Championships crown in 1960, and a semifinal place at the 1966 World Cup. With Moscow Dynamo, Yashin won six league titles and two Soviet Cups. In 1963 he became the first—and still the only—goalkeeper to win the coveted European Player of the Year award.

▲ *Lev Yashin makes a great save at the 1966 World Cup.*

GORDON BANKS
England, 1937–2019
Caps: 73 Goals: 0

"Banks of England" was as reliable a goalie as any nation could call upon in the 1960s. During his ten-year international career he kept 35 shutouts and was on the losing team just nine times. His professional career began at Chesterfield, before a $20,000 move took him to Leicester City. In 1962 Banks made his debut for England, with whom he won the 1966 World Cup. The following year, he moved to Stoke City, but a car accident in 1972 caused Banks to lose the sight in his right eye. The accident ended his career in Great Britain, although he did play in the U.S. for the Fort Lauderdale Strikers in 1977–1978.

FACT FILE
Gordon Banks won FIFA's Goalkeeper of the Year award a record six times.

GAME ACTION

Brazil and England played a tense yet thrilling match in the group stages of the 1970 World Cup, with Brazil winning 1–0. In the tenth minute, Jairzinho slipped a high cross into the English penalty area. Rising high, Pelé headed the ball down fiercely toward the far post, with Gordon Banks seemingly stranded. The ball bounced just short of the line, and a goal seemed certain. Yet Banks showed electrifying reactions, scrambling across his line and clawing the ball almost vertically upward and over the crossbar. Pelé was stunned and later called it "the greatest save I ever saw." Few who witnessed it would disagree.

▲ *Gordon Banks in action for Stoke City in 1972. Throughout his career, Banks trained tirelessly on angles and repeat drills to improve his strength and agility.*

Tommy Wright

Pelé

Banks 2

Banks 1

Alan Mullery

Tostao

PAT JENNINGS
Northern Ireland, born 1945
Caps: 119 Goals: 0

Calm, gentle, and seemingly unflappable, Northern Ireland's Pat Jennings famously received no formal coaching before joining his local team, Newry Town. A short stint with Watford followed before he moved to Tottenham Hotspur in 1964. There he won the FA Cup, two League Cups, and the UEFA Cup. In the 1967 Charity Shield game against Manchester United, a kick from Jennings sailed over the head of the opposing goalie, Alex Stepney, to score a memorable goal. Jennings was sold to Tottenham's north London rivals, Arsenal, in 1977, where he played for eight seasons. He came out of retirement to play his 119th game for his country at the 1986 World Cup.

▲ Pat Jennings tips the ball over the bar during a World Cup qualifying game against England in 1985.

> **FACT FILE** In 2016, Neuer set a record of 557 minutes without conceding a goal in a major tournament.

▶ Dino Zoff organizes Italy's defense during the 1982 World Cup. Voted Italian goalkeeper of the century, Zoff once remained unbeaten in goal for Juventus for ten games.

▲ Manuel Neuer was voted German footballer of the year for the 2014–2015 season, a rare accolade for a goalkeeper.

MANUEL NEUER
Germany, born 1986
Caps: 84 Goals: 0

A dynamic sweeper-keeper, comfortable on the ball and brilliant in one-on-one situations, Neuer joined Schalke 04 in 1991 and didn't leave until 2011 when he moved for a record fee of just under $25 million to Bayern Munich. He made an instant impact, notching up over 1,000 minutes without conceding a goal in a string of games in his first season, winning three Bundesliga titles and the 2012–2013 Champions League. Debuting internationally in 2009, he only conceded one goal in Germany's Euro 2012 campaign. More was to come in 2014 when he became a World Cup winner and was voted goalkeeper of the tournament.

DINO ZOFF
Italy, born 1942
Caps: 112 Goals: 0

A true goalkeeping legend, Dino Zoff was rejected as a 14-year-old by both Juventus and Internazionale for being too small. He finally signed for Udinese before moving to Mantova and then Napoli. In 1972 Zoff was bought by Juventus, where he won six Italian league titles, two Italian Cups, and a UEFA Cup. Zoff's first international call-up came during the 1968 European Championships. He debuted in the quarterfinals and was part of the team that won the final. A model athlete with intense concentration, Zoff broke many goalkeeping records (see page 23), and in 1982, at the age of 40, he captained Italy to their first World Cup success in the modern era. The oldest player to win a World Cup, Zoff retired shortly afterward and went on to coach Italy's Olympic team, Juventus, and Lazio. He coached Italy to the final of Euro 2000, where they lost narrowly to France.

HOPE SOLO
USA, born 1981
Caps: 202 Goals: 0

The United States' best goalie since 2005, Solo started her professional career with Philadelphia Charge in 2003 before having spells in Sweden and France and returning to the U.S. with a succession of WUSA and WPS teams. In 2013 she joined the Seattle Reign in the newly formed National Women's Soccer League. She has won Olympic gold twice (2008, 2012) and was a member of the U.S. team that was the runner-up at the 2011 World Cup. Solo was voted goalie of the World Cup—a feat she repeated four years later as her five shutouts helped her side become 2015 champions.

DEFENDERS

MARCEL DESAILLY
France, born 1968
Caps: 116 Goals: 3

Marcel Desailly is world-famous as one of the French players who won the World Cup and European Championship crowns in 1998 and 2000. He was born in the African nation of Ghana and came to France as a young child. A skilful and commanding central defender, Desailly began his career with FC Nantes and then Olympique Marseille. In 1993 he won the Champions League with Marseille, before moving to AC Milan and winning the Champions League again the following year. After a series of outstanding performances at the 1998 World Cup, Desailly moved to Chelsea, where he proved a popular leader. In 2004, Desailly retired from international soccer and left Chelsea to join Qatar's Al-Ittihad club.

▲ Marcel Desailly hits a long pass during France's 1998 World Cup game against Denmark.

FACT FILE World Cup winner Marcel Desailly became the third player to be sent off in a World Cup final when he was dismissed against Brazil in 1998 after receiving two yellow cards.

▲ In 1978 Daniel Passarella captained Argentina to the World Cup trophy on home soil.

DANIEL PASSARELLA
Argentina, born 1953
Caps: 70 Goals: 22

Passarella was a gifted central defender who made surging runs into midfield to build attacks. He was exceptionally good in the air despite being of average height and struck devastating free kicks. In 298 Argentinian league matches he scored an astonishing 99 goals. Passarella had success with River Plate before a move to Europe in 1982, first to Fiorentina and then to Internazionale. In 1985–1986, he scored 11 goals for Fiorentina, a record for a defender that lasted for 15 years. He won the 1978 World Cup, played in the 1982 tournament and was chosen to play in 1986, but was sidelined through injury. After retiring, Passarella became a coach, managing Argentina at the 1998 World Cup.

ELIAS FIGUEROA
Chile, born 1946
Caps: 47 Goals: 2

This elegant and skilled defender played almost all of his football in the left-back position. Figueroa appeared in three World Cups—1966, 1974, and 1982—and in 1974 he was voted the best defender of the tournament. He won the South American Footballer of the Year award an unprecedented three times in a row (1974–1976). At club level, Figueroa won league titles in three different countries— the Chilean league with Colo Colo twice, the Brazilian league with Internacional on three occasions, and the Uruguayan league with Peñarol five times. He ended his career in the U.S., playing for the Fort Lauderdale Strikers alongside Gerd Müller and Teofilio Cubillas, the great Peruvian striker.

LUCY BRONZE
England, born 1991
Caps: 63 Goals: 7

Starting out in Sunderland's youth team, this tough tackling yet skilful defender made her full team debut at the age of 16. Moving to the USA in 2009, Bronze became the first English player to win the NCAA Cup with the University of North Carolina's Tar Heels side. Time at Everton, Liverpool, and Manchester City followed before she signed for Lyon in 2017 where she won both the French league and the UEFA Women's Champions League in 2018. Arguably the most consistent all-round defender in women's football, her resolute displays and occasional goal threat helped propel England to third place at the 2015 Women's World Cup.

◄ Lucy Bronze at a 2019 Women's World Cup match. She captained England for the first time in 2018.

FACT FILE In 1976 Bobby Moore played for Team America against England, in a game to mark the U.S. bicentenary. One of Moore's teammates was Pelé.

BOBBY MOORE
England, 1941–93
Caps: 108 Goals: 2

England's finest ever defender, Moore appeared to lack the speed and commanding physique to be a great central defender. However, he was blessed with a wonderful eye for the game and always appeared to be one step ahead of opposition attackers. His tackling was clean and precise, and he was very rarely cautioned. One of soccer's truly outstanding captains, Moore led England in 90 games—a record shared with Billy Wright—including the 1966 World Cup triumph. He spent most of his career at West Ham, only joining Fulham (alongside George Best) at the age of 32, before finally moving to the United States to play for Seattle Sounders and San Antonio Thunder. His friendship with Pelé was cemented in 1970 when the two men played out an epic struggle for supremacy in England's World Cup game against Brazil. Pelé called Moore the greatest defender he had played against.

◄ *Bobby Moore, England's captain, celebrates with the 1966 World Cup.*

▲ *Matthias Sammer (left) was the first defender to win the European Player of the Year award since Franz Beckenbauer in 1976.*

MATTHIAS SAMMER
East Germany/Germany,
born 1967 Caps: 74 Goals: 14

Matthias Sammer followed in the footsteps of his father, who played in midfield for East Germany and Dresden. As a midfielder, Sammer led East Germany to victory at the 1986 European Youth Championships. After Germany reunified in 1990, he moved into defense and was a commanding sweeper in the 1994 World Cup and two European Championships. A move to the Italian club Internazionale was short lived and he returned to Germany to join Borussia Dortmund, with whom he won two Bundesliga titles and the 1997 Champions League. In 1996, he became the first player from the former East Germany to win the European Footballer of the Year award.

PAOLO MALDINI
Italy, born 1968
Caps: 126 Goals: 7

One of the best defenders in world soccer, Paolo Maldini was a one-team player. He made his first-team debut for AC Milan in 1985 and played over 900 games for the Italian team, mostly at left-back, although he would also play as a central defender or as a sweeper. Maldini was able to read the game extremely well, tackle cleanly, and move the ball forward accurately. He debuted for Italy in 1988 and soon became a regular in the national team. He played in four World Cups and four European Championships, retiring from international soccer after the 2002 World Cup. Winning seven Serie A titles, Maldini also lifted the Champions League trophy in 2003 and 2007. He eventually retired just before his 41st birthday.

◄ *Paolo Maldini, Italy's longest-serving defender, clears the ball out of his penalty area during the 1994 World Cup final against Brazil.*

FACT FILE Paolo Maldini's father, Cesare, also played as a sweeper for AC Milan, lifting the European Cup at Wembley in 1963. His son repeated that feat for the same club exactly 40 years later. Cesare Maldini also managed his son and the Italian team at the 1998 World Cup.

THIAGO SILVA
Brazil, born 1984
Caps: 61   Goals: 4

Tough and skilful, Silva can play in any position across the defense and actually started out as a midfielder in Brazil but moved to Europe in 2004. After spells at Porto and Dynamo Moscow, where he contracted tuberculosis and nearly quit soccer, Silva joined Fluminense and helped them to win their first ever Copa do Brazil in 2007. AC Milan paid just over $11 million to bring him back to Europe in 2009, where he won the 2010–2011 Serie A before becoming the world's most expensive defender with a move to Paris Saint-Germain. Silva captained Brazil when they won the 2013 FIFA Confederations Cup and has played at two Olympic Games, winning a bronze medal in 2008 and a silver in 2012.

▲ *The Netherland's Ruud Krol at the 1980 European Championships, which were held in Italy.*

FACT FILE
Ruud Krol held the record as the most-capped Dutch player for 21 years. His total was finally overtaken in 2000.

▶ *Franz Beckenbauer at the 1974 World Cup. Sixteen years later, he became the second man— after Brazil's Mario Zagalo —to have won the World Cup as both a player and a manager.*

RUUD KROL
Holland, born 1949
Caps: 83   Goals: 4

Krol was a vital part of the great Ajax and Netherlands "total soccer" sides of the late 1960s and 1970s, comfortable playing in almost any defensive position. With Ajax he won six league titles and two European Cups (1972 and 1973). Krol was the last of the Ajax greats to move away when, in 1980, he played for Vancouver Whitecaps in Canada. He returned to Europe the following year to play for Napoli and later for Cannes in the French second division, where injury forced him to retire in 1987. He has since managed in a variety of countries, including Switzerland, Egypt, and Belgium.

FRANZ BECKENBAUER
West Germany, born 1945
Caps: 103   Goals: 14

Der Kaiser ("The King") made his debut for Bayern Munich in 1964 as an attacking inside-left. Only 27 games later, he was on the national team. At the 1966 World Cup, Beckenbauer played in midfield and scored four goals on the way to the final. By the 1970 tournament, he had moved into defense, where he revolutionized the ultradefensive role of sweeper with his astonishing vision and smooth on-ball skills. Time and again he would turn defense into attack, striding up the field to release teammates or to take a chance himself. With his stylish attacking play, it is sometimes forgotten that he was a masterful defender, always cool under pressure. In 1972 Beckenbauer won the European Championships with West Germany and was European Footballer of the Year. Two years later, he won the first of three consecutive European Cups with Bayern Munich and also captained his country to World Cup glory. In 1977, he made a surprise move to the United States, playing in a star-studded New York Cosmos team before returning to Germany in 1980 with Hamburg. He became West Germany's coach in 1984, leading the team to two World Cup finals and winning one.

HIT THE NET

www.planetworldcup.com/LEGENDS/wcstars.html
A selection of profiles of many great soccer players, including Austria's Hans Krankl, Belgium's Jan Ceulemans, and West Germany's Karl-Heinz Rummenigge.

www.rsssf.com/miscellaneous/century.html
A regularly updated list of players with 100 or more international caps. Clicking on a player's name reveals a list of all their international matches.

www.theguardian.com/football/series/the-100-best-footballers-in-the-world
Profiles of the 100 great players from past World Cups.

▲ *Franco Baresi won three European Cups with AC Milan, including this triumph in 1989.*

FRANCO BARESI
Italy, born 1960
Caps: 81 Goals: 1

A tough, intelligent defender, Baresi made his first-team debut for AC Milan in 1978. He played 716 games for the club, winning six Serie A titles. Baresi had to wait until 1990 to break fully onto the Italian national team. Although part of the 1982 World Cup squad, he was not chosen to play and refused to appear for Italy while Enzo Bearzot remained manager. He played in both the 1990 and 1994 World Cups and superbly wiped out the threat of Brazil's Romario and Bebeto in the 1994 final, which Italy lost only on penalties. Milan paid him the ultimate tribute on his retirement in 1997, dropping the number six shirt from its lineup.

HONG MYUNG-BO
South Korea, born 1969
Caps: 136 Goals: 10

An excellent passer of the ball, Hong played for Pohang Steelers in South Korea and for Bellmare Hiratsuke (now Shonan Bellmare) and Kashiwa Reysol in Japan. He is South Korea's most-capped player and is a veteran of four World Cups. At the 2002 tournament, where South Korea reached the semifinals on home soil, Hong was voted the third-best player of the World Cup behind Oliver Kahn and Ronaldo. In November 2002 he became the first Korean to play in the American MLS when he signed for Los Angeles Galaxy.

LINDA MEDALEN
Norway, born 1965
Caps: 152 Goals: 64

Medalen started her career as a striker, making her debut for Norway in 1987 and going on to win the 1988 unofficial Women's World Cup and the 1993 European Championships. At the 1991 World Cup she was her team's top scorer, with six goals, as Norway finished runner-up. As Medalen's career progressed, she moved into defense, where her skill in the air and strong tackling helped Norway to win the 1995 World Cup, conceding just one goal in six games. Medalen played in the 1999 tournament, but a knee injury kept her out of the 2000 Olympics, which Norway won. At club level, she won five league championships and three cup competitions for the Norwegian team Asker SKK.

◄ *Linda Medalen holds off China's Ying Liu in the 1999 World Cup semi-final. The Norwegian retired a year later.*

JOHN CHARLES
Wales, 1931-2004
Caps: 38 Goals: 21

The gloriously talented Charles was equally skilled as a bustling, powerful center-forward or as a hugely commanding central defender. In both positions, he was world class. Appearing in attack for Leeds United, he scored a record 42 goals in one season, while playing internationally as a central defender. In the Welsh team, Charles was joined by his brother, Mel, and teammates Ivor and Len Allchurch—the first time that any national side had included two pairs of brothers. In 1957 the British transfer record was smashed as he moved to Juventus for $185,000. Charles became a genuine legend in Italy for his towering performances, generous behavior toward fans, and his sportsmanship. In a highly defense-minded league he scored an astonishing 93 goals in 155 matches, helping Juve win three Serie A titles and two Italian Cups. He later moved back to Leeds, then on to Parma, Cardiff City, and Hereford United before retiring.

◄ *John Charles (right) battles for the ball at the 1958 World Cup. Charles' name is still revered by Juventus fans, who nicknamed him Il Buon Gigante— the Gentle Giant.*

MIDFIELDERS AND WINGERS

LANDON DONOVAN
USA, born 1982
Caps: 157 Goals: 57

Donovan came to prominence early when he was voted the best player of the 1999 FIFA Under-17 World Championship and was signed the same year by German team Bayer Leverkusen. Returning to the U.S. on loan with the San Jose Earthquakes, Donovan would later have short loan spells with Bayern Munich and Everton, but in 2005 he joined the LA Galaxy. He has won five MLS Cups, three with LA Galaxy and two with the San Jose Earthquakes, as well as winning the CONCACAF Gold Cup three times with the U.S. team. Two-footed and capable of devastating attacking bursts from midfield, Donovan's eye for a goal has seen him score more than 150 times in the MLS and other U.S. club competitions. His 57 goals make him, far and away, the U.S. national team's most prolific goal scorer.

◀ *Landon Donovan goes to turn with the ball during an MLS game between LA Galaxy and the Portland Timbers.*

STANLEY MATTHEWS
England, 1915-2000
Caps: 54 Goals: 11

The "Wizard of the Dribble" made his first-team debut for Stoke City in 1932 and went on to amaze crowds with his sensational wing play, supreme control, and ability to dribble through a defense at will. Matthews' dedication to physical fitness, years ahead of his time, ensured that his career was one of the longest in British football. He joined Blackpool in 1947 and inspired them to an incredible FA Cup triumph in 1953, in what is remembered as the "Matthews final." His England career ran from 1937 to 1954, although he only played in 54 of the 119 internationals the team strived to win, to the outrage of his many fans. He became the first winner of the European Footballer of the Year award in 1956, and in 1961 he returned to Stoke, for whom he played his last game in 1965, aged 50 years and five days. In the same year, he became the first ever serving player to be knighted.

▲ *Stanley Matthews (left) exhibits supreme poise, balance, and skill on the ball as he takes on Scotland's George Young in 1948.*

FACT FILE Stanley Matthews was praised as one of the most modest and fair players to ever grace the game. In his 33-year-long career, he never received a booking.

CARLOS VALDERRAMA
Colombia, born 1961
Caps: 110 Goals: 10

Famous for his flamboyant style of play and hairstyle, Carlos Valderrama was an exquisite passer of the ball in midfield, who would often link with the attack for a devastating effect. He played for three Colombian teams—Union Magdalena, Millionarios, and Deportiva Cali—before moving to France in 1988, where he won the league title with Montpellier. In 1996 he moved to the United States to play for Tampa Bay Mutiny and then Miami Fusion. Valderrama captained Colombia to three World Cup tournaments in a row (1990–1998) and retired from international soccer after the 1998 tournament. Yet, even past his 40th birthday, Valderrama was still one of the biggest stars in the MLS.

▶ *Carlos Valderrama on the ball during Colombia's 1998 World Cup game against England.*

ALAIN GIRESSE
France, born 1952
Caps: 47 Goals: 6

At 5ft. 3 in. (1.63m) tall and weighing about 130 lbs. (60kg), Giresse was small for competitive soccer, but his tireless work in midfield caught the eye both at club level, for Bordeaux and Olympique Marseille, and with the French national team. Giresse appeared at two World Cups (1982 and 1986) and also won the 1984 European Championships. He played more than 500 games for Bordeaux and scored the winning goal in the 1986 French Cup final against Marseille, whom he joined a few weeks later. Giresse went on to manage Paris Saint-Germain and Toulouse. After coaching for the national teams of Georgia, Gabon, and Mali, in 2013 he took over as head coach for Senegal.

HRISTO STOICHKOV
Bulgaria, born 1966
Caps: 83 Goals: 37

As an attacking midfielder or a striker, the strong, stocky Stoichkov was surprisingly quick over a short distance and possessed unstoppable power, particularly in his left foot. He emerged as a skilled young player at CSKA Sofia before moving to Barcelona. Unpredictable and with a fiery temper, Stoichkovbecame dissatisfied with Barcelona coach Johan Cruyff when he was asked to play out wide. He later moved to Italy's Parma, Japanese team Kashiwa Reysol, and the Chicago Fire in the MLS. He arrived at the 1994 World Cup as the star player on an underrated Bulgarian team that sensationally knocked out Germany before losing the semifinal to Italy. Stoichkov finished the tournament as joint top scorer.

FACT FILE Stoichkov was banned for the 1985–1986 season for his part in a riot involving players and supporters at the 1985 Bulgarian Cup final.

▲ *Stoichkov during the Euro '96 match against Romania. The midfielder's goal won the game.*

DAVID BECKHAM
England, born 1975
Caps: 115 Goals: 17

David Beckham is one of the most recognizable soccer players on the planet. He began his career as a youth-team player at Manchester United and then had a short loan stint with Preston North End, before announcing his arrival in English soccer with a Premiership goal from inside his own half against Wimbledon. At the 1998 World Cup he was heavily criticized for kicking out at Argentina's Diego Simeone and receiving a red card. But Beckham's excellence for team and country, particularly his trademark swerving free kicks, won back public support—notably when he ensured England's qualification for the 2002 World Cup with a last-gasp free kick against Greece. He also won "the triple" of Champions League, Premiership and FA Cup with Manchester United in 1999. When David Beckham joined Paris Saint-Germain, in 2013, he donated his entire salary to a local children's charity. He became the first English player to win the league in four different countries (England, Spain, the U.S., and France).

▶ *In 2006 David Beckham became the first English player to score in three World Cups. He resigned as captain right after the tournament.*

ANDRÉS INIESTA
Spain, born 1984
Caps: 131 Goals: 13

Quick feet and an even quicker soccer brain has enabled this slight midfielder to become one of the most celebrated players in world soccer. Joining Barcelona as a youth team player, Iniesta later formed a formidable central midfield partnership with Xavi Hernández for both team and country. With Barcelona he has won nine Spanish league championships, four Champions Leagues, and six Spanish Super Cups. Internationally, he has been a crucial part of Spain's success, and scored the winning goal in the 2010 World Cup final.

▲ *Spanish midfield legend Xavi Hernández.*

XAVI HERNÁNDEZ
Spain, born 1980
Caps: 133 Goals: 12

Rising through the ranks of youth and reserve teams at Barcelona, Xavi made his first-team debut in 1998 and played over 750 games for the Spanish club before moving to Qatar in 2015 to play for Al Sadd. With Barcelona, he won eight La Liga titles and four Champions Leagues and enjoyed Euro 2008, 2012, and 2010 World Cup glory with Spain. Brilliant at finding space even in the most crowded parts of the fields, Xavi was known as a passing maestro—enabling his team to keep possession and attack.

MICHEL PLATINI
**France, born 1955
Caps: 72 Goals: 41**

A truly great attacking midfielder, Platini was the glittering jewel in a French side that suffered semifinal heartbreak at the 1982 World Cup. Two years later he was top scorer at the European Championships (nine goals) as France won the title. In partnership with Alan Giresse and Jean Tigana, Platini exhibited immense skill and vision. At club level, Platini played for AS Joeuf, Nancy, and Saint-Étienne before turning down a transfer to Arsenal in favor of Italian giants Juventus in 1982. He was Serie A's leading marksman three times and was crowned European Footballer of the Year three times in a row (1983–1985)—a unique feat. Retiring in 1987, he went on to coach France and then led his country's bid to host the 1998 World Cup. In 2007, he became president of UEFA.

▲ Dragan Dzajic (left) and Willie Morgan wave to the crowd after Yugoslavia's 1-1 tie with Scotland at the 1974 World Cup.

FACT FILE Garrincha retired in 1966, after Brazil's loss to Hungary in the World Cup. Amazingly, in his 50 games it was the only time he was on the losing team for Brazil.

GARRINCHA
**Brazil,
1933-1983
Caps: 50
Goals: 12**

Manuel Francisco dos Santos was nicknamed "Garrincha"—meaning "little bird"—at a young age. A small player at only 5 ft. 6 in. (1.69m) tall, a childhood illness had left his legs distorted, with one bent inward and the other 2.4 in. (6cm) shorter. Yet those who saw Garrincha play remember him as the greatest dribbler in the history of soccer. He also perfected the bending banana kick, which he used to great effect for his club team, Botafogo, scoring 232 goals in 581 games. He also played in Colombia, Italy, and in France for Red Star Paris, but it was on the international stage that Garrincha became famous. He starred

DRAGAN DZAJIC
**Yugoslavia, born 1946
Caps: 85 Goals: 23**

A left-winger for his entire career, Dragan Dzajic boasted lightning-fast acceleration and an eye for a delicate pass. He made more than 580 appearances for Red Star Belgrade, scoring 287 goals, winning five Yugoslav league titles and four Yugoslav Cups. Dzajic also spent two seasons in France, where he scored 31 goals for Bastia. He was part of the Yugoslav team that entered the 1964 Olympics and reached the final of the 1968 European Championships, knocking out World Cup holders England along the way. Dzajic finished the tournament as the top scorer. After retiring from football in 1979, he went on to become sports director of Red Star.

▼ England defender Ray Wilson fails to stop the mesmeric Garrincha as he surges down the wing in the 1962 World Cup quarter-final. Brazil won 3-1.

in the 1958 World Cup, which Brazil won, but went on to eclipse those performances at the 1962 competition. Voted player of the tournament, he was joint leading scorer as he struck two goals to knock out England in the quarterfinal, and then two more to beat Chile in the semifinal. Sadly, his life away from soccer was troubled, and he died of alcohol poisoning at the age of 49.

▲ Platini skips a challenge during France's 4-1 win over Northern Ireland at the 1982 World Cup.

CRISTIANO RONALDO
Portugal, born 1985
Caps: 154 Goals: 85

A winger who, in his later years, has played more as a center-forward, Ronaldo began his career on the Portuguese island of Madeira before joining Sporting Clube de Portugal. After impressing in a pre-season friendly, he joined Manchester United in 2003, where he blossomed into one of the world's greatest attackers, bewildering defenders with tricks and speed, outstanding ball control, and masterful free kicks. His team performances helped to propel Manchester United to three successive Premier League titles as well as the Champions League crown in 2008. Ronaldo joined Real Madrid in 2009 for a world-record fee of about $124 million. He made a huge impact, scoring 450 goals in just 438 games as he won four Champions League and two Spanish league titles with the Spanish giants. He also captained Portugal to Euro 2016 glory before moving to Juventus in 2018, the same year he scored in his eighth consecutive World Cup or European Championship tournament.

FACT FILE Cristiano Ronaldo scored 50 or more goals a season for six seasons in a row for Real Madrid. These include a record 34 hat tricks.

▲ Portugal's Cristiano Ronaldo races forward with the ball at his feet. After Euro 2008, he was appointed captain of the national team.

WORLD-RECORD TRANSFERS

PLAYER	FROM	TO	FEE	YEAR
Neymar (Brazil)	Barcelona	Paris Saint-Germain	$240m	2017
Kylian Mbappé (France)	Monaco	Paris Saint-Germain	$192m	2018
Philippe Coutinho (Brazil)	Liverpool	Barcelona	$129m	2018
Ousmane Dembélé (France)	Borussia Dortmund	Barcelona	$118m	2017
Paul Pogba (France)	Juventus	Manchester United	$108m	2016
Cristiano Ronaldo (Portugal)	Real Madrid	Juventus	$107m	2018
Gareth Bale (Wales)	Tottenham	Real Madrid	$132m	2013
Cristiano Ronaldo (Portugal)	Manchester United	Real Madrid	$124m	2009
Gonzalo Higuain (Argentina)	Napoli	Juventus	$98m	2016
Harry Maguire (England)	Leicester City	Manchester United	$97m	2019
Romelu Lukaku (Belgium)	Everton	Manchester United	$91m	2017

ZINEDINE ZIDANE
France, born 1972
Caps: 108 Goals: 31

The son of Algerian immigrants, Zidane grew up in Marseille with posters of his idol, Uruguayan striker Enzo Francescoli, on his wall. His first club was Cannes, followed by Bordeaux, where he won France's Young Player of the Year award in 1992. In his international debut in 1994, he scored both of France's goals in a 2–2 tie with the Czech Republic. In 1995–1996, Zidane played 57 games—more than any other French player—and he appeared jaded as he underperformed at Euro '96. But a move to Juventus in the same year saw him regain his best form, as he helped the Serie A giants win two league titles. Zidane was a key part of the world-beating French team that captured a double of World Cup (1998) and European Championships (2000). As the best midfielder in the world, he won World Player of the Year titles in 1998, 2000, and 2003. Zidane's last tournament, the 2006 World Cup, was memorable as he led France to the final, scoring three goals on the way and being voted FIFA's player of the tournament. He was sent off in the final, however, for a headbutt to the chest of Italy's Marco Materazzi.

ENZO SCIFO
Belgium, born 1966
Caps: 84 Goals: 18

One of only a handful of players to have taken part in four World Cups, Vicenzo "Enzo" Scifo (see page 87) was born to Italian parents and became a Belgian citizen at the age of 18. He was a teenage soccer prodigy, scoring a staggering 432 goals in just four seasons as a junior. After joining Anderlecht in 1980, his smooth midfield skills helped the club win three Belgian league titles in a row (1985–1987), while with the national team he reached the semifinals of the 1986 World Cup. Scifo's moves to Internazionale and then Bordeaux were both failures, but his career was reignited at Auxerre. He went on to enjoy stints in Italy, before rejoining Anderlecht toward the end of his career.

LUIS FIGO
Portugal, born 1972
Caps: 127 Goals: 32

A darting wide midfielder, Luis Figo won the European Cup-Winners' Cup in 1997 and back-to-back Spanish league titles in 1998 and 1999 with Spanish giants Barcelona. He moved for a world-record fee to Barcelona's fiercest rivals, Real Madrid, winning two league titles and the Champions League in 2002. Figo played at three European Championships, reaching the semifinals in 2000 and the final four years later. In 2005, he came out of international retirement to help Portugal qualify for the 2006 World Cup, where they reached the semifinal.

▲ Hagi pushes forward at the 1994 World Cup.

GHEORGHE HAGI
Romania, born 1965
Caps: 125 Goals: 34

Moody, unpredictable, and outstandingly skillful, Hagi played for Steaua Bucharest from 1987, either in midfield or in a free role in attack. His superb ball skills and vision helped his club to three league titles in a row, as well as to the 1989 European Cup final. Hagi then played for Real Madrid, Brescia, Barcelona, and Galatasaray, with whom he won the 2000 UEFA Cup. A linchpin of the Romanian team, Hagi scored a sublime goal from 115 ft. (35m) out against Colombia at the 1994 World Cup, but he was sent off in his final international match, at Euro 2000.

▲ Boniek scored all three goals in this 3–0 victory for Poland over Belgium at the 1982 World Cup.

ZBIGNIEW BONIEK
Poland, born 1956
Caps: 80 Goals: 24

A hardworking attacking midfielder, Boniek won two league titles with Widzew Lodz and starred when the Polish team knocked Juventus out of the 1980 UEFA Cup. He joined the Italian team two years later and formed a deadly midfield partnership with Michel Platini. At Juventus, he won Italian league and cup titles, the European Cup-Winners' Cup, and the 1985 European Cup (scoring the two winning goals). A member of three World Cup teams, Boniek scored four goals in 1982, with Poland finishing third. After joining Roma in 1985, he operated deeper and deeper in midfield, and he played as a sweeper in the 1986 World Cup.

> **FACT FILE** Michael Laudrup is the only player to have appeared for Real Madrid in a 5–0 win over Barcelona and also for Barcelona when they have beaten Real 5–0.

▶ Michael Laudrup challenges for the ball during Denmark's Euro '96 match with Portugal.

SOCRATES
Brazil, 1954–2014
Caps: 60 Goals: 22

Named after the Ancient Greek scholar, Brazil's Socrates played as an amateur for Botafogo while studying to become a doctor. He turned professional with Corinthians in 1977. The tall, elegant midfielder became a firm favorite with the fans, scoring spectacular goals and threading superb passes around the field. He captained two hugely talented Brazilian World Cup sides in 1982 and 1986, but neither team did its talent justice.

> **FACT FILE**
> In November 2004, at the age of 50, Socrates played for English nonleague side Garforth Town in the Northern Counties League.

MICHAEL LAUDRUP
Denmark, born 1964
Caps: 104 Goals: 37

The peak of Michael Laudrup's international career came in the quarterfinals of the 1998 World Cup, where Denmark lost narrowly to Brazil 3–2—despite his younger brother, Brian, scoring a goal. Laudrup was much in demand as an attacking midfielder, playing for Lazio and Juventus in Italy and winning five league titles in Spain with Barcelona and Real Madrid. Sadly, he missed out on Denmark's finest hour—its Euro '92 championship triumph, when he argued about tactics with the coach and was dropped from the team.

▲ *Lothar Matthäus appeared at five World Cups.*

LOTHAR MATTHÄUS
West Germany / Germany, born 1961 Caps: 150 Goals: 23

Matthäus began his career at Borussia Mönchengladbach before moving to Bayern Munich in 1984. A powerful midfielder with great stamina, Matthäus could play as a midfield anchor or be more creative, using his passing and vision to bring others into the game. He won six Bundesliga titles at Bayern Munich, plus the Serie A title with Internazionale. A veteran of five World Cups, Matthäus played a record 25 tournament games. He led West Germany to World Cup glory in 1990 and in the same year he was voted World Footballer of the Year. He retired from international football after Euro 2000.

LUKA MODRIC
Croatia, born 1983 Caps: 118 Goals: 14

A finalist with Croatia at the 2018 World Cup, where he was voted the tournament's best player, Modric is a skilled playmaker with an eye for the perfect pass. After long stints with Dinamo Zagreb and Tottenham Hotspur, Modric joined Real Madrid in 2012 with whom he has won four Champions Leagues. In 2018, following his enduring excellence, he won the Ballon D'Or as the world's best soccer player.

SUN WEN
China, born 1973 Caps: 152 Goals: 106

A legend in women's soccer, Sun Wen won seven regional championships with Chinese team Shanghai TV, before moving to the United States in 2000 to play for Atlanta Beat. Playing in midfield or attack, she has become one of the world's leading international goalscorers, thanks to her strong shooting, vision, and eye for a goal. Sun Wen won both the Golden Boot (top scorer) and the Golden Ball (top player) awards at the 1999 Women's World Cup, where China was narrowly beaten on penalties in the final by the United States. In 2000, she was named FIFA World Player of the Century alongside the U.S. player Michelle Akers. After China's surprise World Cup exit at the hands of Canada in 2003, she retired.

▲ *Sun Wen goes past Ghana's Mavis Danso at the 2003 World Cup. China won the game 1–0, courtesy of a goal from Sun.*

JAIRZINHO
Brazil, born 1944 Caps: 82 Goals: 34

Jair Ventura Filho, better known as "Jairzinho," was an electrifying right-winger in a similar mold to his childhood hero, Garrincha. First capped for Brazil in 1964, he was moved to the left wing to accommodate Garrincha in the 1966 World Cup. At the 1970 tournament Jairzinho was moved back to his favored right side, where he shone, scoring in each of the six rounds of the competition—a record to this day. At club level, Jairzinho spent most of his career at Brazil's Botafogo, also having short stints with Marseille in France, Portuguesa in Venezuela, and the Brazilian side Cruzeiro, with whom he won the Copa America in 1976.

◀ *Jairzinho surges forward during the third-place play-off at the 1974 World Cup. Brazil were defeated 1–0 by Poland.*

STRIKERS

JOHAN CRUYFF
Holland, 1947–2016
Caps: 48 Goals: 33

Cruyff was one of the game's finest ever players and a pivotal part of the Dutch "total soccer" revolution. Blessed with great vision and remarkable ball skills, he is the only player to have a move named after him—the Cruyff turn. He won three European Cups in a row at Ajax, before following his ex-boss, Rinus Michels, to Barcelona in 1973 and helping them to win Spanish league and cup titles. Cruyff played as a center-forward, but would drift around the field, creating confusion among defenders. His total of 33 goals for the Netherlands would have been higher were it not for his refusal to play in the 1978 World Cup (see page 112). Cruyff later managed both Ajax and Barcelona to success in Europe.

► *Johan Cruyff was European Footballer of the Year three times.*

PAOLO ROSSI
Italy, born 1956
Caps: 48 Goals: 20

As a teenager, Paolo Rossi was released by Juventus due to a knee injury, but he went on to star for Italy at the 1978 World Cup. Juve tried to buy him back from Vicenza, but was outbid by Perugia, who paid a world-record fee of $6.6 million. A two-year ban for alleged game-fixing ended just before the 1982 World Cup, by which time Rossi was back at Juventus. After failing to score in the first four games of the tournament, the pressure was mounting. He responded with a fine hat trick against Brazil, followed by two goals in the semifinal and one in the final to emerge as a World Cup winner and the tournament's leading scorer. Sadly, he was overcome by injuries and he retired in 1987, aged 30.

▼ *Puskas (left) fires in a shot in the 1954 World Cup final against West Germany. His goalscoring ratio at international level—almost one goal per game—was extraordinary.*

FACT FILE In his distinguished career, Puskas won five Spanish league titles, four Hungarian league titles, an Olympic gold medal (1952), and three European Cups.

FERENC PUSKAS
Hungary, 1927–2006
Caps: 84 (4 for Spain)
Goals: 83

A star for his club, Kispest (which became Honved), and his country, Puskas was short, stocky, and an average header of the ball. But his sublime skills, vision, and thunderbolt of a left-foot shot made him a devastating striker. After the Hungarian revolution in 1956, Puskas searched for a club in western Europe for more than a year. In his thirties and overweight, he was eventually signed by Real Madrid in 1958. He repaid Real's faith by heading the Spanish goalscoring table four times, netting four goals in the 1960 European Cup final and a hat trick in the 1962 final. In 1966 he began a coaching career, which saw him take Greek side Panathinaikos to the 1971 European Cup final. In 1993 an emotional Puskas was welcomed home to act as caretaker manager of the national team.

FACT FILE George Best made 466 appearances for Manchester United between 1963 and 1974, scoring 178 goals. He was a substitute only once.

GEORGE BEST
Northern Ireland, 1946–2005
Caps: 37 Goals: 9

Best was only 17 when he made his first-team debut for Manchester United. He was the most gifted player to emerge from the British Isles—and its first superstar. A free spirit both on and off the pitch, Best's goalscoring exploits and his eye for an outrageous pass or move quickly made him a legend. He was also a fearless tackler and great dribbler and was Manchester United's leading scorer five seasons in a row. Sadly, he was denied the biggest stage of all as Northern Ireland failed to qualify for the World Cup during his playing career. In 1974 Best sensationally retired from the game. He made a series of comebacks in England, the U.S., and, finally, Australia, where he appeared for the Brisbane Lions in 1983.

◄ *George Best was first capped for his country, Northern Ireland, at the tender age of 17.*

LIONEL MESSI
Argentina, born 1987
Caps: 128 Goals: 65

Locals in the Argentinian city of Rosario knew they were seeing a special talent when Messi, not yet in his teens, powered his local children's soccer team to lose just one game in four years. Moving from Argentina to Spain at the age of 13, Messi was schooled on Barcelona's youth sides before making his official debut for the first team at the age of 17. He has already won ten Spanish league and four UEFA Champions League titles with Barcelona, as well as over ten Spanish cup competitions and a 2008 Olympic gold medal with Argentina. His close control, vision, and flair is almost unparalleled in the modern game. The 2009–2010 season saw Messi score 47 goals, including all four goals in Barcelona's Champions League mauling

of Arsenal, and the following season he upped this to a staggering 73 goals in all competitions. Messi has not let up since and in March 2018 scored his 600th career goal for Barcelona and is La Liga's all-time leading goalscorer.

▶ Lionel Messi controls the ball during the 2012–2013 season, in which he scored 60 goals.

DENNIS BERGKAMP
Holland, born 1969
Caps: 79 Goals: 37

Named after the Scottish striker Denis Law, Bergkamp was a product of the famous Ajax youth academy. He played in the Dutch league for the first time in 1986. The most technically gifted Dutch soccer player since Cruyff, Bergkamp often played in the space between midfield and attack, where he used his eye for an unexpected pass, plus world-class technique, to create as many goals as he scored. After an unsuccessful spell at Internazionale, Bergkamp moved to Arsenal for $12 million in 1995. In his 11 years at the club, he won three Premier League titles and scored or set up more than 280 goals. He retired in May 2006 after the final of the Champions League against Barcelona.

▲ Dennis Bergkamp brings the ball down moments before his sublime goal against Argentina at the 1998 World Cup.

FACT FILE
Dennis Bergkamp's fear of flying caused the striker to miss many international matches and European games for Arsenal.

Roa

Bergkamp 1   Bergkamp 2

Ayala 2

Ayala 1

GAME ACTION

Dennis Bergkamp broke the deadlock in a tense 1998 World Cup quarterfinal against Argentina with a sensational goal. On the stroke of 90 minutes, Frank de Boer hit a 164-ft. (50-m) pass into the penalty area. Controlling the ball with one delicate touch of his right boot, Bergkamp took a second touch to turn Argentinian defender Roberto Ayala, before shooting powerfully past goalie Carlos Roa. The goal saw Bergkamp become the Netherland's leading international scorer.

JUST FONTAINE
France, born 1933
Caps: 21 Goals: 30

Fontaine was born and brought up in Morocco before coming to France in 1953 to play for Nice. A relatively slight center-forward with a real eye for goal, he scored 45 times in three seasons at Nice before moving to Stade de Reims, where he achieved 116 goals in only four years. Yet going into the 1958 World Cup finals, Fontaine was third-choice striker behind Raymond Kopa and René Bliard. An injury to Bliard allowed Fontaine to start the first game against Paraguay, in which he scored a hat trick. He followed this with a further ten goals in five games. His record of 13 goals at a single World Cup is unlikely to be beaten. In 1962 Fontaine retired after suffering the second double fracture of his right leg. The following year, he became the first president of the French footballers' union.

ROBERTO BAGGIO
Italy, born 1967
Caps: 57 Goals: 27

Blessed with great skill and vision, Roberto Baggio made his professional debut with Vicenza (in the Italian third division) at just 15 years of age. He broke into Italy's Serie A with Fiorentina in 1985, and when Baggio was transferred to Juventus in 1990, three days of rioting by Fiorentina fans ensued. The fee of $13 million made him the world's most expensive player at that time. Crowned World Footballer of the Year in 1993, Baggio scored spectacular goals for his country and his clubs, AC Milan, Bologna, Inter Milan, and Brescia. In 2004, while playing for Brescia, he scored his 200th Serie A goal. He appeared in three World Cups and scored five out of Italy's eight goals in the 1994 competition. However, Baggio will always be remembered for his costly penalty miss in the final of the tournament (see page 32). The striker was given an emotional sendoff in 2004 when he played for Italy for the first time in five years, in an exhibition game against Spain.

RAÚL
Spain, born 1977
Caps: 102 Goals: 44

Raúl González Blanco made his debut for the Real Madrid first team at 17—their youngest ever player—and went on to score six times in his first 11 games. In the years that followed, Raúl became the biggest star in Spanish soccer and the country's all-time leading goalscorer. At club level, he has won two Spanish league championships and three Champions League titles with Real Madrid. Twice the top scorer in the Spanish league, Raúl's goals in the 2003–2004 Champions League campaign saw him become the first player to score more than 40 times in the competition.

GERD MÜLLER
West Germany, born 1945
Caps: 62 Goals: 68

"The Bomber," as Gerd Müller was nicknamed, holds a series of goalscoring records. From 1963, he scored a club record 365 goals in 427 league matches for Bayern Munich. During 16 years with Bayern, he won four Bundesliga titles, four German Cups and three European Cups. For his country, Müller held one of the greatest international striking records, scoring more than a goal every game. His two strikes against the Soviet Union helped West Germany win the 1972 European Championships. Müller's tally of 14 World Cup goals remained a record until 2006, while his final international goal won West Germany the 1974 World Cup on home soil.

▼ *Gerd Müller shoots during West Germany's win over Morocco in the 1970 World Cup.*

▲ *Spain's Raúl was the top scorer during the qualifying rounds for Euro 2000, with ten goals from eight games. Here, he chases down the ball during Euro 2004.*

ZICO
Brazil, born 1953
Caps: 72 Goals: 52

The youngest and smallest of three soccer-crazy brothers, Artur Antunes Coimbra (known as Zico) was given a special diet and training regime to build him up when he first arrived at the Brazilian club Flamengo. Sharp, quick-witted, and with the ability to hit an explosive shot or take a deadly, curling free kick, Zico won four Brazilian league titles with Flamengo, as well as the Copa Libertadores and the World Club Cup (both in 1981). He scored a staggering 591 goals in his first 11 seasons with Flamengo and returned to the club in 1985 after a spell at the Italian Serie A side Udinese. Zico retired from international soccer after the 1986 World Cup final, but went on to play in Japan for Kashima Antlers. In 2002, he became manager of the Japanese national team.

BOBBY CHARLTON
England, born 1937
Caps: 106 Goals: 49

Apart from a final season with Preston North End, Charlton was a one-team player with Manchester United, for whom he made his debut in 1956. Known around the globe for his trophy-winning exploits in both the World Cup and the European Cup, Charlton was one of the few survivors of the devastating Munich, Germany, airplane crash, which claimed the lives of many of his Manchester United teammates. As a player he showed great sportsmanship and dedication—in training, he even wore a slipper on his right foot to encourage him to pass and shoot with his weaker left foot. Operating as a deep-lying center-forward with a phenomenal shot from either foot, Charlton remains the record goalscorer for both England and Manchester United, scoring 245 times and making 751 appearances in total for the club. He was knighted in 1994.

▼ Bobby Charlton's 1970 World Cup campaign was his fourth in a row as part of the England squad.

◄ Roger Milla challenges for the ball during Cameroon's second-round victory over Colombia at the 1990 World Cup.

FACT FILE In 1990, Andriy Shevchenko played for the Kiev under-14 team in a youth tournament in Wales. Welsh striker Ian Rush was so impressed, he gave the young Ukrainian his soccer cleats.

ROGER MILLA
Cameroon, born c.1952
Caps: 81 Goals: 42

Roger Milla's celebratory corner-flag dance remains the most memorable image of the 1990 World Cup, as his four goals helped Cameroon to become the first African side to reach the quarterfinals. In the same year, the veteran striker was voted the African Footballer of the Year. He had won the award before, in 1976, the year he moved from Cameroon's Tonnerre Yaoundé to play for Valenciennes in France. Milla went on to play for Monaco, Bastia, and Saint-Etienne, and won the African Nations Cup twice with Cameroon (1984 and 1988). At the age of 42, he came out of retirement for the 1994 World Cup to become the oldest-ever player and scorer in the competition.

ANDRIY SHEVCHENKO
Ukraine, born 1976
Caps: 111 Goals: 48

Shevchenko scored just one goal in 16 games in his first season at Dynamo Kiev, but his perfect blend of speed and power propelled Kiev to five Ukrainian league titles and strong showings in the Champions League. A multimillion-dollar transfer to AC Milan followed in 1999. On three occasions Shevchenko scored 24 goals per season in the ultratough Italian league. In 2004 he was voted European Footballer of the Year. Two years later he moved to Chelsea for just over $57 million but returned to Milan on loan for the 2008–2009 season. He then returned to Kiev, where he made more than 80 appearances before retiring in 2012.

▲ Andriy Shevchenko shoots for Ukraine against England during a friendly international in 2000.

CAROLINA MORACE
Italy, born 1964
Caps: 153 Goals: 105

Italy's finest female player, Morace made her international and Women's Serie A debut at the age of only 14. She went on to win 12 league titles with eight different clubs, and scored more than 500 goals. A lethal finisher, Morace was twice runner-up with Italy in the European Championships. After retiring in 1999, she became the first female coach of an Italian men's professional team, Viterbese in Serie C. She later became coach of the Italian women's national side.

▲ Ruud Gullit shoots against England at Euro '88.

RUUD GULLIT
Netherlands, born 1962
Caps: 66 Goals: 17

In 1978 the dreadlocked Gullit started out as a sweeper for Dutch side Haarlem. He possessed great attacking flair, stamina, a tough tackle, and a powerful pass. He was the subject of feverish transfer activity, moving to Feyenoord, PSV Eindhoven, and AC Milan, with whom he won European Cups in 1989 and 1990. After a season at Sampdoria he moved to Chelsea, and in 1996 he was appointed player-coach of the London club. By winning the 1997 FA Cup he became the first non-British coach to obtain a major domestic trophy in England.

KENNY DALGLISH
Scotland, born 1951
Caps: 102 Goals: 30

The only player to have scored more than 100 goals for both English and Scottish top-division clubs, Dalglish gave defenders nightmares. He became a legend at Celtic—where he won four league titles and four Scottish Cups—thanks to a quicksilver turn and an icy coolness in front of goal. In 1977 Liverpool signed Dalglish as a replacement for Kevin Keegan. He became Liverpool's player-coach in 1985, winning three league titles. He won a fourth in 1995 with Blackburn Rovers to become one of the few coaches to win the English league with different clubs.

DIEGO MARADONA
Argentina, born 1960
Caps: 91 Goals: 34

Diego Armando Maradona was a phenomenal soccer player. Stocky and with a low center of gravity, he conjured mesmeric, weaving runs through the tightest defenses, lightning turns that left opposition players kicking at thin air, and sublime shots, chips, and flicks. Maradona debuted at the age of 15 for Argentinos Juniors. Calls for his inclusion in the 1978 World Cup team were ignored by Argentina's coach, Cesar Luis Menotti, but he would appear at the next four tournaments. His finest hour came in 1986, when Maradona was the player of the tournament as he skippered an unremarkable side to World Cup victory (see pages 56–57). Maradona captained Argentina at the 1990 World Cup, where he reached the final, but the following year he failed a drugs test and was banned for 15 months. A further failed test during the 1994 World Cup saw him sent home after playing the first two games. His international career was over. Since then Maradona has battled with drug addiction, but in 2000 he was the joint winner of FIFA's Footballer of the Century award with Pelé.

▲ As well as appearing for Real Madrid (pictured) and Spain, Di Stefano also played seven unofficial games for Argentina and four for Colombia.

FACT FILE Diego Maradona's moves to Barcelona in 1982 (for $7 million) and then to Napoli in 1984 (for $8.7 million) were both world-record transfers. After nine years at Napoli and a spell at Sevilla, he returned to Argentina with Newell's Old Boys and Boca Juniors.

▼ The magical Maradona brings the ball under control at the 1986 World Cup.

ALFREDO DI STEFANO
Spain, 1926–2014
Caps: 31 Goals: 23

To many people, Di Stefano was the "complete" player, years ahead of his time. His astonishing energy helped him play all over the field—defending, tackling, unselfishly distributing the ball, and creating chances for others as well as for himself. Born in a poor suburb of Buenos Aires, he played for his father's old club, River Plate, in a relentless forward line known as *La Máquina* ("the Machine"). A move to Europe in 1953 saw him become part of the legendary Real Madrid team that dominated Europe in the 1950s and early 1960s. Di Stefano formed a deadly partnership with Ferenc Puskas, scoring in five European Cup finals in a row. Real Madrid player and coach Miguel Muñoz explained: "The greatness of Di Stefano was that with him in your side, you had two players in every position."

JÜRGEN KLINSMANN
**West Germany/Germany,
born 1964 Caps: 108 Goals: 47**

Sharp and athletic around the penalty area and an outstanding goal poacher, Klinsmann was German Footballer of the Year in his first spell at VfB Stuttgart. He then moved to Internazionale, where he won the 1989 Serie A title. He was part of West Germany's 1990 World Cup-winning side, scored five goals in the 1994 competition, and captained the team at the 1998 tournament. Klinsmann enjoyed spells with Monaco and, in 1994, the first of two stints with Tottenham Hotspur. The British media and some supporters were suspicious of a player who had a reputation for diving to win free kicks and penalties. But in his first Premiership season, Klinsmann's performances and 29 goals won the support of many fans, and in 1995 he was voted England's Footballer of the Year. The striker moved to Bayern Munich, Sampdoria, and Tottenham once again before retiring in 1998. In 2004 he was appointed Germany's manager and coached an exciting side to third place at the 2006 World Cup.

▲ *Jürgen Klinsmann surges forward with the ball during Germany's Euro '96 qualifying campaign.*

FACT FILE Luigi Riva had such a fearsome shot that he once broke the arm of a spectator.

EUSEBIO
**Portugal, 1942—2014
Caps: 64 Goals: 41**

Eusebio da Silva Ferreira was the first African soccer superstar. Lethal in the air and equipped with a power-packed right-foot shot, he scored an incredible 727 goals in 715 professional games. Eusebio played his early soccer for Sporting Lourenço Marques in his home country of Mozambique— a Portugese colony at the time. The striker was at the center of one of the fiercest transfer disputes when he arrived in Portugal. He was virtually kidnapped by Benfica to keep him away from rivals Sporting Lisbon. Benfica's $21,000 purchase proved to be one of the buys of the century. Over a 15-year career with Benfica, Eusebio scored at an awe-inspiring ratio of more than a goal per game. He was the Portuguese league's top goalscorer seven times, twice the leading goalscorer in the whole of Europe and the 1966 World Cup's top scorer, with nine goals for Portugal.

CARLI LLOYD
**USA, born 1982
Caps: 266 Goals: 105**

A livewire attacker with stamina, speed, and a lethal shot, Lloyd played for W-League team New Jersey Splash while still at High School. She made her international debut at age 23 and became a fixture in the U.S. women's team that won two Olympic gold medals and the 2015 World Cup. In that competition, Lloyd was at her best, scoring six times, including a hat trick in the final that featured a goal from the halfway line. Lloyd was made player of the tournament and was also voted the world's best female soccer player in both 2015 and 2016. In 2017, after having played for nine American clubs, including Chicago Red Stars and Western New York Flash, she crossed the Atlantic to move to Manchester City, returning to U.S. club Sky Blue FC in 2018.

▲ *Benfica's Eusebio (right) competes for the ball with Cesare Maldini of AC Milan during the 1963 European Cup final.*

GEORGE WEAH
**Liberia, born 1966
Caps: 61 Goals: 22**

In 1988 the Monaco manager Arsène Wenger, shrewdly plucked the young, raw Weah from Cameroon side Tonnerre Yaoundé. Weah exploded onto the European scene, winning the French league with Monaco in 1991 and Paris Saint-Germain in 1994, before moving to AC Milan. A truly devastating finisher, Weah scored many spectacular goals to help AC Milan win two Serie A titles. He was voted African Footballer of the Year four times, and also won European and World Player of the Year awards in 1995 and FIFA's Fair Play Award the following year. He had short spells at Chelsea, Manchester City and in the United Arab Emirates late in his career, before retiring in 2002. A UNICEF ambassador since 1997, Weah has invested much time and money helping to build schools and clinics in his war-torn home country, Liberia.

FACT FILE In 1996 George Weah paid for his teammates' kit and expenses so that Liberia could enter the African Nations Cup.

RONALDO
Brazil, born 1976
Caps: 98 Goals: 62

Ronaldo Luis Nazario de Lima became a hot commodity as an 18-year-old by scoring 58 goals in 60 games for Brazil's Cruzeiro. Ronaldo moved to PSV Eindhoven and then Barcelona, where his close control and devastating bursts of speed helped him become Europe's top scorer in 1996–1997, with 34 goals. He was sold to Internazionale and was its top scorer in his first season. He then endured four injury-ravaged years, and, after a disappointing performance in the 1998 World Cup final, many doubted his ability, but he bounced back in 2002 as the tournament's top scorer. One month later, Real Madrid paid $46.6 million for the Brazilian, and in 2006 Ronaldo became the highest scorer in World Cup history, with 15 goals. In 2007, he moved to Italian giants AC Milan, and in 2009 to Brazilian team Corinthians.

FACT FILE
Ronaldo's ex-wife, Milene Domingues, broke the world record for keeping a soccer ball off the ground in 1995. She kept the ball in the air for nine hours and six minutes, making 55,187 touches in the process.

▼ Ronaldo shows his speed against Italy. In 2002 he won his third FIFA World Player of the Year award.

MIA HAMM
USA, born 1972
Caps: 276
Goals: 158

Born with a partial club foot that had to be corrected by casts, Mia Hamm went on to become the world's most famous female soccer player. She was the youngest player ever for the U.S. women's team when she debuted against China at the age of 15, and the youngest member of the U.S. team that won the 1991 World Cup. Hamm played in three more World Cups and won two Olympic gold medals and one silver. A phenomenal all-round player with an icy-cool finish, she was the leading scorer in the history of women's international soccer for a decade. Hamm was also a founding member of WUSA, playing for Washington Freedom when the league began in 2001.

HENRIK LARSSON
Sweden, born 1971
Caps: 104 Goals: 37

A goalscoring predator, Larsson played in Sweden before being signed by Feyenoord coach Wim Jansen in 1993. Four years later Jansen, by then the manager of Celtic, signed him again. Larsson became the Scottish Premier League's most feared striker, with 28 or more goals in five of his seven seasons. He retired from internationals in 2002, but changed his mind to help Sweden qualify for Euro 2004. Larsson then moved to Barcelona. In his final match for the Spanish side, the 2006 Champions League final, he came on as a substitute to play a key role in Barcelona's win. The striker returned to his former side, Helsingborg, before moving to Manchester United on loan in 2007.

◄ The legendary Mia Hamm playing for the United States at the Women's Gold Cup in 2002. In the final against Canada, her "golden goal" in extra time secured the trophy.

MARTA VIEIRA DA SILVA
Brazil, born 1986
Caps: 133 Goals: 110

Short for a striker, at under 1.6m tall, Marta is a goal-scoring dynamo who was voted the world's best female player five years in a row (2006–10). She played her early football for several Brazilian clubs before two spells in Sweden, either side of three seasons in the USA, where she won the Women's Professional Soccer (WPS) championship twice with two different clubs – FC Gold Pride and Western New York Flash. A truly prolific finisher, she averages close to a goal per game for club and country. Marta has also won four Swedish league titles with Umeå IK, one with Tyresö FF and the 2014 title with FC Rosengård.

◄ Barcelona's Henrik Larsson battles for the ball in a friendly against Japan's Kashima Antlers.

PELÉ
Brazil, born 1940
Caps: 92 Goals: 77

Edson Arantes do Nascimento simply had it all. Considered the finest soccer player of all time, Pelé was a masterful attacker with seemingly limitless skills, creativity, and vision. He was magnificent in the air, lethal on the ground, could dribble, pass, and take swerving free kicks, and saw passes and opportunities that other players could not. His father had been a striker for Fluminense, and at 11 years of age Pelé was spotted by a former Brazil player, Waldemar de Brito, who took him to Clube Atletico Bauru. Four years later, Pelé trialled at Santos, for whom he made his debut at age 15. He would play for the São Paulo side for the next 18 years. Pelé was only 17 when he appeared at the 1958 World Cup, scoring a hat trick in the semifinal and two superb goals in the final as Brazil won their first World Cup. A pulled muscle cut short Pelé's involvement in the 1962 competition, and he had to be content with winning the World Club Cup for Santos. Injured by brutal tackling in the 1966 World Cup, Pelé was outstanding at the 1970 tournament. He retired from international football in 1971—in front of around 180,000 fans at the Maracana Stadium—and from club soccer in 1974. In tribute, Santos removed the number ten shirt from its team lineup.

Pelé later came out of retirement to play in a star-studded lineup at New York Cosmos. He went on to become Brazil's minister of sports and a United Nations (UN) and UNICEF ambassador. He remains one of the most respected figures in world soccer, and in 1999 he was voted Athlete of the Century by the International Olympic Committee.

▶ Pelé battles for the ball with an Italian defender at the 1970 World Cup.

FACT FILE Pelé's father once scored five headed goals in one game, a feat Pelé never managed. However, his header in the 1970 World Cup final was Brazil's 100th World Cup goal.

GAME ACTION

Against Uruguay in the 1970 World Cup semifinal, Pelé came close to scoring what would have been one of the greatest goals ever seen. A through pass from Gerson saw Pelé and the Uruguayan goalie Ladislao Mazurkiewicz racing for the ball just outside the penalty area. Pelé made an outrageous dummy to the left, letting the ball run to the other side of the bewildered keeper. The striker sprinted to collect the ball and hit a first-time shot from a tight angle. The ball sped past Uruguayan defender Atilio Ancheta, only to flash mere inches wide of the left post.

▲ Germany's Birgit Prinz is challenged by Norway's Anneli Giske during the UEFA Women's Euro 2009.

BIRGIT PRINZ
Germany, born 1977
Caps: 214 Goals: 128

Apart from a stint in the United States in 2002, where her 12 goals in 15 games helped Carolina Courage to win the WUSA championship, Prinz played all her club soccer for FFC Frankfurt. Here, she won six German league titles and eight German cups, and scored over 250 goals (at a rate better than a goal a game). With Germany, she won two World Cups (2003, 2007), five European Championships, and three Olympic bronze medals—a staggering haul. She was also awarded the FIFA World Women's Footballer of the Year on three occasions and finished second a further four times, the last in 2010, a year before she announced her retirement.

Pelé 2

Ancheta

Mazurkiewicz

Pelé 1

GABRIEL BATISTUTA
Argentina, born 1969
Caps: 77 Goals: 56

Batistuta played one season for each of his home country's three biggest clubs—Newell's Old Boys, River Plate, and Boca Juniors—before moving to Italy in 1991, the year of his international debut. In nine seasons and 269 games at Fiorentina the striker was rarely not at his best, scoring 168 goals. He even stayed with the club after relegation, helping them win promotion back into Serie A. In 2000 he joined Roma for the huge fee of $32 million. There, Batistuta finally won the Serie A title in 2001. A winner of two Copa Americas, Batistuta scored five goals at the 1998 World Cup as Argentina made the quarterfinals. The 2003–2004 season saw him make a lucrative move to Qatar, where he played for Al-Arabi.

MARCO VAN BASTEN
Holland, born 1964
Caps: 58 Goals: 24

One of the coolest finishers in world football, van Basten was just 29 when an ankle injury in the 1993 European Cup final effectively ended his playing career—although he struggled on until 1995. Renowned for spectacular goals in crucial contests, van Basten was European Footballer of the Year three times (1988, 1989 and 1992) and in 1988 he hit the headlines as Holland won the European Championships. He scored a hat-trick against England in the quarter-final, the semi-final winner versus Germany and a breathtaking volley from the tightest of angles in the final against the Soviet Union. With Ajax he won three league titles, scoring 128 goals. He then moved to AC Milan, hitting 90 goals in 147 games and winning three Serie A titles and two European Cups.

▶ *Marco van Basten on the rampage in Holland's 3–1 win over England at Euro '88.*

LEADING INTERNATIONAL GOALSCORERS (TO MAY 2019)

PLAYER	COUNTRY	CAPS	GOALS
Ali Daei	Iran	149	109
Cristiano Ronaldo	Portugal	154	85
Ferenc Puskas	Hungary	84	83
Godfrey Chitalu	Zambia	111	79
Hussein Mohammed	Iraq	137	78
Pelé	Brazil	92	77
Bashar Abdullah	Kuwait	134	75
Sandor Kocsis	Hungary	68	75
Majed Abdullah	Saudi Arabia	139	71
Miroslav Klose	Germany	113	71
Kiatisuk Senamuang	Thailand	134	71
Kinna Phiri	Malawi	115	71

▲ *Argentina's all-time top scorer, Batistuta began the 1994–1995 season by scoring in each of Fiorentina's first 11 games, a Serie A record.*

HUGO SANCHEZ
Mexico, born 1958
Caps: 57 Goals: 26

Mexico's most famous player, Sanchez spent the peak of his playing career in Spain, scoring more than 230 goals for Atlético Madrid and Real Madrid. He formed a lethal partnership with Emilio Butragueno at Real as they won five league titles in a row. Sanchez was La Liga's top scorer in five different seasons and in 1990 he won the European Golden Boot award for a record 38 goals in one season. Sadly, his commitments to European soccer and frequent problems with Mexican soccer officials meant that he appeared in only a fraction of the international games played by his home country. He had a disappointing finish at the 1986 World Cup on home soil, scoring just one goal.

FACT FILE Playing for Manchester City in 1974, Denis Law scored a spunky back-heeled goal but did not celebrate—because the goal relegated his former team, Manchester United.

▲ *Denis Law unleashes a shot during a 1974 World Cup game against Zaire.*

DENIS LAW
Scotland, born 1940
Caps: 55 Goals: 30

In 1962, Manchester United paid $322,000—a world record at the time—to bring the former Huddersfield Town, Manchester City, and Torino striker Denis Law to Old Trafford. The money was well spent, as the quick-witted Scot formed a magnificent forward line with Bobby Charlton and George Best, scoring 160 goals in 222 games for the club. Fast over the ground and brave in the air, Law won the 1964 European Footballer of the Year award, as well as league titles and the European Cup with Manchester United, before moving to Manchester City and then retiring in 1974.

MARADONA'S WORLD CUP

Diego Maradona, the Argentinian striker with magical balance and touch, ended the 1986 World Cup with his hands on the trophy and a highly impressive five goals and five assists. Yet these statistics do not tell the story of his true impact, for Mexico '86 was Maradona's tournament. He roused a fairly ordinary Argentinian side into recapturing soccer's biggest prize (the South Americans had won the trophy on home soil in 1978) and wiped out the memory of a disappointing tournament in 1982.

In a tense quarterfinal against England, controversy raged over Maradona's infamous "hand of God" goal (see right), but his second and winning goal was pure genius. The Argentinian collected the ball in his own half, then dribbled, twisted, and turned through the English defense to score what was later voted the goal of the century. He would score a goal of similar brilliance in the semifinal versus Belgium. At this point, at the age of only 25, Maradona was without doubt the greatest soccer player on the planet.

Diego Maradona, clutching the World Cup after his team's epic 3–2 victory over West Germany in the 1986 final, is carried around the Azteca Stadium on the shoulders of ecstatic Argentinian fans.

► Maradona uses his hand to get the ball past England goalkeeper Peter Shilton to score Argentina's first goal in a 2–1 victory.

THE BRAIN GAME

Soccer is a sport that calls for speed, power, stamina, and skill, but it also demands mental agility. Players with the ability to think one step ahead of the opposition are highly prized, and such skills can win a game for their team. The same applies to managers and coaches. In the run-up to a game they have several key decisions to make. They must decide who to select, which formation to play, and which tactics they will use in their bid to outwit the opposition.

TEAM SELECTION

To a casual spectator, team selection appears simple—just pick the team's best 11 players. With large teams of players, the truth is much more complex. Teams need flair, skill, composure, aggression, sound defensive skills, and goalscoring abilities—all in the right quantities. Some players, despite being soccer superstars, may not play well with each other or work with the rest of the team, while other, less famous players may actually perform a more effective job in a particular game. The way the opposition plays can dictate which players are selected, as can the fitness and performances of individuals. Star players, who would normally be first on the team sheet, may not be picked if they are recovering from injuries or suffering from a lack of confidence. Both young, talented players emerging from the reserve team and experienced veterans at the end of their careers will have strong cases for a place in the team. It all adds up to a complex

▲ In the past, club teams were much smaller. In 1983–1984, Liverpool's league- and European Cup-winning team (above) played 66 games with a squad of just 16. Bruce Grobbelaar, Alan Kennedy, Sammy Lee, and Alan Hansen played in every game.

▼ West Germany manager Josef "Sepp" Herberger (right) is chaired off the field as his team wins the 1954 World Cup. Early in the competition he sent out a weakened team that lost to favorite Hungary. Having already beaten Turkey, Herberger's gamble meant that his team got an easier opponent, meeting Turkey again in a play-off that the Germans won 7–2.

puzzle that coaches must solve. As the legendary Ajax and Netherlands coach Rinus Michels said, "It is an art in itself to compose a starting team, finding the balance between creative players and those with destructive powers, and between defense, construction, and attack—never forgetting the quality of the opposition and the specific pressures of each match."

PICKING AND PLAYING

Picking the right players for the game ahead can be a tricky task. Coaches are often criticized by fans for dropping a favorite player or not playing him or her in the player's favored position. But they have to hold their nerve and go with what they feel is their best team for a particular game. Cesar Luis Menotti was criticized by the Argentinian public and media for refusing to include the teenage prodigy Maradona in his 1978 World Cup team, fielding veteran striker Mario Kempes instead. But Menotti proved himself to be a strong-willed and clever coach, who surprised opponents with an exciting, attacking game, and his team went on to win the tournament by beating the Netherlands in the final.

With large teams, coaches at the top teams often rotate and rest key players. In games against supposedly weaker opposition, they might field an understrength team. While resting your best players and giving young players first-team experience can bring benefits, it is a risky tactic. Liverpool manager Jurgen Klopp rested key players and made nine changes for his side's 2017 FA Cup game against Wolves, who were playing in a division lower. Liverpool were knocked out of the competition, 2-1.

FACT FILE FIFA changed its rules on substitutions in international exhibition games in 2004, limiting a team to six subs. The move was prompted, in part, by the mass substitutions of England coach Sven-Goran Eriksson. In 2003 he made 11 substitutions during a game that Australia won 3-1.

SUBSTITUTIONS

Although they were allowed in some exhibition games, substitutes were not a feature of competitive games until the 1960s. Before this time the lack of subs resulted in all sorts of heroics, from outfield players going in goal to players persevering in spite of a serious injury. One of the most famous examples is that of Manchester City's German goalkeeper Bert Trautmann, who continued playing in the 1956 FA Cup final even though he had broken his neck. Today's coaches have the chance to alter their team selection and tactics by making up to three substitutions in most competitions (more in exhibition games). The timing and choice of substitutes can be crucial. They can bolster a winning team's momentum, help a defense to hold on to a lead, or turn a losing team's fortunes around. In the 2018 World Cup, for example, Belgium were facing an exit with Japan leading 2–0. Belgium manager Roberto Martínez brought on Marouane Fellaini and Nacer Chadli, both of whom scored as Belgium turned the game around and won a thrilling encounter 3–2.

◄ Substitutes can make an immediate impact in some games. Kamil Kopunek celebrates after coming on as substitute and scoring with his very first touch for Slovakia, in their shock win over Italy at the 2010 World Cup.

▼ With Manchester United losing 1–0 to Bayern Munich in the 1999 Champions League final, Alex Ferguson brought on Norwegian striker Ole Gunnar Solskjaer in the 81st minute. After another substitute, Teddy Sheringham, had equalized, Solskjaer scored this memorable winner in injury time.

▲ After leading South Korea to the semifinals of the 2002 World Cup, Dutchman Guus Hiddink— a firm believer in attacking tactics—was made an honorary citizen of South Korea.

FORMATIONS

The way in which a team lines up on the field is known as its formation. The first international soccer game, in 1872, saw two teams field heavily attacking formations. Scotland began playing in a 2-2-6 formation, with two backs, two halfbacks (similar to midfielders), and six attackers. England went even further, playing 1-1-8 (eight forwards), but crowded goal areas saw the game end 0–0.

EVOLVING TACTICS

Although England's eight forwards quickly became a thing of the past, attacker-heavy formations such as 2-3-5 persisted for more than 50 years. A change to the offside law in 1925 (see page 19) reduced the number of players needed between an attacker and the goal from three to two. It gave attackers more scoring chances and forced a rapid rethink for coaches. None was quicker than Arsenal's Herbert Chapman, who, two days after a 7–0 loss to Newcastle, debuted his W-M formation (so named for the shapes the two groups of five players made). The change resulted in a 4–0 win over West Ham. The W-M formation was effectively 3-2-2-3 and was adopted by many sides. Other teams played the *metodo* formation, devised by World Cup-winning Italian coach Vittorio Pozzo. It was also based on 2-3-5, but was effectively 2-3-2-3, with two of the forwards pulled back to link between midfield and attack and to defend against breaks by the opposition.

FOUR AT THE BACK

The arrival of four defenders at the back sounds like a negative formation, but it was first unveiled by the marvellous attacking Brazil team that won the 1958 World Cup. The Brazilian formation was actually 4-2-4, with two wingers up front feeding two central strikers. By the next World Cup, Brazil and many other sides were opting for a slightly less attacking 4-3-3 with an extra player to stop the midfield from being overrun. This formation can work with a single winger who switches flanks at will or it can feature two genuine wingers feeding a single striker. England won the 1966 World Cup playing 4-4-2 with no out-and-out wingers, but they had midfielders with the energy and stamina to add width to an attack, as well as defending

◄ Playing as a wingback, Germany's Philipp Lahm holds off Portugal's Cristiano Ronaldo. Wingbacks play on the flanks. They act like fullbacks in defense, but also make attacking runs up the field.

when necessary. This formation is still widely used today. Ahead of the four-person defense, a coach has plenty of options. He may opt for three attackers upfront (4-3-3) or split strikers (4-4-1-1), or no strikers at all. At the final of Euro 2012, Spain did away with out-and-out strikers, starting the game with three attacking midfielders—David Silva, Cesc Fabregas, and Andrés Iniesta—instead of a regular center-forward. The team beat Italy convincingly, 4–0.

◄ As a coach, Pep Guardiola has won league championships in three countries: Spain, Germany, and England.

▲ The Serbia and Montenegro international Sinisa Mihajlovic enjoyed six glorious seasons at Lazio as a powerful sweeper, strong in defense but with an eye for goal, especially from set pieces.

SWEEPING UP

At many clubs around the world—and in Italian soccer—a different system is used at the back, with a sweeper (also known as a *libero* or "free man") in the center of defense. Sweepers tend to play behind the main line of defenders, literally sweeping up loose balls and acting as a last line of defense if an opposition attack breaks through. In some formations a sweeper can be too negative. This was seen as the case with the *catenaccio* system, invented by Padova coach Nereo Rocco in the early 1950s and popularized by Helenio Herrera's Internazionale side of the 1960s.

▲ Celebrated coach José Mourinho has won league titles in four countries: Portugal, Italy, England, and Spain, but success is not always guaranteed. He was fired from Manchester United after a trophyless season in 2017–2018.

Effectively a 1-4-3-2 or 1-4-4-1 system, *catenaccio* aimed to stifle attacks with large numbers of defenders, relying on counterattacks by a few forwards. Italy has produced a long line of world-class sweepers including Giovanni Facchetti, Gaetano Scirea, and Franco Barcsi. But it took a German, Franz Beckenbauer, to show a different side

▲ A team often alters its formation after a sending off. This team has lost its left midfielder (shown by the red arrow) and switches from a 3-2-3-2 system with wingbacks to a 4-3-1-1 formation with a flat back four, three in midfield, and split strikers up front.

to the sweeper's art. Beckenbauer linked play going forward and would often surge ahead of his defense, creating an extra

player in attack and opening up the game.

Today the sweeper is often replaced by one or more deep-sitting midfielders, one of whom can drop back into defense if a defender pushes forward. These "anchor" or defensive midfielders—such as Spain's Sergio Busquets or France's N'Golo Kanté—are highly prized.

TOTAL SOCCER

"Total soccer" was never quite formation-free soccer, but it did involve players switching positions and roles within the team with amazing frequency. Under Rinus Michels, defenders would crop up in attack, strikers in midfield, and midfielders just about everywhere. It proved a hard system to defend against, but few teams could boast the quality of player to make it work since it relied on excellent ball skills and very high energy levels. Today players switch positions with remarkable ease and regularity, so much so that one might wonder why "total soccer" caused such a stir. Formations in the past were more rigid, however, with fullbacks staying in their half and strikers staying upfield throughout the game. While this gave a team a shape and structure, it could also make it easier for opponents to mark dangerous players and defend.

FORMATIONS

A formation is the way in which a team lines up for a game. This is usually shown in terms of the numbers of outfield players from the defense forward. In reality, soccer is a dynamic game and players move around the field. Sometimes, they are drawn out of position by an opposition attack. At other times, players choose to move out of position. For example, a central striker may drift out wide or drop back to find space.

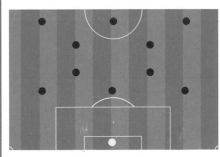

3-2-2-3 formation

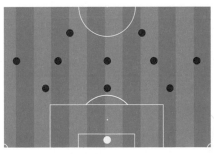

3-5-2 formation

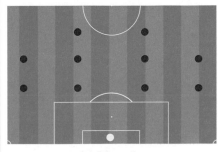

4-4-2 formation

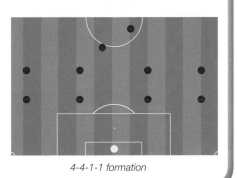

4-4-1-1 formation

TACTICS

Teams may start a game in one of several common formations, but there can be great variation in how they play within that formation and in the tactics they use. For example, a team that lines up as a 4-4-2 side may choose to play defensively, with midfielders helping out, or aggressively, with one or more midfielders joining the strikers in attack.

▲ Clint Dempsey heads the ball during the 2011 CONCACAF Gold Cup final between the U.S. and Mexico. Versatile players such as Dempsey, who could play up front or in several positions in midfield, give a coach more options to change formations and tactics during a game.

TAILORING TACTICS

Coaches start a game with what they feel are the best tactics for the players available and the opposition they face. They closely watch how a game unfolds, knowing that they can change tactics at any time in order to exploit an opponent's weakness or to fix problems in their own team's play. Most top players can play in several positions. A coach may switch formations using the same players or may bring on a substitute with different attributes and skills. In the 2014 World Cup, Netherlands coach Louis van Gaal brought on substitute goalkeeper Tim Krul especially for the penalty shootout with Costa Rica. Krul saved two penalties and the Netherlands won. A year later, at the 2015 Women's World Cup semifinal against Germany, U.S. coach Jill Ellis changed her usual 4-4-2 formation, switching to a 4-2-3-1, which helped her side triumph 2–0.

TACTICS IN DEFENSE

Teams have several choices about how they defend. Some coaches prefer defenders to patrol areas of space that overlap, a system known as zonal marking. This tactic is often used by Argentinian clubs and many national teams. It requires good communication between defenders. Alternatively, each defender marks an individual player, tracking his or her opponent's attacking runs throughout the game. Manchester United's Ander Herrera, for example, man-marked Chelsea's Eden Hazard during their April 2017 league game, restricting Hazard's time on the ball and earning United a 2-0 win. When an opposing team features a dangerous playmaker positioned behind the strikers, a team may nominate an extra central defender to man mark him or her.

▶ The offside trap is a defensive tactic in which the back three or four players move upfield in a straight line to catch an opponent offside. It can be very effective, but may be beaten by a player dribbling through the line or by a well-timed through pass combined with an attacking run.

Jorgensen
Camara
Diouf
Diao 1
Heintze
Fadiga 1

GAME ACTION

One goal down and under pressure from a Danish attack down its right wing, Senegal scored a superb counterattacking goal at the 2002 World Cup. Senegal's Henri Camara made a firm tackle on Martin Jorgensen and played a quick pass down the wing to El Hadji Diouf. Diouf, closely marked by Jan Heintze, spotted Salif Diao's run and back-heeled the ball into his path. Diao hit a perfect pass to Khalilou Fadiga, who was sprinting into the center circle. As Diao continued his run, Fadiga took the ball into the Danish half before playing a perfectly timed through pass. Racing between two defenders, Diao latched onto the ball and coolly sent it into the corner of the goal.

LONG OR SHORT

All teams seek to pass and move the ball into the attacking one third of the field, where goal-scoring chances can be made. The way in which they get the ball there can vary greatly. For many decades British teams favored a direct style with few passes. Coaches believed that hitting long balls toward tall target strikers in the opponent's penalty area created more goal chances, often through a defensive mistake. In continental Europe and elsewhere, a shorter, passing-and-moving game was often preferred, with teams keeping possession for fairly long periods of time as they looked for an opening in the opposition defense. Another tactic, originally favored by many Central and South American teams, is to rely on precise passing and skillful dribbling to get into the opposition penalty area. Some teams play a counterattacking game, defending in large numbers and soaking up pressure. When they retrieve the ball, they move it rapidly out of defense with a long pass or by running with the ball. Fast, accurate counterattacking can catch the opposition off guard and outnumbered but requires players with good speed and awareness. Many coaches alternate their passing and movement tactics—if their team is behind with only minutes to go, for example, they may switch to a direct style, pushing extra players up into the opposition penalty area to look for headers and knockdowns.

◀ *Cristiano Ronaldo practices free kicks at a Portuguese training camp. Attacking set pieces are often planned and worked on hard in practice sessions because they offer a good chance of scoring.*

HIT THE NET

www.fourfourtwo.com/performance/tactics
A collection of great tactical tips and videos from leading coaches.

www.thefalse9.com/category/football-tactics-for-beginners
A great series of articles on different aspects of tactics, from keeping compact in defense to how to counterattack and the role of fullbacks.

www.football-lineups.com/tactic/4-3-1-2
Diagrams and comments on more than 20 different formations used by teams.

Fadiga 2

Diao 2

FACTFILE
Barcelona lost the first leg of their 2017 UEFA Champions League quarterfinal versus Paris Saint-Germain 4-0. In an astonishing comeback, they won the second leg, 6-1, to go through.

▶ *Liverpool's Mohamed Salah dribbles at speed around Manchester City's Aymeric Laporte. Salah can play on the wing, as a second striker, or central attacking midfielder and can even switch positions throughout a match.*

THE COACH'S ROLE

A successful team needs more than great tactics. It needs to be prepared, instructed, and inspired in order to produce a great performance. Motivating players, directing them, and giving them the confidence to perform is all part of a coach's job. Crucially, coaches can determine the tone, style, and attitude of their team through the players they hire and send out onto the field, as well as through their work during training.

THE TEAM BEHIND THE TEAM

Behind the players on a major team is a large team of staff. At the forefront is the coach and his or her assistants, some of whom may specialize in training goalkeepers or strikers or may specifically work with younger players and youth teams. A top club will also include a fitness coach, a dietician, and one or more physiotherapists and medical staff to help with players' preparation and recovery from injury.

▲ José Mourinho oversees a practice session before Real Madrid's 2013 Champions League quarterfinal against Galatasaray. Head coaches like Mourinho are in charge of an array of coaches and physiotherapists, as well as fitness and diet experts.

Videos of games that interest the management are studied in detail, while scouts are employed to check out and report on forthcoming opposition teams and to watch potential transfer targets in action. Many teams also arrange visits from temporary personnel such as sports psychologists, balance and coordination specialists, as well as inspirational figures from other sports.

INS AND OUTS

With soccer teams becoming increasingly big businesses, a coach's ability to deal profitably and successfully in the transfer market is essential. Some coaches are highly prized for their ability to hire players cheaply and sell them for profit or to put together a team on a limited budget that can seriously challenge anyone. European Cup-winning coach Brian Clough was famous for working wonders with bargain buys. Scottish legend Archie Gemmill only cost Clough's Derby team about $160,000. Many clubs today still have an eye for a bargain. Leicester City, for example, bought Riyad Mahrez for $500,000 and N'Golo Kante for $6.9 million. They sold Kante to Chelsea for $39 million and Mahrez to Manchester City for $75 million. Tottenham Hotspur profited after buying Gareth Bale from Southampton $9 million in 2007 and selling him in 2013 to Real Madrid for $109 million. Other managers are rated for their ability to bring promising youngsters through from their youth set-ups or training

▶ In 2011 Porto bought Radamel Falcao from Argentinian club River Plate for less than $8 million. After three seasons, in which he scored 72 goals in 87 games, they sold him on to Atlético Madrid for approximately ten times what they had originally paid.

> **FACT FILE** Irishman Tony Cascarino was sold in 1982 by Crockenhill FC to Gillingham for a new team uniform and some corrugated iron to patch up the ground. The total cost was said to be about $345.

academies, and to attract good players on loan from other clubs to help strengthen their side at key stages of the season.

UNDER PRESSURE

Few people in sport are under as much pressure as the coach of a major club or national team. Coaches stand or fall by their results. In the past some coaches stayed with their teams for season after season. Miguel Munoz, for example, managed Real Madrid for 417 games during the 1960s. At the top level today few coaches stay in charge of the best teams for more than a handful of seasons. In the 2015-2016 season, 66 of the 92 professional English league clubs changed managers. In 2007 Leroy Rosenior became coach of Torquay United, but new owners arrived at the same time. As a result, he was fired after just 10 minutes in charge. Even recent success does not guarantee a long stay. Real Madrid's Vicente del Bosque had delivered two Spanish league titles, two Champions League trophies, and other cups to the Spanish giants in only four years, but he was dismissed in June 2003. In 2008, Roberto Mancini was fired as the head coach of Internazionale right after delivering the team its third Serie A title in a row. In such an unforgiving climate, Alex Ferguson's record of more than 1,500 games in charge of Manchester United is remarkable.

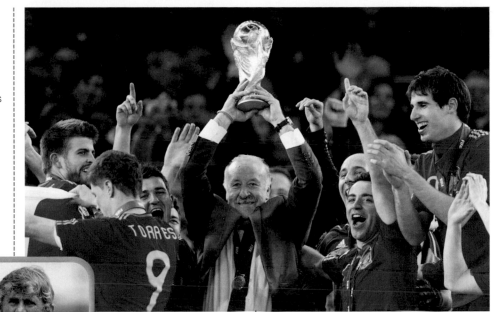

▲ *Vicente del Bosque holds the World Cup after guiding Spain to victory in 2010. A former Real Madrid player and coach, he was voted World Coach of the Year in 2012.*

◄ *Bora Milutinovic led five different countries to successive World Cups—a unique feat in soccer coaching. In 2009 he was appointed coach of Iraq.*

FACT FILE
In a 1999 Spanish second division game, Leganes coach Enrique Martin ran onto the field to run down an opposition player who was clean through on goal. Martin received a ten-game ban.

MANAGERIAL MIGRATIONS
Like modern players, top coaches often move overseas in order to further their coaching careers. While teams such as Germany and Italy have never had a foreign coach, more and more have, including England with Sven-Goran Eriksson and Fabio Capello. In the past British coaches were influential abroad. Willy Garbutt helped shape Genoa into a powerful team, while Fred Pentland coached Athletic Bilbao to Spanish league success in 1930 and 1931. Jimmy Hogan, who used pass-and-move tactics years ahead of his time, worked with Austrian coaching legend Hugo Miesl to set up the Vienna school of soccer. This created the Austrian *Wunderteam* that remained unbeaten in 14 internationals

and narrowly missed out on glory at the 1934 World Cup and 1936 Olympics. Today, managers and coaches switch countries and continents frequently. Dutch coach Guus Hiddink led many European teams as well as the national teams of the Netherlands, South Korea, Australia, Russia, and Turkey, while Italian coach Fabio Capello has led England and, from 2012, the Russian national team. Globetrotting Luis Felipe Scolari has managed 21 clubs all over the world from China and Qatar, to England and Uzbekistan. He has also coached Portugal, Kuwait, and Brazil twice.

▼ *Jürgen Klinsmann was appointed head coach of the U.S. men's team in 2011 and led them to nine wins in 2012, including a victory over Italy. The former German striker has coached a club team for only one season (Bayern Munich, 2008–2009).*

▲ *Jurgen Klopp (right) encourages his Liverpool players during their triumphant 2018–2019 UEFA Champions League campaign. Klopp's team also won the 2019 UEFA Super Cup.*

GREAT COACHES

There have been dozens of truly great managers and coaches in soccer. Some have been masters at discovering new talents and putting together successful teams on tight budgets; others are soccer visionaries who have helped to improve the skills and playing of the world's biggest stars. Below are profiles of eight of the finest coaches in the history of soccer.

HERBERT CHAPMAN
1878-1934

Only four teams have won the English league three seasons in a row, and Chapman created two of them. After arriving at Huddersfield Town in 1921, he won the league in 1924 and 1925. By the time Huddersfield made it three in a row, Chapman had left for Arsenal. They were in 20th place when he took over, but finished the season second, behind his former team. Arsenal went on to win a hat trick of league titles, the first two under Chapman. The Englishman took tactics very seriously, and his W-M formation (see page 60) was used by many teams. He pioneered large-scale youth coaching, undersoil heating, top-class medical facilities, and professional training regimes. Some of his proposals, such as numbered shirts and playing regular evening games under floodlights, were adopted only long after his death.

GIOVANNI TRAPATTONI
Born 1939

Trapattoni's managerial career got off to a flying start when he won the 1973 European Cup Winners' Cup as caretaker coach of AC Milan, for whom he had played as a fearsome center-back. After moving to Milan's great rival Juventus, he enjoyed an unmatched run of success, winning six Serie A league titles, two UEFA Cups and, in 1985, a European Cup. Trapattoni won a further Serie A title with Internazionale in 1989 before moving to Bayern Munich in the 1990s, where he became the first foreign manager to win the Bundesliga. His teams were based on strong defenses, usually with three central defenders linked to exciting attackers who were often bought from overseas. He was finally given a chance to coach the Italian national side at 63 years of age, but the team fell short at the 2002 World Cup and Euro 2004, after which Trapattoni had stints at Benfica, Stuttgart, and Salzburg. Between 2008 and 2013, he was coach of the Republic of Ireland national team.

▲ *Trapattoni argues with the officials during Italy's match against Bulgaria at Euro 2004.*

BELA GUTTMANN
1900-1981

The only coach to have won the top club trophy in both South America and Europe, Guttmann is a coaching legend. He was a gifted amateur player for MTK Budapest and appeared at the 1924 Olympics for Hungary. After retiring in 1935, he embarked on a 40-year-long coaching career that took him to Switzerland, Uruguay, Greece, Portugal, Brazil, Romania, Italy, and Austria. He won national league titles in five different countries, including the 1955 Serie A title with AC Milan; he won the European Cup twice as coach of Benfica and also lifted the Copa Libertadores with Peñarol. He was a great influence on Gusztav Sebes, the coach of the magical Hungarian sides of the 1950s, and his forward-thinking 4-2-4 formation and styles of play are believed to have inspired Brazil to become the great attacking force of the late 1950s onward.

JOCK STEIN
1922-1985

Jock Stein began his coaching career as the assistant coach at Celtic. In 1960 he moved to Dunfermline and beat his old team in the following season to win the Scottish Cup. In 1962 Dunfermline caused a major upset, knocking out top Spanish team Valencia from the Inter-Cities Fairs Cup. Stein moved on to Hibernian for one season before being appointed as the coach of Celtic. He quickly built one of British soccer's finest and most entertaining teams. Under Stein, Celtic won 11 Scottish league titles and, in 1967, overturned the mighty Internazionale to become the first British team to lift the European Cup. The "Big Man" left Celtic in 1977 for an ill-fated stint at Leeds United, but later became Scotland's coach, guiding them to the 1982 and 1986 World Cup tournaments.

FACT FILE In the 1970s, two coaching legends, Jock Stein and Brian Clough, both had stints at Leeds United that lasted only 44 days.

◄ *Herbert Chapman (right) watches an Arsenal match in 1932 alongside trainer Tom Whittaker (left) and star player Alex James.*

SIR ALEX FERGUSON
Born 1941

As European soccer's longest-serving top-class coach, Sir Alex Ferguson took Manchester United to a record 13 Premier League titles and the 1999 and 2008 Champions League crowns. A ruthless and highly driven player, Ferguson carried those attributes into his coaching career, first with East Stirling and then at St. Mirren and Aberdeen. He broke the monopoly of Celtic and Rangers to win three Scottish league titles; in 1983, his team defeated Real Madrid to lift the European Cup Winners' Cup. Ferguson also served as assistant Scotland coach under Jock Stein, taking over in 1985. At Manchester United, Ferguson developed young talents such as David Beckham and Ryan Giggs and proved to be a masterful player of mind games with rival coaches. Knighted in 1999, for his services to the game, Sir Alex announced his retirement from club coaching at the end of the 2012–2013 season, after 26 years with Manchester United.

> **FACT FILE** Alex Ferguson has only been fired once, in 1978, when Scottish club St. Mirren dismissed him for a range of offenses that included "unpardonable swearing at a lady."

RINUS MICHELS
1928-2005

The man behind "total soccer," which revolutionized both Ajax and the Dutch national team, Marinus "Rinus" Michels had been a center-forward as a player, winning five caps for the Netherlands in the 1950s. As coach of Ajax in the mid-1960s, he gave 17-year-old Johan Cruyff his debut. Michels later managed Cruyff at Spanish giants Barcelona and in the Dutch team that finished runner-up at the 1974 World Cup. Michels returned to Ajax in 1975 and became coach of German side Cologne five years later. He rejoined the Dutch national team in 1984 and, with a star-studded team, won the 1988 European Championships—the Netherland's first major trophy. Michels' achievements were acknowledged in 1989, when he was named FIFA's Coach of the Century.

VALERY LOBANOVSKY
1939-2002

A gifted mathematician, Valery Lobanovsky viewed soccer as a science, and was one of the first coaches to analyze the performances of teams and players. His management style was strict, yet it enabled creative talents such as Oleg Blokhin and Andriy Shevchenko to flourish. After four years in charge of Dnipro Dnipropetrovsk, he was appointed coach of Dynamo Kiev, guiding them to five Soviet league titles between 1974 and 1981 and two European Cup Winners' Cup victories (1975 and 1986). He also coached the Soviet Union three times, reaching the 1988 European Championships final, only to be defeated by Rinus Michels' Dutch team. After spells with the United Arab Emirates and Kuwait, he returned to Kiev in 1996, taking them to five Ukrainian league titles in a row (1997–2001) and reaching the semifinals of the Champions League in 1999.

▶ Rinus Michels with Johan Cruyff during their time at Barcelona.

HELENIO HERRERA
1917-1997

The well-traveled Argentinian Helenio Herrera was a tough coach who liked to control almost every aspect of a team. At Spain's Atlético Madrid, he won consecutive league titles. After stints with Malaga, Valladolid, and Sevilla, he joined Barcelona. Under his management, they won two Spanish titles and two Inter-Cities Fairs Cups. Internazionale liked what they saw and hired him in 1960. Herrera's reign and his use of *catenaccio* tactics (see page 60) coincided with Inter's most glorious era, in which they won three Serie A titles, two European Cups, and two World Club Cups. Herrera was also in charge of the Italian national team during qualification for the 1962 World Cup, but by the time the tournament began, he was the coach of Spain.

◀ In November 2004 Alex Ferguson celebrated his 1,000th game in charge of Manchester United by beating Lyon in the Champions League.

▶ Helenio Herrera poses with two soccer balls in 1971, when he was coach of Italian team Roma.

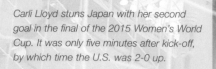

Carli Lloyd stuns Japan with her second goal in the final of the 2015 Women's World Cup. It was only five minutes after kick-off, by which time the U.S. was 2-0 up.

SNAPSHOT
A HAT TRICK OF WINS

In 2015, the U.S. women's national team had long been the powerhouse of women's international football, winning four Olympic gold medals, two Women's World Cups, and all bar one of the CONCACAF Championship and Gold Cups it had entered. But it hadn't won the World Cup for 16 years, and lost to Japan in the 2011 final. At the 2015 tournament, the U.S. eased past Colombia, China, and Germany in the knockout stages to reach the final... against old rivals Japan. Despite being favorite against a talented Japanese side, no one expected such a wildly entertaining opening. Captain Carli Lloyd, who had scored in both the quarter and semifinals, exploded to score twice in the first five minutes. After Lauren Holiday extended the U.S. team's lead in the 14th minute, Lloyd completed her hat trick with a stunning strike from the halfway line that sailed over the Japanese goalkeeper, Ayumi Kaihori, to record the first hat trick in any World Cup final since England's Geoff Hurst in 1966. The U.S. won the game 5-2, securing its third Women's World Cup.

GREAT TEAMS

What makes a great team? Great players, playing with spirit and supported by passionate crowds—with the help of excellent coaches—often win. Yet assembling a team of superstars does not guarantee success. Sometimes, unheralded players gel together to win against the odds. Over the last 15 years Japan, Chile, Burkina Faso, and Iraq have lit up world soccer by triumphing over more powerful countries. Similar surprises occur at club level—from provincial team Toluca's rise to win the Mexican league, to Leicester City escaping relegation in 2015 to become unexpected English Premier League champions the following season. This chapter looks at some of the world's great teams over the years. There are dozens of other successful teams, such as Olympiacos, who in 2017 won their 19th Greek league title in 20 years. The focus in this section is on teams that at one point in their history were especially exciting, revolutionary, or dominant in the soccer competitions in which they played.

NATIONAL TEAMS

► Hungarian goalkeeper Gyula Grosics gathers the ball under pressure from England's Stan Mortensen. Hungary's 6–3 win condemned England to their first home defeat to a team from Europe.

FACT FILE The team was still at its peak when the Soviet Union invaded Hungary in 1956. Many of its star players were on tour with their club, Honved, and chose not to return home. Puskas signed for Real Madrid, while Kocsis and Czibor joined Real's great rivals, Barcelona.

HUNGARY
Founded: 1901

The Hungarian national team of the 1950s was exceptional and was one of the few teams at club or international level to change the way soccer is played. Organized at the back by the dependable Jozsef Bozsik, Hungary brimmed with attacking talent thanks to Zoltan Czibor, Sandor Kocsis, Nandor Hidegkuti, and Ferenc Puskas. At a time when almost every team played the W-M formation (see page 60), coach Gusztav Sebes devised a simple but devastating alternative. Hidegkuti was the team's center-forward, but he played very deep, allowing Puskas, Kocsis, and other teammates to raid forward into space.

Opposition teams simply did not know how to play against a team that swept all before it, winning the 1952 Olympics and scoring 220 goals in 51 matches during the first half of the decade. In 1953 the team earned its nickname—the "Magnificent Magyars"—by beating a stunned England 6–3 at Wembley Stadium. That memorable win was followed by a 7–1 knockout of the English team in Budapest. From June 1950 to November 1955, Hungary's international record read: played 50, won 42, tied seven, lost one. The defeat was heartbreaking, however, as it came in the final of the 1954 World Cup. After taking a 2–0 lead against a West German team they had thrashed 8–3 in the group stages, Hungary—fielding an unwell Puskas—lost 3–2. That single defeat should not detract from one of the finest teams ever to grace the international stage.

WEST GERMANY
Founded: 1900

West Germany staged a major shock when they courageously toppled the favorite, Hungary, to win the 1954 World Cup thanks to two goals from Helmut Rahn. Their team of the mid-1960s finished runner-up at the 1966 tournament and third in 1970. Manager Helmut Schön then rebuilt the team shrewdly, keeping the superb

Sepp Maier in goal and moving Franz Beckenbauer from midfield into defense, where he played alongside Hans-Georg Schwarzenbeck and one of the best fullbacks of the 1970s, Paul Breitner. Schön incorporated the talented Günter Netzer into midfield and often played a 4-3-3 formation, with Uli Hoeness in attack alongside goal machine Gerd Müller. West Germany's players had a very strong team spirit because they came almost exclusively from just two clubs—Bayern Munich and Borussia Mönchengladbach. Their self-confidence was evident as they powered to the 1972 European Championships title and then went a step further, winning the 1974 World Cup on home soil. By this time the talented but outspoken Netzer had been replaced by Wolfgang Overath, while midfielder Rainer Bonhof had also played his way onto the team. A defeat to Czechoslovakia in the 1976 European Championships final signaled the end of a remarkable period in which West Germany had become the first team to hold the European and World crowns at the same time.

◀ *West German defender Berti Vogts holds the World Cup aloft in 1974, with Hans-Georg Schwarzenbeck (number 4) and Rainer Bonhof (16) to his left.*

UNITED STATES (WOMEN)
First international game: 1985

Women's international soccer came of age during the 1990s and early 2000s, with the arrival of World Cup and Olympic competitions. The period's most successful nation was the United States who won two Olympic titles (1996 and 2004) and two Women's World Cups (1991 and 1999). Their record in World Cup games during the 1990s was remarkable, with 20 wins, two ties, and just two defeats. Mia Hamm was considered to be the world's finest female striker, while Kristine Lilly became the first female player to pass 300 international caps in 2006. For a number of the U.S. women's team, 2004 proved a successful swan song, with victory over Brazil to win Olympic gold—a feat that a new generation of U.S. players such as Carli Lloyd, Christie Rampone, and Abby Wambach repeated in 2008 and 2012. The team has dominated the Women's World Cup in recent years, finishing as runner-up in 2011, lifting the trophy for the third time in 2015, and going unbeaten in 2019 when it defeated the Netherlands 2-0 to become world champion for the fourth time.

▶ *Abby Wambach of the United States is fouled from behind by Homare Sawa of Japan in the second half of the Women's World Cup 2015 final.*

FRANCE
Founded: 1919

France has a long and illustrious soccer pedigree. It has produced several superb teams, particularly in the late 1950s—the era of Raymond Kopa and Just Fontaine—and in the early 1980s, with an impressive team led by Michel Platini. But it was the team of the late 1990s that finally translated great promise into World Cup success. As world champion, France entered Euro 2000 with the majority of its key players still at their peak, including flamboyant goalie Fabien Barthez and strong, skilled defenders in Marcel Desailly, Lilian Thuram, and Bixente Lizarazu. In midfield, a blend of flair and dynamism was headed by the world's best attacking midfielder, Zinedine Zidane. Up front, young livewires such as Sylvain Wiltord and Thierry Henry were intent on making their mark. Five players scored two or more goals in their six-match Euro 2000 campaign, which ended with France beating Italy 2–1 to become the second team (after West Germany in 1974) to hold European and World titles at the same time.

▲ France celebrate its Euro 2000 triumph after a "golden goal" from David Trezeguet (center, with Fabien Barthez's hand on his head) sealed victory.

SOUTH KOREA
Founded: 1928

At the 2002 World Cup, cohost South Korea were given little chance of success by many people. In truth, the country boasted an improving team and had qualified for the previous three World Cups. Under the guidance of Guus Hiddink—a former Real Madrid and Netherlands coach—the South Koreans beat Poland 2–0 to record their country's first win at the World Cup. After a 1–1 tie with the United States, South Korea knocked a strong Portugal team out of the tournament thanks to Park Ji-Sung's goal. An extraordinary second-round game versus Italy saw South Korea miss a penalty, then fall behind, only to tie two minutes before the final whistle. Urged on by an entire country, the hardworking team defended resolutely and attacked with energy, skill, and surprise. A "golden goal" three minutes before the end of extra time knocked Italy out of the tournament and sent the country into raptures. The drama was not over, however. A tense quarterfinal against Spain ended in a thrilling penalty shoot-out, with keeper Lee Woon-Jae pulling off a magnificent save from Joaquin before captain Hong Myung-Bo slotted home the winning penalty. A narrow 1–0 defeat to Germany in the semifinals did not dampen the cohost nation's enthusiasm, and attendances at club level rocketed in the following seasons.

FACT FILE Ahn Jung-Hwan struck the goal that knocked Italy out of the World Cup. Ahn played for Italian side Perugia, whose president was so enraged that he terminated the South Korean midfielder's contract.

HIT THE NET

www.fifa.com/associations
A list of all the national associations linked to FIFA. Clicking on a country gives news and details about their national team.

www.worldfootball.net
A large website with information and fixtures for all leading league and international competitions.

www.fifa.com/fifa-world-ranking
See the world rankings for women's and men's international teams. Click through to the ranking tables for more details and select a country for that team's FIFA information page.

▲ South Korea's Lee Chun-Soo (number 14), Choi Jin-Cheul (4), Hwang Sun-Hong (18), and Park Ji-Sung (21) celebrate their team's penalty shoot-out victory over Spain in the quarterfinals of the 2002 World Cup.

SPAIN
Founded: 1904

Spain had been the perennial underachievers on the international stage, producing dozens of world-renowned players—from Ricardo Zamora and Andoni Zubizarreta in goal to Raul and Emilio Butragueño in attack—yet rarely producing the goods at major tournaments. The 2000s, however, saw a major change with the arrival of a clutch of supremely talented, technically gifted players, many from Barcelona, who thrived on a style of play—dubbed *tika-taka*—where control of the ball, frequent short passing, and quick, nimble movements are paramount. Players like Xavi Hernández and Andrés Iniesta in midfield kept possession of the ball in front of no-nonsense defenders such as Carles Puyol and Gerard Piqué. It yielded great results. Between November 2006 and June 2009, Spain went unbeaten in 35 international games—until suffering a shock defeat by the U.S. at the Confederations Cup. Spain won Euro 2008 and became the first champions to successfully defend their European title in 2012. In between came Spain's first World Cup triumph ever, achieved after qualifying with a perfect record (ten wins out of ten) and victories over Portugal, Paraguay, Germany, and the Netherlands at the tournament.

◀ *Xavi Hernández unleashes a shot during Spain's comprehensive 4–0 victory over Italy in the final of the 2012 European Championships.*

ITALY
Founded: 1898

Italy and Uruguay emerged as the leading teams during the first decade of the World Cup. The Italians chose not to enter the first tournament, in 1930, but were hosts of the second, where they were managed by Vittorio Pozzo, who was nicknamed the "Old Maestro." Pozzo deployed several *oriundi*—Argentinians of Italian descent—including Raimundo Orsi and the captain, Luisito Monti. His side also included one of the world's finest attackers of the inter-war years in Giuseppe Meazza. Italy won the 1934 World Cup under Pozzo's leadership and also triumphed at the 1936 Olympics. Recognizing the fact that his team was aging, the wily Pozzo introduced more and more young players, so that by the time of the 1938 World Cup, only two members of the 1934 team, Meazza and Giovanni Ferrari, remained. Pozzo's overhaul of the team proved a triumph, as Italy beat the popular French, Brazilian, and Hungarian teams to reclaim the trophy and make Pozzo the only coach in history to have won two World Cups.

FACT FILE In the semifinal of the 1938 World Cup the string of Giuseppe Meazza's shorts broke, and they fell to the ground just as he went to take a penalty shot. Holding his shorts up with one hand, Meazza calmly hit the penalty home past the bemused Brazilian goalkeeper, Valter.

▲ *Italy's national team, including star striker Giuseppe Meazza (front row, center) pose before the 1938 World Cup. The Italians comfortably beat Hungary 4–2 in the final.*

ENGLAND
Founded: 1863

As an England player, Alf Ramsey's last game had been the 6–3 demolition by Hungary in 1953—the game that punctured English belief in its soccer superiority. Ramsey was made England coach in 1962 and for the 1966 World Cup he had assembled a powerful team with a strong spine—Gordon Banks in goal, Jackie Charlton and Bobby Moore in central defense, Bobby Charlton in midfield, and, up front, Roger Hunt and the free-scoring Jimmy Greaves (who was injured during the tournament and replaced by Geoff Hurst). Propelled by goals mainly from Hunt and Bobby Charlton, and by a prudent defense that did not concede a goal until the semifinal, England beat Mexico, France, Argentina, and Portugal. In the final at Wembley Stadium a memorable hat trick by Geoff Hurst and a goal from Martin Peters saw England beat West Germany 4–2 to win the trophy. After reaching the semifinals of the 1968 European Championships, England was one of the favorites for the 1970 World Cup. In the quarterfinal they were leading 2–0 with just 20 minutes left to play, before West Germany struck back to win 3–2. They would only reach two semifinals in the next 12 World Cups (1990 and 2018).

▼ England captain Bobby Moore (left) and goalie Gordon Banks hold up the World Cup at Wembley.

▲ German striker Birgit Prinz powers away from a North Korean defender during the 2007 Women's World Cup.

▶ Nigerian midfielder Sunday Mba.

NIGERIA
Founded: 1945

In 1985 Nigeria's youngsters captured the World Under-17 Championship to become the first African nation to win a world tournament. Eleven years later, the "Super Eagles" were the stars of the Atlanta Olympics thanks to their attacking verve, team spirit, and will to win. Featuring talented players such as Celestine Babayaro, Emmanuel Amunike, and Daniel Amokachi, Nigeria beat Hungary 1–0 and Japan 2–0, before losing to Brazil 1–0 in the group stages. They then beat Mexico 2–0 in the quarterfinals, setting up a second meeting with Brazil. That match is considered to be the finest in Olympic history. With 13 minutes to go, Nigeria were losing 3–1, but they pulled back one goal before their captain, Nwankwo Kanu, scored a last-gasp goal to tie. In a frenetic period of extra time, Kanu struck again to seal a 4–3 victory. Another great comeback in the final saw Nigeria win gold by defeating Argentina 3-2.

GERMANY (WOMEN)
First international game: 1982

Germany struggled to be competitive in the 1980s, but received a huge boost in 1989 when they won the first of their eight European Championships. The 21st century proved remarkably fruitful for the side as they won the 2003 Women's World Cup and continued their European dominance with their sixth championship crown in a row in 2013. Before retiring in 2011, Germany's goal machine, Birgit Prinz, scored an incredible 128 goals for her country. In the 2007 World Cup, Germany's 11–0 spectacular defeat of Argentina—and feat of not conceding a goal throughout the tournament—were undoubted highlights. The Olympics eluded this talented side until Brazil 2016, when the team defeated China, Canada, and Sweden to win the gold medal.

▶ Johan Neeskens evades the tackle of Argentina's Americo Gallego during the 1978 World Cup final.

NETHERLANDS
Founded: 1889

Rinus Michels, a former center-forward for the Netherlands, masterminded a revolution in Dutch soccer in the mid-1960s. First at club side Ajax, and then with the national team, he developed a system in which all his players were comfortable on the ball and would switch positions, often with devastating results. Called "total football" (see page 61), the system revolved around such world-class talents as Johan Cruyff, Johan Neeskens, and Ruud Krol. With Michels at the helm, the Dutch powered to the 1974 World Cup final, scoring 14 goals and conceding only one in qualifying. They soared through the rounds, demolishing Argentina 4–0 and beating Brazil 2–0 on the way to the final against West Germany. Despite taking a one-goal lead within 80 seconds, the Netherlands suffered heartbreak, losing 2–1. Two years later, they reached the semifinal of the 1976 European Championships, going out to the eventual winners, Czechoslovakia, in extra time. The Dutch entered the 1978 World Cup without Cruyff, but could still call upon many of the 1974 squad, including Neeskens, Krol, and strikers Johnny Rep and Robbie Rensenbrink. They reached the final again, this time losing 3–1 to Argentina. Considered the most talented team never to win the World Cup, the Dutch enthralled millions of fans with their exploits and flair.

MEXICO
Founded: 1927

Having reached the quarterfinals of the two World Cups it has hosted (1970 and 1986), the soccer-crazy nation of Mexico had much to cheer about in the 1990s, when its national team dominated the continental championships, the CONCACAF Gold Cup. In the inaugural competition of 1991, Mexico lost to the United States at the semifinal stage, but in the next three competitions it was unstoppable. It was rampant in 1993, beating Canada 8–0 and Jamaica 6–1, before humbling the United States 4–0 in the final. At the 1996 Gold Cup, it defeated invited guests Brazil to win the title and, four years later, beat the United States again to secure a hat trick of wins. At the heart of Mexico's authoritative displays was the defender Claudio Suarez, nicknamed the "Emperor" for his commanding performances. Suarez made his national debut in 1992 and played his 177th game in 2006 against the Netherlands. A new generation of Mexican talent has added to this success, winning the Gold Cup in 2009 and 2011, and beating Brazil to grab more gold at the 2012 London Olympics.

FACT FILE
Mexico striker Javier Hernandez, who has grabbed 52 goals from 109 games, was timed as the fastest player at the 2010 World Cup—reaching a speed of 20 mph (32.15km/h).

▶ Mexico's Luiz Hernandez is tackled by Dietmarr Hamann of Germany. His record of 35 goals has since been overtaken by Javier Hernandez (52 goals) and Jared Borgetti (46).

BRAZIL
Founded: 1914

The 1958 World Cup signaled the arrival of Pelé and the start of a magnificent era for Brazil, which enchanted fans of the "beautiful game" as they won three out of four World Cups. The team that claimed the 1970 World Cup is considered by many people to be international soccers greatest team. In attack, few countries before or since have been able to field a team so blessed with flair, composure, and skill on the ball, as well as superb vision and movement. Opposition teams sometimes tried to mark Pelé out of the game, but this would only give space and opportunities to marvelous players such as center-forward Tostao, the bustling Roberto Rivelino (who had one of the most fearsome shots in world soccer), the midfield general Gerson, or the powerful winger Jairzinho. At the back, top-class players such as Carlos Alberto and center-back Wilson Piazza maintained a solid defense, but this team was all about attack. After going a goal down to Czechoslovakia in its first game at the 1970 World Cup, Brazil responded by scoring four times. It scored three to beat Uruguay in the semifinal and four in the final, in which it beat a strong Italian side with one of the greatest-ever displays of attacking soccer. Brazil dazzled with its wit and invention, and the 4–1 scorecard was completed by a fantastic team move ending in a thunderous shot by Carlos Alberto (see below). In his last game for

▲ *Brazil's team that beat England at the 1970 World Cup. Back row, left to right: Carlos Alberto, Brito, Wilson Piazza, Félix, Clodoaldo, Everaldo, Mario Zagalo (coach); front row: Jairzinho, Roberto Rivelino, Tostao, Pelé, Paulo Cesar.*

Brazil, Pelé was chaired off the field by his teammates owing to his part in the victory. The departure of other members of the team meant that, by the 1974 World Cup, only Rivelino and Jairzinho remained from the team that had captured the imagination of millions.

FACT FILE In 1970, Brazil's coach, Mario Zagalo, became the first person to have both played in and coached a World Cup–winning team. He had played in Brazil's 1958 and 1962 World Cup triumphs.

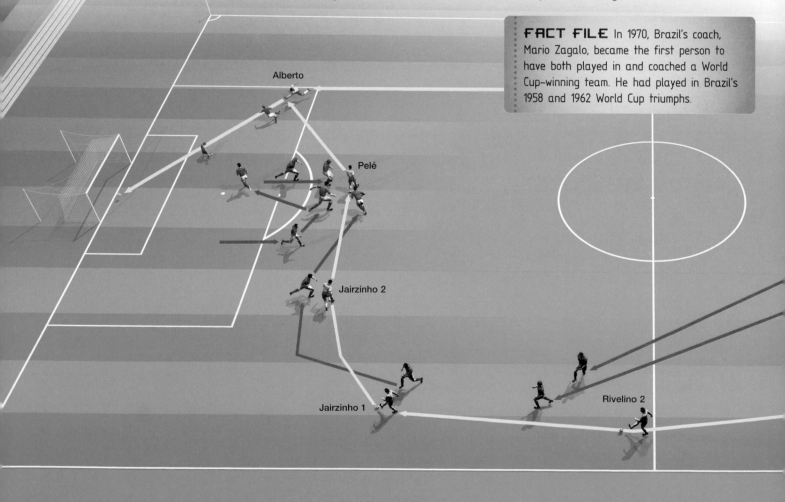

Alberto

Pelé

Jairzinho 2

Jairzinho 1

Rivelino 2

FACT FILE Idriss Carlos Kameni was only 16 when he played goalkeeper for Cameroon in the 2000 Olympic final. He was a hero as early as the fifth minute, when he saved a Spanish penalty. Cameroon went on to win gold in a penalty shoot-out, making the coach, Jean-Paul Akono, the first African coach to win a major world soccer competition.

▶ *Roger Milla runs past Colombian goalie Jose Higuita on his way to scoring during Cameroon's 2–1 victory in the second round of the 1990 World Cup. Cameroon was the talk of the tournament, defeating World Cup holders Argentina in the group stage.*

GAME ACTION

In the 1970 World Cup final against Italy, right-back Carlos Alberto scored one of the best team goals ever. The move started in the Brazilian half with a series of passes and some highly skilled dribbling from defender Clodoaldo. He released Roberto Rivelino, who fired a pass down the touchline. Jairzinho controlled the ball instantly and cut infield, shielding the ball from Italian defenders before feeding Pelé. Pelé spotted a run by a teammate on his right and nonchalantly rolled the ball diagonally into the penalty area. Marauding down the right flank, Carlos Alberto met the pass with a booming right foot shot that sent the ball crashing low into the corner of the net.

FACT FILE Brazil's first international game was in July 1914, when they played English league team Exeter City. In 2004 the 1994 Brazilian World Cup-winning side played a rematch against Exeter, winning the game 1–0.

Clodoaldo 1

Clodoaldo 2

Rivelino 1

CAMEROON
Founded: 1960

Cameroon threatened a major shock at the 1982 World Cup, drawing against Italy (the eventual winners) and Poland, yet narrowly failing to reach the second round. In 1990 a team led by Roger Milla lit up the tournament, winning a tough group containing the Soviet Union, Argentina, and Romania, beating Colombia in round two, and taking England to extra time before losing 3–2. Recently many of Cameroon's players have played for Europe's top clubs—Geremi at Real Madrid, Samuel Eto'o at Barcelona, and Salomon Olembe at Marseille, for example. After a disappointing 1998 World Cup, Cameroon roared back in 2000. They won the African Nations Cup, beating Nigeria. They then triumphed at the Olympics, stunning Brazil in the quarterfinals, Chile in the semis, and Spain in the final to win gold.

LONGEST UNBEATEN INTERNATIONAL RUNS (IN GAMES)

36	Brazil 1993–96	28	South Korea 1977–79
35	Spain 2007–09	27	Colombia 1992–94
31	Argentina 1991–93		Spain 2016–18
	Spain 1994–98	26	Spain 2011–13
30	France 1994–96	25	Italy 2004–06
	Hungary 1950–54		Netherlands 2008–10
29	Brazil 1970–73		

CLUB TEAMS

BARCELONA
Spain
Founded: 1899
Stadium: Nou Camp

With their own bank, radio station, and one of the most impressive stadiums in the world, Barcelona can easily claim to be one of the world's largest soccer clubs. Barcelona's domestic achievements are impressive— their sixth-place finish in the Spanish league, La Liga, in 2003 was their worst since 1942. The club have won 26 league titles, finished runner-up 25 times, and tops the list of Spanish Cup winners, with 30 victories. They have also won the European Cup Winners' Cup four times—more than any other team. Barcelona smashed the world transfer record in 1973 when they paid $2 million for Dutch maestro Johan Cruyff. Fifteen years later, he returned as the club's coach. In his first season, Cruyff steered the club to second place in La Liga and to victory over Sampdoria to collect the European Cup Winners' Cup. Dutchman Ronald Koeman and Denmark's Michael Laudrup were signed to play alongside Spanish stars such as goalie Andoni Zubizarreta and midfielder José Bakero. In 1991 Barcelona won the first of four league titles in a row and one year later won their first European Cup, beating Sampdoria.

▲ *Barcelona's captain, Carles Puyol, lifts the trophy after his team's 2–1 victory over Arsenal in the final of the 2006 Champions League.*

Their second triumph in the competition came in 2006 along with the Spanish league title. Barcelona have won the prized double of La Liga and Champions League three times in 2008–2009, 2010–2011, and 2014–2015.

KASHIMA ANTLERS
Japan
Founded: 1991
Stadium: Kashima Soccer Stadium

The former factory team of Sumitomo Metals Industries, the Kashima Antlers were formed in time to enter the inaugural J-League competition in 1993. Their name comes from the literal translation of "Kashima," meaning "deer island." Little was expected of the side, which lacked the pedigree of Japanese teams such as Yokohama Marinos and Verdy Kawasaki. The Antlers' management team was ambitious, however, recruiting Brazilian World Cup star Zico, as well as Mazinho and Jorge "Jorginho" de Amorim Campos (also from Brazil) and talented Japanese stars such as Tomoyuki Hirase and Yasuto Honda. They took the Antlers to four J-League titles between 1996 and 2002. They have won four more since— the latest in 2016.

▲ *Kashima's Yasuto Honda celebrates with the J-League trophy in 2000.*

AL-AHLY
Egypt
Founded: 1907
Stadium: Mukhtar El-Tetsh

Cairo-based Al-Ahly are the dominant soccer club in Egypt and one of the most successful teams in North Africa. Having won the first Egyptian league competition in 1949, they held on to the title until 1960, when they lost to fellow Cairo team and fierce rival Zamalek. The 1980s were glorious for Al-Ahly. At home, they won five of the seven Cup of Egypt trophies and seven out of a possible ten league titles between 1980 and 1989. Overseas, Al-Ahly won the African Champions League twice, in 1982 and 1987, and also won the African Cup Winners' Cup three times in a row. Al-Ahly was named as the CAF African Club of the 20th Century before going on to win the African Champions League in 2001, 2005, 2006, 2008, 2012, and 2013, and winning 12 out of 13 Egyptian league titles (2005–2019).

FACT FILE Two of Al-Ahly's youngest stars during the 1990s were the twins Hossam and Ibrahim Hassan, the most-capped players in Egyptian soccer. The brothers were idolized as they helped Al-Ahly to four league titles, but turned from heroes to villains when they sensationally quit the club to join rival Zamalek in 2000.

FLAMENGO
Brazil
Founded: 1895
Stadiums: Gávea, Maracana

Brazil is full of famous soccer sides, including Vasco da Gama, São Paulo, Botafogo, and Corinthians. Flamengo are the most heavily supported of them all, having recorded 42 attendances of 100,000 or more at their games. Many gifted players have worn the side's distinctive black-and-red striped shirts. One of the greatest was Léonidas da Silva, known as the "Black Diamond" and the star of the 1938 World Cup. After a successful period in the 1950s, when the team won three Rio state league titles and earned the nickname the "Steamroller," Flamengo had to wait more than 25 years for their next great era. Inspired by Zico and his strike partner, Nunes, the side won the Rio Championship (the Carioca) in 1978, 1979, and 1981, and the Brazilian National Championship in 1980, 1982, and 1983. In 1981 it captured the Copa Libertadores and one month later went on to claim the World Club Cup, beating Liverpool 3–0.

▲ Flamengo's Ze Carlos da Silva performs a spectacular overhead kick during the 2003 Brazilian Cup final against Cruzeiro.

MANCHESTER UNITED
England
Founded: 1878
Stadium: Old Trafford

Sir Alex Ferguson, the Premiership's longest-serving and most successful coach, led Manchester United to a unique triple in English soccer when it won the Premiership, the FA Cup, and the Champions League in 1999. Forty years earlier a Manchester United team coached by Sir Matt Busby—another Scot who became a knight—had captured the hearts and minds of fans everywhere. The story began in the mid-1950s. Great things were expected of the young "Busby Babes" side that had won two league titles (in 1956 and 1957) and included, among other talents, the young England stars Roger Byrne and Duncan Edwards. But in 1958 a tragic plane crash in Munich,

◀ Bobby Charlton (left) celebrates after scoring the opening goal in Manchester United's defeat of Benfica to win the European Cup in 1968.

Germany, killed 23 people on board, including eight members of the Manchester United first team. Busby had to build a new team, which contained tough defenders like Nobby Stiles, young midfielders such as Brian Kidd, and two survivors from the Munich crash, Bobby Charlton and central defender Bill Foulkes. Although often playing in midfield, Charlton formed a glittering attacking trio with Denis Law and George Best. Busby's team won the league title in 1965 and 1967, but the pinnacle of their achievements came in the 1968 European Cup. After beating Real Madrid in the semifinal, Manchester United faced Benfica in the final. Two goals from Charlton, one from Best, and one from the 19-year-old Kidd secured a memorable 4–1 victory. The "Red Devils," as the team is nicknamed, had become the first English team to win the European Cup.

◀ Ryan Giggs (left) in action during a friendly match in 2009. Giggs played four Champions League finals (1999, 2008, 2009, and 2011) and scored in each of the first 21 seasons of the English Premier League.

INTERNAZIONALE (INTER MILAN)
Italy
Founded: 1908
Stadium: Giuseppe Meazza (San Siro)

Also known as Inter Milan, Internazionale was formed by a group of former AC Milan players. During the rule of dictator Benito Mussolini, the club was forced to change its name to Ambrosiana-Inter, but switched it back in 1942. Argentinian coach Helenio Herrera joined Inter in 1960 and pioneered a new tactical system, playing a sweeper behind a back four and using fast-moving defenders to build attacks. Known as the *catenaccio* (door bolt) system, it was seen as negative and defensive by some. But Inter won Serie A in 1963, 1965, and 1966 and also triumphed over Real Madrid in 1964 and the mighty Benfica in 1965 to win the European Cup twice. They added the World Club Cup to their list of honors in 1964 and 1965, but it did not add to its European tally until the 1990s, when it won the UEFA Cup three times. In 2006, Inter were controversially awarded the Italian league title when Juventus were stripped of the trophy. They followed up with four further Serie A titles in 2007, 2008, 2009, and 2010.

▲ *Sparta Prague's Radoslav Kovac is challenged by Michael Chrysostomos of Cypriot side APOEL Nicosia during a Champions League qualifier.*

SPARTA PRAGUE
Czech Republic
Founded: 1893
Stadium: Letná

One of the grand clubs of Eastern European soccer, Sparta has been known by a series of different names, from Kralovske Vinohrady (King's Vineyard) through AC Sparta, Spartak Sokolovo, and Sparta Bratrstvi. The club have dominated the domestic game, winning over 30 league championships, the latest being in 2013–2014 with the side finishing runner-up in 2014–2015 and 2015–2016. The first great Sparta team competed admirably in Europe in the late 1920s and 1930s, winning the Mitropa Cup (the forerunner of the European Cup) in 1927 and 1934. A number of Sparta players also featured in the Czechoslovakia team that finished runner-up in the 1934 World Cup. These included star striker Oldrich Nejedly, who was the tournament's leading scorer with five goals. Sparta had several more great eras, notably in the early 1960s and the beginning of the 1990s, when it competed in the first Champions League competition in 1991–1992. Despite memorable victories over Olympique Marseille, Dynamo Kiev, and Barcelona, Sparta narrowly failed to qualify for the final.

◀ *Luiz Suarez, Inter Milan's elegant midfielder, on the ball in 1967. Inter broke the world transfer record to buy the Spaniard, paying $400,000 in 1961.*

SANTOS
Brazil
Founded: 1912
Stadium: Vila Belmiro

Santos are most famous as being Pelé's club. They had won few honors before he began playing for the team in 1956, aged only 15. During Pelé's 19 years at the club, Santos won the São Paulo Championship ten times and the Copa Libertadores twice, in 1962 and 1963. It also won the World Club Cup in those years, the first with an extraordinary 5–2 win away at Benfica, which included a sensational hat trick from Pelé. Santos has fared less well in the years since, but a number of bright young stars emerged in this century. The club took a gamble on many of these players in the 2002 Brazilian National Championship, fielding a side with an average age of only 22. With 17-year-old midfielder Diego and 18-year-old striker Robinho especially prominent, Santos rolled back the years and delighted many neutral fans by winning the competition.

◄ *Brazilian star Neymar runs with the ball for Santos during a 2012 Brazilian league match versus Palmeiras. Neymar scored more than 130 goals for Santos by the time he was 21 years old. In 2013 he transferred to Barcelona for $63.4 million.*

BOCA JUNIORS
Argentina
Founded: 1905
Stadium: La Bombonera

Best known in Europe as the club for which Diego Maradona played, Boca Juniors were founded by a group of Italian immigrants and an Irishman, Patrick MacCarthy. With their Buenos Aires neighbors River Plate, they form one of the fiercest rivalries in world soccer. Boca have the edge in the derby games and has won two more Copa Libertadores than River. Boca had a strong resurgence at the end of the 1900s. Beginning in May 1998 it went 40 league games unbeaten to set an Argentinian record. The run helped them to win the Clausura and Apertura league titles in 1999, a feat that was followed by an incredible four Copa Libertadores triumphs in 2000, 2001, 2003, and 2007, as well as two Intercontinental Cups in 2000 and 2003.

DICK, KERR LADIES
England
Founded: 1917
No stadium

W. R. Dick and John Kerr owned a railroad and tram equipment-making factory in Preston, northwest England. During World War I, women began to work in factories, taking the jobs of the men serving in the war. In 1917 the women at Dick, Kerr challenged their male coworkers to a game of soccer and went on to organize games against male and female opponents to raise money for war charities. By 1920 Dick, Kerr Ladies were playing matches to sell-out crowds. One game against St. Helen's Ladies attracted 53,000 spectators to Everton's Goodison Park. In 1921, at the peak of their popularity, Dick, Kerr Ladies played 67 games, and a tour of the United States the following year saw the team win three and tie three out of nine games against male teams. The Football Association felt threatened by a team that, in some cases, was attracting bigger crowds than the men's game. In 1921 the FA banned all women from playing soccer on the fields of its member clubs. Incredibly, the ban remained in force for 50 years. As a result, support for women's soccer dwindled, and by 1926 Dick, Kerr Ladies had disbanded. Yet the team left an important legacy by showing that women could play soccer in a competitive, entertaining way.

◄ *The Dick, Kerr Ladies attack the penalty area during a floodlit game against Heys of Bradford in 1919.*

AC MILAN
Italy
Founded: 1899
Stadium: Giuseppe Meazza (San Siro)

AC Milan's first period of notable success came in the 1950s, when a trio of Swedish stars—Gunnar Gren, Nils Liedholm, and Gunnar Nordahl—followed by Uruguayan striker Juan Alberto Schiaffino, helpedit win four Serie A titles. Nordahl remains the club's highest scorer, with an amazing 210 goals in 257 games. The 1960s saw AC Milan emerge as one of the leading clubs in Europe, winning two European Cups and a Cup-Winners' Cup trophy. A period of decline followed, which included an enforced relegation in 1980 as a result of a betting scandal. Milan's fortunes were revived by the arrival of a new chairman, Silvio Berlusconi, in 1986. The wealthy media tycoon and future Italian prime minister appointed Arrigo Sacchi as coach the following year. An exciting team was assembled, which included the superb Dutch trio of Ruud Gullit, Marco van Basten, and Frank Rijkaard, alongside the homegrown talents of Franco Baresi, Roberto Donadoni, and Paolo Maldini. Milan won Serie A in 1988 and went on to win it five times during the 1990s. Starting in 1991, Milan went unbeaten in Serie A for an incredible 58 games, a run that included thrashings of Foggia (8–2) and Fiorentina (7–3). The side also put five goals past Sampdoria, Lazio, Pescara, and

▲ *Kaka sprints away from Liverpool's defence during the 2007 Champions League final. Milan beat Celtic, Bayern Munich, and Manchester United on the way to the final.*

Napoli (twice). In Europe, Milan beat Real Madrid 5–0 and then Steaua Bucharest 4–0 in the final to collect the European Cup in 1989—a competition it also won in 1990, 1994, and 2003, and in which it was runner-up in 1993, 1995, and 2005. AC Milan won its seventh Champions League title in 2007. In Italy, Milan claimed the Serie A title for the 18th time in 2011.

RIVER PLATE
Argentina
Founded: 1901
Stadium: Monumental

River Plate are one of Argentina's leading teams. In the late 1930s it moved to a wealthy suburb of Buenos Aires which, along with a team of expensive players, led to their nickname, the "Millionaires." River is renowned for its attacking style. In the late 1940s its powerful forward line became known as *La Maquina* (the Machine), and the club has produced a succession of world-class attackers, including Omar Sivori, Mario Kempes, Hernan Crespo, Javier Saviola, and the legendary Alfredo di Stefano. River Plate have won a total of 36 Argentinian league titles, yet it was not until 1986 that they triumphed in the Copa Libertadores. The team had made the final twice previously (in 1966 and 1976) before a side featuring Norberto Alonso, Juan Gilberto Funes, and the great Uruguayan striker Enzo Francescoli beat America Cali of Colombia. River has enjoyed three further Copa Libertadores triumphs, the latest in 2018, in which it beat fierce rivals Boca Juniors 5–3 in the final.

◀ *Paraguayan striker Nelson Cuevas (left) is congratulated by Gaston Fernandez after scoring River Plate's first goal in a 3–2 victory over Colón in 2004.*

KAIZER CHIEFS
South Africa
Founded: 1970
Stadium: Johannesburg Athletics Stadium

Kaizer Motaung played for South Africa's oldest and most famous club for black players, the Soweto-based Orlando Pirates. In 1968 he moved to the United States to play for the Atlanta Chiefs in the newly formed NASL. After returning to South Africa, he founded the Kaizer Chiefs (named after Motaung and his former U.S. team) with ex-Orlando Pirates teammates Zero Johnson, Ratha Mokgoatlheng, Msomi Khoza, and Ewert Nene. Featuring a mixture of promising young players and experienced veterans, the Chiefs soon made their mark. The team won the Life Cup in 1971 and 1972 and the BP Top Eight Cup in 1974. In the same year, it claimed its first South African league title. Tragedy struck in 1976, with the death of captain Ariel Kgongoanc in the Soweto uprising and the killing of Ewert Nene, but the Chiefs went on to win the league in 1977 and 1979. It has won the Premier Soccer League four times—the latest in 2014–2015.

▲ *Patrick Mabedi (left) of Kaizer Chiefs tackles Vikash Dhorasoo of Olympique Lyonnais during the 2003 Peace Cup competition, held in South Korea.*

▼ *Eluding Red Star Belgrade's Miodrag Belodedici (left), Jean-Pierre Papin of Marseille powers upfield during the 1991 European Cup final.*

MOST CONSECUTIVE LEAGUE CHAMPIONSHIPS

15	Tafea FC (Vanuatu)	1994–2008
14	Lincoln (Gibraltar)	2003–2016
14	Skonto Riga (Latvia)	1991–2004
13	Al-Faisaly (Jordan)	1959–66, 1970–1974
13	BATE Borisov (Belarus)	2006–2018
13	Rosenborg (Norway)	1992–2004
11	Al-Ansar (Lebanon)	1988, 1990–1999
11	Dinamo Zagreb (Croatia)	2006–2016
11	Loto Ha'apai FC (Tonga)	1998–2008
11	Nauti (Tuvalu)	1980–1990

OLYMPIQUE MARSEILLE
France
Founded: 1899
Stadium: Vélodrome

One of France's biggest teams, Olympique Marseille boasts an intensely passionate fan base. After a flurry of league titles at the start of the 1970s (helped by Yugoslavian striker Josip Skoblar, who scored a record 44 goals in the 1970–1971 season), Marseille found success hard to come by. New chairman Bernard Tapie arrived in 1985 and invested heavily, bringing in expensive stars

such as Enzo Francescoli, Jean-Pierre Papin, Didier Deschamps, and the Ghanaian midfielder Abedi Pele. Papin had the greatest impact, showing an incredible appetite for goals and becoming the French league's leading scorer for an astonishing five consecutive seasons from 1988 to 1992.

The team rampaged through the domestic league, winning five championships in a row from 1989 to 1993. Marseille were agonizingly close to becoming the first French club to win the European Cup, going out in the semifinals to Benfica in 1990 and losing on penalties in the final to Red Star Belgrade the following year. In 1993 a header by Basile Boli sent Marseille fans into ecstasy as they beat AC Milan 1–0 to win the trophy. Then it all went very wrong, as Marseille were found guilty of game-fixing a French league game against Valenciennes. The team was stripped of its 1993 league title and relegated, as well as being denied the right to defend the Champions League trophy the following season. Tapie was eventually imprisoned for corruption. Marseille had to battle hard to regain its former glory, finishing French league runner-up five times and winning the title in 2010.

FLUMINENSE

Brazil
Founded: 1902
Stadiums: Laranjeiras, Maracanã

Founded in 1902, Fluminense has traditionally been supported by the middle classes, while its fierce Rio de Janiero rival, Flamengo, drew support from the working class. Derby games between the two always guarantee big crowds. One "Flu v. Fla" derby in 1963 attracted a world-record attendance for a club game, with 177,656 fans crammed inside the enormous Maracanã Stadium. Fluminense also competes in Rio's oldest derby, the *Classico Vovô* (Grandpa Derby), with Botafogo, cofounders of the Rio league. Despite being the home club of a series of Brazilian soccer legends, including Didi during the 1950s and Carlos Alberto and Roberto Rivelino in the 1960s and 1970s, Fluminense has always disappointed on the international stage. It has never won a major South American competition. However, it has achieved a lot in Brazil, winning the Rio Championship title 31 times. One of its most impressive runs came when the Tricolores—so nicknamed for their green, red, and white colors—won three Rio Championships in a row from 1983 to 1985. Fluminense has also won the Brazilian National Championship four times, and won the inaugural Primeira Liga in 2016.

◀ *Brazilian legend Romario (right), in Fluminense colors, celebrates with his teammates during a league game against Goias in 2004.*

ARSENAL

England
Founded: 1886
Stadium: Emirates

First known as Dial Square FC, Arsenal were formed by workers from the Royal Arsenal munitions factory in Woolwich, south London— hence their nickname, the "Gunners." After a move to the north of the city in 1913, the club's rise to the top of the English game coincided with the appointment of Herbert Chapman as coach in 1925. Chapman was highly innovative both on and off the field, and he built a counterattacking team featuring inside-forwards Alex James and David Jack and winger Cliff Bastin, whose 178 goals for the club remained a record for more than 50 years. Arsenal was league runner-up in Chapman's first season and won the title in 1931 with a point total that would not be beaten for 30 years. Runners-up in 1932, they then claimed three league titles in a row (1933–35) and two FA Cups (1930 and 1936). Despite a league and FA Cup double in 1971,

FACT FILE Under Herbert Chapman, "The Arsenal" became just "Arsenal," allegedly to make them appear at the top of an alphabetical list of Division One clubs. Chapman also successfully campaigned for Gillespie Road subway station, close to the ground, to be renamed "Arsenal."

▲ *Arsenal players congratulate Thierry Henry after his goal against Fulham. Henry scored 37 goals in all competitions in both 2002–2003 and 2003–2004.*

the closest Arsenal have come to their earlier dominance has been under French coach Arsène Wenger. With a team boasting Thierry Henry, Dennis Bergkamp, and Patrick Vieira, it won three Premier League titles and four FA Cups from 1998 to 2005. Arsenal were unbeaten through the 2003–2004 season, recording a total of 49 league games without defeat, a record in English soccer. It has won the FA Cup a record 13 times in total.

▲ *Alessandro del Piero lines up an overhead kick. He spent 20 years at Juventus before moving to A-League side, Sydney FC, in 2012.*

JUVENTUS
Italy
Founded: 1897
Stadium: Delle Alpi

Formed by a group of high-school students in the city of Turin, Juventus used to play in pink shirts until they switched to black-and-white striped ones in 1903. The team has enjoyed successful periods, including five consecutive league titles from 1931 to 1935 and a 1980s team that won Serie A four times. Juve beat Liverpool to win the 1985 European Cup, but the victory was overshadowed by the Heysel Stadium tragedy in which 39 fans died. Financed by the wealthy Agnelli family, the owners of the Fiat car company, Juventus spent lavishly on world-class players in the 1990s, including Roberto Baggio, Gianluca Vialli, Attilio Lombardo, Angelo di Livio, Fabrizio Ravanelli, and Christian Vieri. After capturing the UEFA Cup twice in the early 1990s, Juve won an Italian league and cup double in 1995 and beat Ajax to win the Champions League in 1996. The team lost the final of that competition in 1997 and 1998, but its fans could console themselves with Serie A titles in both years. Following a game-fixing scandal, Juventus was stripped of the 2005 and 2006 Serie A titles and relegated to Serie B for the first time. The team bounced back into Serie A in 2009 and built a new era of dominance, winning its eighth Serie A championship in a row in 2018–19 and reaching the Champions League final in 2015 and 2017.

STEAUA BUCHAREST
Romania
Founded: 1947
Stadium: Ghencea

Formed by the Romanian Army, Steaua Bucharest had built a formidable team by the mid-1980s. The side included the superb goalkeeper Helmut Ducadam, Miodrag Belodedici (one of the finest sweepers in Europe), goal machine Marius Lacatus in attack, and Romania's greatest player, Gheorghe Hagi. In August 1986 the club began an unbeaten run that is unique in Romanian soccer. It did not suffer a defeat for three league seasons, conceding 63 goals but scoring a staggering 322. The team made history overseas, too, beating Spanish giants Barcelona in the final of the 1986 European Cup to become the first East European club to lift the prestigious trophy. In the early 1990s, after three seasons as runner-up in the Romanian league, Steaua began another incredible run, winning six consecutive domestic titles between 1993 and 1998.

GALATASARAY
Turkey
Founded: 1905
Stadium: Ali Sami Yen

Turkey's three biggest clubs—Galatasaray, Fenerbahçe, and Besiktas—are all based in Istanbul and their passionate fans are fierce and occasionally violent rivals. Galatasaray has won the league title 22 times (three more than Fenerbahçe), the latest being in 2019, as well as the Turkish Cup 18 times, including victory over Akhisarspor in 2019. It is the best-known Turkish club overseas, partly because of its competitive performances in Europe during the 1990s. Visiting foreign teams often encounter an intimidating atmosphere—from "Welcome to Hell" banners displayed at the airport by fans, to a stadium that turns into a cauldron of color and noise on game nights. Galatasaray went unbeaten at home in Europe from 1984 to 1994, the year in which it tied 3–3 at Old Trafford to knock Manchester United out of the Champions League. In 2000 the team won its first major European trophy by beating Arsenal to win the UEFA Cup.

▲ *Striker Hakan Sükür made more than 500 appearances for Galatasaray, scoring more than 290 goals.*

BAYERN MUNICH
Germany
Founded: 1900
Stadium: Allianz Arena

Germany's most famous club was formed in 1900 by rebels who had split from their former club, MTV 1879. The new team beat their old side 7–1 in the first game between the clubs. Although Bayern won a league title in 1932, by the early 1960s they were one of West Germany's less popular clubs and did not achieve a place in the Bundesliga when it was formed in 1963. But it earned promotion soon after and by the late 1960s was a dominant force in the domestic game. At the forefront were future soccer legends such as Sepp Maier, Franz Beckenbauer, and Gerd Müller, who was the Bundesliga's top scorer in seven seasons (1967, 1969–1970, 1972–1974, and 1978). With that squad, Bayern won German Cups in 1966 and 1967 and a European Cup-Winners' Cup in 1967. In the early 1970s Bayern's stars were joined by more world-class players such as Paul Breitner and Uli Hoeness. The team won three Bundesliga titles in a row and three consecutive European Cups from 1974 to 1976. Success has continued with 2012–2013 proving a stellar season—including a notable Bundesliga, German Cup, and Champions League triple under outgoing coach Jupp Heynckes. In 2018–19 Bayern celebrated winning their 29th Bundesliga title, their seventh in a row.

▶ *This header by Jerome Boateng helped give Bayern Munich one of their 29 wins out of 34 games in the 2012–2013 Bundesliga.*

▲ *Werner Roth rounds the Atlético Madrid goalkeeper as Bayern Munich powers to a 4–0 victory to win the 1974 European Cup final replay. Bayern had salvaged a 1–1 tie in the first game with a goal in the last minute of extra time.*

BENFICA
Portugal
Founded: 1904
Stadium: Estadio da Luz

Benfica remains Portugal's most famous and successful club, despite the long periods of glory enjoyed by rivals Porto and Sporting Lisbon. Its greatest era was undoubtedly the 1960s, which began under the management of Hungarian Bela Guttmann. The side played with a mix of speed, power, and skill, typified by the midfielder Mario Coluna and the brilliant Eusebio. Benfica began the decade by defeating Barcelona 3–2 to win the 1961 European Cup. The following year, facing the mighty Real Madrid in the final, they found themselves 3–1 down to a Ferenc Puskas hat trick but fought back to beat the Spanish giant 5–3. Benfica featured in five European Cup finals during the 1960s and won eight out of ten league championships. Defending another league title in the 1972–1973 season, Benfica went unbeaten through 30 league games, scoring 101 goals in the process.

▲ *Benfica pose before the 1968 European Cup final, having beaten Juventus in the semifinals. Amazingly, their toughest opponents were Northern Irish team Glentoran in the first round—Benfica sneaked through on the away goals rule.*

ZENIT SAINT PETERSBURG
Russia
Founded: 1925
Stadium: Petrovsky Stadium

Founded by a group of local metal workers, Zenit originally played in the Soviet league, and in the 1950s they could count on the support of famous classical composer Dmitri Shostakovich in the stands. The breakup of the Soviet Union saw Zenit, known as the Blue-and-Whites, enter the Russian league, which it won for the first time under Dick Advocaat in 2007—with Andrei Arshavin the team's standout performer. Four further league titles came in 2010, 2011–12, 2014–15, and 2018–19. In Europe, the club frequently plays in the Champions League, and in 2008 Zenit won the UEFA Cup for the first time and beat Manchester United later the same year to lift the UEFA Super Cup.

LOS ANGELES GALAXY
USA
Founded: 1995
Stadium: Dignity Health Sports Park

A founder member of Major League Soccer (MLS), the Los Angeles Galaxy is one of its most successful teams, with five MLS Cups (2002, 2005, 2011, 2012, 2014) and four MLS Supporters' Shields trophies (1998, 2002, 2010, 2011). In addition, the team has won the Lamar Hunt U.S. Open Cup twice (2001, 2005) and, in 2000, the CONCACAF Champions League. Attracting homegrown talents such as Cobi Jones and Landon Donovan, the Galaxy has also bought in foreign stars, including David Beckham and, in 2015, Steven Gerrard. The Galaxy previously played at the Rose Bowl and Titan Stadium, but since 2005 the team's games have been held at the Dignity Health Sports Park, a ground it shares with CD Chivas USA.

◀ Mexican midfielder Jonathan dos Santos joined L.A. Galaxy in 2017. He scored the winning goal against the United States in the 2019 Gold Cup.

ANDERLECHT
Belgium
Founded: 1908
Stadium: Constant vanden Stock

It took 39 years from the club's formation for Anderlecht to win its first Belgian league championship. Since then the Brussels-based team has made up for lost time, winning a staggering 34 league titles— 19 more than the second most successful side in Belgium, Club Brugge. In addition, Anderlecht has been runner-up 20 times. Such consistency saw the club qualify to play in a major European competition every year from 1964 to 2007. The 1970s were a golden era for Anderlecht. It was the runner-up in the 1970 Inter-Cities Fairs Cup, losing 4–3 over two stages to Arsenal. By the mid-1970s, under the management of Raymond Goethals, Anderlecht's team boasted many high-quality players. A strong midfield, featuring Frankie van der Elst, Ludo Coeck, and Arie Haan, played behind talented attacking duo Benny Nielsen and Robbie Rensenbrink. The club contested three European Cup-Winners' Cup finals in a row, beating West Ham 4–2 in 1976 but losing to Hamburg the following year. Anderlecht bounced back to knock the same German team out of the 1977–1978 competition on its way to the final, where the team thrashed Austria Vienna 4–0. The team also added two European Supercups to its trophy cabinet by beating Bayern Munich in 1976 and Liverpool in 1978.

▲ Belgian striker Enzo Scifo on the ball for Anderlecht against PSV Eindhoven— the team for which Luc Nilis, Scifo's World Cup teammate, played.

HIT THE NET

www.soccerlinks.net/pages/index.html
A huge collection of web links to more than 5,000 official and unofficial club websites, searchable by continent and country.

www.eurotopfoot.com/indexgb.php3
This website ranks 475 soccer teams according to their performances in European competitions and provides profiles of each of the featured teams.

www.soccerbase.com/teams/home.sd
A great database of club and national teams that is searchable by competition or region and gives details of teams, including their players and game results.

ESPERANCE SPORTIVE TUNIS

Tunisia
Founded: 1919
Stadium: El-Menzah

With a distinctive uniform that gave the team its nickname— the Blood and Golds—Esperance has long been one of the leading clubs in Tunisia and North Africa. Consecutive Tunisian league wins in 1993 and 1994 paved the way for its 1994 African

▲ *Esperance's Issam Jomaa vies with Nigerian team Enyemba's Musa Aliyu in the semi-finals of the 2004 African Champions League.*

Champions League triumph, where, in front of a delirious home crowd, it beat the Egyptian holders Zamalek 3–1. In 1997 Esperance began a record-breaking league run. Seeing off the challenge of leading rivals such as Etoile Sportive du Sahel and Club Africain, the team captured an incredible seven straight league championships. No Tunisian club had won more than three in a row before. It also won four more league titles in a row (2009–12), further titles in 2014, 2017, 2018, and 2019, and its fourth African Champions League in 2019. Many of the team's best players were part of the Tunisian national team that won the 2004 African Nations Cup on home soil.

▼ *Peñarol players celebrate their winning goal against fierce rivals Nacional to claim the 1999 Uruguayan Championship.*

OLYMPIQUE LYONNAIS FÉMININ

France
Founded: 1970
Stadium: Parc Olympique Lyonnais

Aligned to Olympique Lyonnais since 2004, this team has become known for pacy, powerful, and skilful women's football. OL Féminin has been dominant in France with a record 17 league titles from 1991 to 2019. It has also won ten Coupe de France Féminine. In 2011, it secured its first Women's Champions League title. Propelled by a free-scoring attack led by prolific Norwegian striker Ada Hegerberg and anchored by a tough defense, OL Féminin has won five further Champions League titles and finished runner-up twice, to make it the most successful women's club in Europe.

▲ *Olympique Lyonnais Féminin celebrate winning the 2018 Women's Champions League after a 4–1 win against Wolfsburg in extra time.*

PEÑAROL

Uruguay
Founded: 1891
Stadium: Centenario

Along with Nacional, Peñarol dominate Uruguayan football. Peñarol are marginally the most successful with 50 titles, the latest in 2018, leaving them four ahead of their rivals. In addition, they have finished league runners-up 41 times. The club's first golden era came in the 1960s. Led by Ecuadorian striker Pedro Spencer, the team won three Copa Libertadores (1960, 1961, and 1966) and two World Club Cups (against Benfica in 1961 and Real Madrid in 1966). Peñarol's team of the 1980s added to this tally, winning two more Copa Libertadores and, in 1982, beating Aston Villa to win a third World Club Cup. Peñarol hold a number of Copa Libertadores records: the largest win (11–2 against Valencia of Venezuela in 1970), the highest aggregate win (14–1 versus Everest of Ecuador in 1963) and the most consecutive participations in the competition (15 between 1965 and 1979).

AJAX
Netherlands
Founded: 1900
Stadium: Amsterdam ArenA

Coach Rinus Michels arrived at Ajax in the 1964–1965 season, just in time to save it from relegation. (The team finished 13th out of 16). Michels went on to develop the concept of "total soccer" (see page 61), which would have a major impact at both club and international levels. Signs of a renaissance at Ajax began to show as early as 1966, when the team won the Dutch league and beat Liverpool 5–1 in the European Cup. Three years later Ajax became the first Dutch team to reach the final of that competition, where it lost to AC Milan. Spurred on by Dutch rivals Feyenoord winning the European Cup in 1970, Ajax went on to claim the trophy for the next three years with the help of such legends as Johan Cruyff, Arie Haan, Ruud Krol, and Johan Neeskens. Playing an electric style of fluid soccer with the emphasis firmly on the attack, the team was crowned Dutch league champion six times in eight seasons (1966–1968, 1970, 1972–1973) and won the European Supercup and World Club Cup, both in 1972. Ajax also supplied most of the players for the Dutch team that finished runner-up at the 1974 World Cup. By the mid-1970s, however, Neeskens, Cruyff,

and Michels had moved to Spain, and Ajax entered a period of decline. But through a comprehensive and much-copied youth system, the team was eventually able to replace its former stars with several new waves of talent, including Dennis Bergkamp, Jan Vertonghen, Wesley Sneijder, and Christian Eriksen.

▼ *Twins Frank and Ronald de Boer, together with strikers Nwankwo Kanu and Finidi George, take a victory lap after Ajax's 1–0 win against AC Milan in the final of the 1995 Champions League.*

LIVERPOOL
England
Founded: 1892
Stadium: Anfield

In 1959 Liverpool was struggling in the English second division and had been knocked out of the third round of the FA Cup by amatour team Worcester City. Then Bill Shankly arrived as the coach.

He was a passionate, no-nonsense Scot who went on to build a successful Liverpool team that won the league championship three times and lifted the UEFA Cup in 1973. One year later he resigned, and Bob Paisley—Shankly's assistant for 15 years—was promoted to coach. Paisley's Liverpool won 19 major trophies in nine years, making him the most successful British coach of the 1900s. The club won six league titles and three League Cups owing to a watertight defense, a quick, accurate passing game, and intelligent attacking by players such as Kevin Keegan, Steve Heighway, John Toshack, and Kenny Dalglish. A UEFA Cup win in 1976 was followed by European Cup triumphs in 1977 and 1978, making Liverpool the first British side to successfully defend the trophy. In 1981 the club beat Real Madrid to win the European Cup for a third time, and a fourth win came (after penalties) in 1984 against Italian team Roma.

> **FACT FILE**
> Between January 1978 and January 1981, Liverpool set an all-time record of 85 home games unbeaten in all competitions. Included in this run were an incredible 63 home league games in a row.

◄ *Liverpool's Ray Kennedy (far left), Graeme Souness, and Alan Hansen close down Flamengo star Zico during the 1981 World Club Cup.*

CELTIC
Scotland
Founded: 1888
Stadium: Celtic Park

With 50 league titles, Celtic has dominated Scottish soccer
for decades alongside its Glasgow-based rival
Rangers. However, Celtic had not
won the league title for 11 years
before Jock Stein's arrival as
coach in 1965. Stein developed
a homegrown team, all of whom
hailed from Glasgow and the
surrounding area. The team was full of youth and
speed and had an adventurous style of play. These qualities
were typified by the tricky winger Jimmy Johnstone, marauding
fullback Tommy Gemmell, prolific strikers Steve Chalmers, Bobby
Lennox, and Willy Wallace, and a defensive rock in Billy McNeill,
the captain. Celtic began an astonishing run from 1966, winning
nine Scottish league championships in a row and achieving a
Scottish Cup and league double five times during that period. Yet
they contested the 1967 European Cup final as underdog to a
powerful Internazionale team that had won two of the previous three
European Cups. Against the odds, Celtic recovered from one goal
down to beat the Italians 2–1, becoming the first British team to win
the biggest club prize in European soccer. The "Lions of Lisbon"
narrowly failed to repeat their achievement when they reached the
1970 European Cup final, going down 2–1 to Dutch team Feyenoord.
It would be 33 years before the Scottish club reached their next
European final, losing 3–2 to Porto in the 2003 UEFA Cup final.

▶ *Winger Jimmy
Johnstone (left)
scored 130 goals
for Celtic on the way to
nine league championships,
five League Cups, and four
Scottish Cups with the club.*

▲ *Colo Colo's Jose Domingo Salcedo gets ahead of Sebastian Battaglia of
Argentinian team Boca Juniors during a Copa Libertadores game in 2008.*

COLO COLO
Chile
Founded: 1925
Stadium: David Arellano

With around 60 percent of the country's soccer fans following
the team, Colo Colo are easily the most popular and successful of
all the Chilean club teams. The team has won a record 32 league
championships (14 more than fierce rival Universidad de Chile) as
well as the Chilean Cup—the *Campeonato de Copa*—11 times.
Under their coach Arturo Salah, Colo Colo captured league titles
in 1986 and 1989 before former Yugoslavia under-20 coach
Mirko Jozic became the coach during the 1990 season. The
team won a sequence of three league titles in a row in 1991,
the same year that they enjoyed fantastic success overseas.
In 1973 Colo Colo had been the first Chilean team to contest
a final of the top South American club cup competition, the
Copa Libertadores. In 1991 the club went one stage further,
beating the mighty Argentinian team River Plate in the semifinals
and the cup holders, Olimpia, 3–0 on aggregate to win the trophy.
While further international success has been restricted to a
runner-up spot in the Copa Sudamericana in 2006, the club
won five league titles between 2006 and 2015.

▲ *Dynamo Kiev pose with the 2003 Ukrainian Cup after beating the holders— and Kiev's most competitive rival in Ukrainian soccer—Shakhtar Donetsk.*

DYNAMO KIEV
Ukraine
Founded: 1927
Stadium: National Sport Komplex Olimpiyskiy

Originally the soccer team of the Soviet secret police, Dynamo Kiev was the first club outside of Moscow to win the Soviet league championship. A player in that 1961 side, Valery Lobanovsky, became Kiev's coach 13 years later. He led the club through its greatest era, which began spectacularly with consecutive Soviet league titles. In 1975 Kiev won the Cup Winners' Cup, becoming the first Soviet side to win a European competition. They also beat Bayern Munich 3–1 to win the European Supercup. In total, Lobanovsky (in three separate periods) coached Kiev to win eight league titles, six Soviet Cups, and two European Cup Winners' Cups. In 1991, after the breakup of the Soviet Union, Kiev played in the newly formed Ukrainian league. The team has dominated there, winning 15 league titles including the 2015–2016 competition.

REAL MADRID
Spain
Founded: 1902
Stadium: Bernabeu

Real Madrid is one of the world's most famous and successful teams. It has won 33 Spanish league titles, seven more than rivals Barcelona and 23 more than its neighbor, Atlético Madrid. It has also captured 13 European Cups and three World Club Cups. In the 1940s and 1950s, Real's president, Santiago Bernabeu, began to transform the club with foreign players and a huge desire to win the newly formed European Cup competition. Real did not disappoint, capturing not only the first European Cup in 1956 but the next four as well. The team included two of the world's outstanding attacking talents in Ferenc Puskas and Alfredo di Stefano, as well as pacy winger Paco Gento, central defenders Marcos Marquitos and Juan Zarraga, and attacking midfielder Hector Rial. From 1957 to 1965, Real remained unbeaten at home in 121 Spanish league games and won five La Liga titles in a row (1961–1965). A transformed team captured the European Cup for a sixth time in 1966.

Today, Real is one of the world's richest clubs, with a habit of buying soccer's most famous and expensive players, such as Zinedine Zidane, James Rodriguez, Cristiano Ronaldo, and Gareth Bale. With stars such as these, Real has won four La Liga titles in the 21st century, including the 2016–2017 competition, and have taken their European Cup and Champions League triumphs to a total of 13.

▲ *Real Madrid's victorious team pose with the 1960 European Cup after one of the greatest displays of attacking soccer ever (see pages 14–15).*

▼ *Pepe and Ronaldo hold the Supercopa trophy after Real Madrid won it for the ninth time in 2012.*

The French team, captained by their goalkeeper, Hugo Lloris, celebrate with the 2018 World Cup trophy after their victory over Croatia in front of over 78,000 fans at Moscow's Luzhniki Stadium.

SNAPSHOT

LES BLEUS TRIUMPH AGAIN

France was where the idea of a World Cup was formed, yet the country had never won the competition until 1998. That triumphant team, featuring global superstars such as Zinedine Zidane, had been captained by the hardworking defensive midfielder Didier Deschamps. Twenty years later in 2018, Deschamps was head coach of the French team, packed full of outstanding attacking flair, but with questions about their ability to perform on the biggest stage of all. Doubts also surrounded Deschamps' selection as he left talented attackers Karim Benzema, Anthony Martial, and Alexandre Lacazette out of the squad. After topping their group, France defeated Argentina 4-3, with two goals from striker Kylian Mbappé ,who finished as the tournament's second-highest scorer alongside his strike partner, Antoine Griezmann. Victories over Uruguay and Belgium took France to the final where they prevailed over Croatia, 4-2.

SOCCER DREAMS

From Beijing to Buenos Aires, Manchester to Mexico City, millions of children, teenagers, and adults play soccer for fun, exercise, and as a sport. Many are content to take part at an amateur level, but for some, the dream of emulating the stars they read about and watch is a passion.

YOUNG DREAMS

Promising players often emerge at an early age in school and local teams. In most countries, young players can play at a regional, county, or state level in organized youth team competitions. Major soccer clubs run youth sides and soccer academies, and also send scouts to watch games in the hope of spotting new talent. Young players may be invited to an open day or trial, where scouts and coaches can observe them in action at close hand. A club may then offer a contract or a place in its youth academy to a promising player. Famous academies exist at clubs such as Bayern Munich, Manchester United, and Porto. The most famous is De Toekomst, the youth academy of Dutch side Ajax. It has been responsible for producing truly great players such as Johan Cruyff, Marco van Basten, Dennis Bergkamp, and—more recently—Wesley Sneijder, Christian Eriksen, Toby Alderweireld, and Luis Suarez.

▲ In the first two years since his debut for Palmeiras in 2015, Brazilian teenager Gabriel Jesus won an Olympic gold medal and moved to Manchester City for a fee of $35 million.

YOUTH TEAMS AND COMPETITIONS

As young players approach the pinnacle of the game, there are international matches for schoolboys and schoolgirls as well as under-17 and youth competitions. These reach a peak with FIFA's Under-17 World Championship and the FIFA U-20 World Cup. The latter competition began in 1977; at the 1991 tournament, Portugal swept to the title with a midfield containing teenagers João Pinto, Rui Costa, and Luis Figo. Argentina won five of the ten competitions held between 1993 and 2011 thanks to goals from players such as Javier Saviola, Lionel Messi, and Sergio Aguero, who was top scorer at the 2007 tournament. Serbia won the 2015

> ### FACT FILE
> In 2015 Vanuatu's U23 soccer team beat Micronesia by a record scoreline of 46–0. It was the second heavy defeat for Micronesia which earlier that year lost 38–0 to Fiji.

tournament, beating Brazil in the final. FIFA's Under-17 World Cup has also thrown up a number of stars. Landon Donovan was the 1999 tournament's Most Valuable Player, an award given to Cesc Fàbregas in 2003, Anderson in 2005, and England midfielder Phil Foden in 2017. Some young players are thrown into action with the adults in the reserve team or first team at a professional club. One of the youngest was Freddy Adu, who, in 2004, came on as a substitute for U.S. club DC United in its game against San Jose Earthquakes. He was only 14 years old.

HANDLING REJECTION

For millions of hopefuls, the desire to play professional soccer remains just a dream. As players rise through the soccer ranks, their talents are surpassed by others, and they are unable to progress further. Some talented young players are rejected because coaches believe that their slight builds or lack of height would put them at a disadvantage. As young players, Kevin

▲ Young Chinese players perform wheelbarrow exercises. According to FIFA, there are more than 28 million registered players in China with the numbers of young players rising.

Keegan and Allan Simonsen were rejected by major clubs for being too small, yet both went on to star for their countries and win the coveted European Footballer of the Year award. Other players are turned down because their levels of fitness are not high enough. As a 16-year-old, the great Michel Platini was rejected by French club Metz after medical checks revealed he had poor breathing and a weak heart.

Rejection is hard to take for many junior players, but some are able to use such a setback to spur themselves on and prove their doubters wrong. The great Dino Zoff tried out at Internazionale, whose coaches were unimpressed. The same thing happened at Juventus, but the young goalie was not discouraged—he worked hard at his game and was eventually signed by Udinese. More than 20 years later he captained Italy to the World Cup trophy. In 2002 a very young Harry Kane was released from Arsenal's youth academy. He joined Tottenham Hotspur's youth academy two years later and went on to become one of the world's most feared center-forwards.

► In the final of the men's blind soccer tournament at the 2004 Paralympics, held in Greece, Argentina's Oscar Moreno (right) holds off Sandro Soares of Brazil.

◄ Brazil's Oscar (left) competes at the FIFA U-20 World Cup. He later set an Asian record transfer fee of $73.4 million.

SOCCER FOR ALL

Football can be enjoyed in all climates and conditions and by people of all ages and abilities. It is also played competitively by people with disabilities that range from being wheelchair-bound to having impaired hearing. In 2014, Russia, Ukraine, and Germany were the medal winners at the Deaflympics, held in Bulgaria. Amputee soccer is played by outfield players using crutches, but no artificial leg, and by goalkeepers who are single-arm amputees. Since 1984 the Paralympics has included a seven-on-seven soccer competition for people suffering from cerebral palsy and brain injuries. The game is played largely according to FIFA's seven-on-seven rules, but with bigger goals, no offsides, and two 30-minute halves. Soccer for blind and visually impaired athletes uses a special ball. It contains a noise-making device that makes a distinctive sound as the ball moves. Teams consist of four blind outfield players, a goalie (who can be partially sighted), and five substitutes. In 2004 the sport made its debut at the Paralympics. Brazil has proven to be the true master of this 50-minute-long game at the Paralympics, winning all four events so far, including the 2016 tournament, beating Iran in the final.

FACT FILE
In 2014 Gloriana Villalobos made her debut for Costa Rica at the age of 14. The following year she appeared at the 2015 Women's World Cup.

► Eric Cantona controls the ball during a beach soccer game. The sport has its own FIFA World Cup. The 2013 tournament, held in Tahiti, was won by Russia. It beat Spain 5–1 in the final.

A PRO'S LIFE

Viewed from the outside, a professional soccer player's life seems glamorous, exciting, and rewarding. But behind the appearances in top games, on television shows, and at celebrity events lies a lot of hard work and sometimes frustration and disappointment.

MAKING THE FIRST TEAM

Signing as a young player for a big club is every aspiring soccer star's dream, but, in truth, a young player in this position is only halfway toward his or her goal. Competition for one of the 11 starting places is intense. Many young players do not make the grade and have to move elsewhere—often down a division or two—to play first-team soccer. "If you're good enough, you're old enough" is a motto used by some coaches who have thrust exceptionally talented young players into first-team action for their team or country. Cameroon striker Samuel Eto'o, for example, first played for his country the day

◀ Colombian attacker James Rodriguez joined Real Madrid in 2014 for $78 million. In 2017, he moved to Bayern Munich on a two-year loan.

before his 16th birthday. In 2012 Fabrice Olinga, a product of Samuel Eto'o's soccer school in Cameroon, became the Spanish La Liga's youngest goalscorer ever, at 16 years and 98 days. Four days later he found himself playing in a UEFA Champions League game for Malaga, and within two months he was playing and scoring for his national team, Cameroon. Most young players have to wait far longer for their first-team debut.

LOANED OUT

Increasingly young players are loaned to other teams in order to gain experience. In January 2019, Juventus had more than 20 players out on loan including Gonzalo Higuain signed for 18 months to play at Chelsea. Times on loan can be relatively short and to a lower-division team in the same country, as in David Beckham's six-week stint at Preston North End when he was a Manchester United youngster. They can also be for longer periods and to a team in a different country, as with Fernando Torres who in 2015 went on an 18-month loan to Atlético Madrid. Many players who are frustrated by a lack of opportunities seek a loan or permanent move elsewhere to play first-team soccer. This is not just limited to young, inexperienced players. In 2018, MLS side Los Angeles FC obtained Brazilian defender Danilo Silva on loan. Others agree to a loan move to put them in the "store window" for a future permanent transfer, either to the team that has taken them on loan or to another in the same league.

TRAINING, INJURIES, AND RECOVERY

A typical week for a soccer player involves training, resting, going to team functions, and traveling to one or more games. Training usually involves a mixture of fitness, strength, and flexibility exercises to boost a player's stamina, speed, and alertness. Players also practice skills and tactics—improving their heading or working on free kicks, for example. In continental Europe, players have eaten a healthy, scientifically managed diet for years. Great Britain, in contrast, was slow to catch on. Even in the 1970s and 1980s, a pregame meal was often as heavy as steak and fries.

Injuries occur fairly often in soccer. An English FA study of the 1997–1998 and

FACT FILE Spanish goalkeeper Santiago Canizares missed the 2002 World Cup after dropping a bottle of aftershave on his foot.

▲ Romelu Lukaku practices with Chelsea. He was loaned to West Bromwich Albion for the 2012–2013 season and then Everton for 2013–2014.

▲ While playing for Malaga in 2012, Fabrice Olinga became La Liga's youngest goalscorer, at the tender age of 16 years and 98 days.

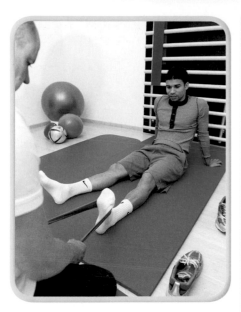

▲ Eduardo da Silva works with a physiotherapist in the gym to help him recover from a broken leg. Recovery from an operation or a serious injury can be a difficult time, as players miss key games and face a long period of training.

1998–1999 seasons recorded more than 6,000 injuries, mostly to knee and ankle joints or leg muscles. In April 2017, more than 80 players were out injured in the 18-team Bundesliga and around 50 in Italy's Serie A league. Arsenal suffered 25, Everton 37, and Manchester United 39 significant injuries to players during the 2014–2015 season.

Injured players are treated by a club's doctor and physiotherapist. They are sent to the best consultants and surgeons to ensure as quick a recovery as possible. This can take weeks or months and usually involves long days in the gym, gentle training, and intensive sessions with the physiotherapist. Injured players are painfully aware that their place on the team has been filled. A young player may have seized the chance, making it even harder for the injured player to return.

A soccer career can be short, with players retiring by their early 30s (although goalies can play into their late 30s). Serious injuries are what pro players most fear. Every year an average of 50 English league players are forced to retire because of injuries.

REWARDS AND RESPONSIBILITIES

Soccer's top players are paid well and are treated as celebrities like music and movie stars. Some use their celebrity to publicize good causes, to help coach and inspire young people, or to visit hospitals, schools, and charities. Just like movie stars, players have to deal with the media. A club may ask players to give interviews for website features or to cooperate with newspapers and television companies to promote an upcoming game or new uniform, for example. What can be harder for young players to handle is the way in which the press can invade their private lives. Photographers and reporters may besiege a player's home and follow their family and friends. Soccer players are seen as important role models for young people, and any wrongdoing, such as being fined for speeding, snubbing autograph hunters, or partying, attracts a lot of negative television and newspaper attention.

FACT FILE In 2004 QPR manager Ian Holloway took his team to train with ballet dancers. The aim was to improve the players' flexibility and balance, helping them avoid injuries.

◄ Top players are constantly in the public eye. Here, David Beckham signs autographs at an open training session. To attend, each fan donated about $6 to charity.

▼ Lionel Messi holds the FIFA Ballon d'Or trophy, awarded to the world's best player each year. The sumptuous skills and goal scoring exploits of the mesmerizing Argentinian helped him win the award five times (2009–2012 and 2015).

FACT FILE Blackburn Olympic spent a week at a health spa before the 1883 FA Cup final. The players' daily diet included a glass of port and two raw eggs for breakfast, a leg of mutton for lunch, and 12 oysters for dinner.

THE PLAYERS' STAGE

Without stadiums, soccer would still be played, but games would be far quieter, less passionate and exciting affairs. Stadiums spring into life on game days, when they are transformed from empty, silent steel and concrete structures into a seething sea of noise and color.

GREAT STADIUMS

England and Scotland boasted the world's first great stadiums. Glasgow's Hampden Park was built in 1903; in 1937 almost 150,000 spectators were admitted to watch an international game between Scotland and England. The biggest crowd at London's Wembley Stadium—which was built in only 300 days—was its first, for the 1923 FA Cup final. More than 150,000 people crammed inside, spilling onto the field and forcing the kickoff to be delayed.

The mighty Maracanã Stadium in Rio de Janiero, Brazil, is almost completely round. It holds the official world record for a soccer crowd—in 1950, around 199,850 people watched a World Cup game there between Brazil and Uruguay. In 2014 Brazil's Maracanã Stadium joined Mexico

▲ A staggering 114,000 spectators, all standing, cram into London's Crystal Palace to watch the 1901 FA Cup final between Tottenham Hotspur and Sheffield United.

City's Azteca stadium as the only venues to hold World Cup final games twice. Many of the world's biggest soccer arenas were built to host the World Cup or European Championships—from the Centenario in Uruguay, the venue for the first World Cup in 1930, to Poland's National Stadium,

which hosted Euro 2012 games. Twelve venues, both new and old, were used for the 2018 World Cup in Russia, from the 81,000-capacity Luzhniki Stadium (completed in 1956) to five new stadiums opened shortly before the beginning of the tournament.

BEHIND THE SCENES

The forgotten people of soccer are often the staff who run a stadium and ensure that a game day goes smoothly. We tend to think of them only when there is a problem such as crowd trouble or a field that is unfit for play. The team or stadium owner liaises with police and local authorities and employs stewards to prevent field invasions, violence, and other problems. Box office staff do their best to ensure that tickets are sold and distributed correctly, and turnstile operators, program sellers, and food and drink vendors all work at a ground on a game day. At the 2006

▼ At Euro 2004, Fabien Barthez saves a David Beckham penalty in the Estadio da Luz in Lisbon, Portugal. The 65,000-capacity arena is Benfica's home ground.

► *Ground staff in traditional dress prepare the goal nets at the National Stadium in Lagos, Nigeria, before the opening game of the 1999 World Youth Championship.*

World Cup, tickets contained tiny microchips that could be read by scanners, easing crowd congestion and helping to prevent ticket fraud.

The ground staff are in charge of the goals and the field and its markings. They work especially hard when the field is in poor condition because of bad weather—clearing snow, thawing out the field, or soaking up excess moisture. On the day of the game—or sometimes earlier—the game referee examines the field carefully and talks to the ground staff before deciding whether the game can go ahead.

▲ *A groundskeeper gives the field a close cut at Newcastle United's St. James' Park stadium. Field care is vital at all top-level stadiums.*

STADIUM INNOVATION

Stadium tragedies have occurred all over the world (see pages 104–105), prompting many governments and soccer authorities to bring in far stricter rules on stadium design, capacities, and crowd control. In the past 30 years, new safety laws and innovations in architecture have led to major changes in the design of soccer stadiums. Despite fans' strong emotional attachment to stadiums, dozens of teams have abandoned their old stadiums in or near the center of a town or city. The money raised from the sale of the land is used to build a new stadium on the outskirts. Many of these stadiums form part of a hotel, entertainment or shopping complex. A famous example is the Stade

FACT FILE The Timsah Arena stadium is green and shaped like a giant crocodile's head. Completed in 2015, it's the home of Turkish club Bursaspor and seats about 45,000.

FACT FILE At the 1986 World Cup, eagle-eyed officials spotted that the field markings at the edge of the penalty area for the France-Hungary game were in the wrong place. They had to be hastily repainted.

de France in Paris, which was built to host the final of the 1998 World Cup. It features 17 stores and 43 cafes and restaurants for its 80,000 spectators.

Notably, the United States staged the first indoor World Cup qualifier (at the Seattle Kingdome) and the first indoor World Cup finals game (at the Pontiac Silverdome). Stadiums with a sliding roof have become more and more popular, allowing the venue to host music concerts and other indoor events. The Amsterdam ArenA was opened in 1996 as Ajax's new ground. The first European stadium with a retractable roof, it seats 51,859 spectators. The Millennium Stadium in Cardiff, Wales, and London's Wembley Stadium also have sliding roofs. Inside a new stadium, fans may find a removable field, corporate boxes for business entertaining, and giant screens that replay action from the game. Germany's Arena Auf Schalke, opened in 2001, has 540 video screens throughout the stadium and a giant video cube suspended from the roof. With four 387.5 sq. ft. (36m²) video screens, it is the first of its type in Europe.

TOP TEN LARGEST SOCCER STADIUMS

POPULAR NAME	LOCATION	CAPACITY
Nou Camp	Barcelona, Spain	99,354
Azteca	Mexico City, Mexico	95,500
FNB Stadium	Soweto, South Africa	94,736
Wembley Stadium	London, England	90,000
Gelora Bung Karno	Jakarta, Indonesia	88,083
Borg El Arab	Alexandria, Egypt	86,000
Santiago Bernabéu	Madrid, Spain	85,454
Azadi	Tehran, Iran	84,412
Signal Iduna Park	Dortmund, Germany	80,667

▲ *The Estádio do Maracanã (Maracanã Stadium), refurbished for the 2014 World Cup. In June 2013 the 78,800-capacity stadium hosted its first official game, an exhibition game between Brazil and England that ended 2–2.*

FANS AND TEAMS

Dreams are not only held by players and coaches. Everyone connected to a club or national team dreams that his or her team will achieve glory and success, and this especially includes the most loyal, passionate, and vocal group of all—the fans.

FOLLOWING A TEAM

For millions of fans, following their club or national team is a lifelong passion. Fans may chant for a coach to leave or be unhappy with certain players or the team's current ranking, but their love of the team tends to remain. Dedicated fans go to great lengths to follow their team, putting up with poor weather and long hours of traveling to away games. Many fans spend a lot of their income every season on getting to as many games as possible and buying jerseys and other merchandise—from T-shirts and scarfs to team-branded toothpaste and credit cards. Do these supporters get a fair deal for their time, effort, and expenditure? To many casual or nonfans, the answer appears to be "no." Entertainment and the "right" result are never guaranteed, and ticket prices have soared, sometimes pricing ordinary fans out

▼ Mascots are a feature at many soccer games. These British mascots are taking part in the 2002 Mascot Grand National, which was won by Oldham Athletic's Chaddy the Owl.

TOP-TEN AVERAGE ATTENDANCES IN EUROPE (2017–18)

1	Borussia Dortmund	79,496
2	Bayern Munich	75,000
3	Manchester United	74,976
4	Tottenham Hotspur	67,953
5	Barcelona	66,603
6	Real Madrid	66,161
7	FC Schalke 04	61,197
8	Arsenal	59,323
9	Inter Milan	57,529
10	Celtic	57,523

of the game. Yet, being a loyal soccer fan is rarely a decision made with the head. It is all about heart and emotions. Loyal fans love to feel the rush of excitement as they approach their home ground, chant with the crowd, and witness the start of a game. What comes next is a 90-minute roller-coaster ride of highs and lows, ending at the final whistle and followed by a postgame discussion of what went right and wrong, before hope and expectancy build for the next game.

◄ A facepainted Croatian fan shows support for her team at the 2018 World Cup.

HIT THE NET

www.stadiumguide.com
Information on the leading football stadiums around the world, including the venues for the 2022 World Cup in Qatar.

http://expertfootball.com/wp/?p=754
A webpage looking at some of the world's greatest derby games.

www.fifa.com/worldcup/destination
A clickable map which takes you to each of the stadiums used at the 2018 World Cup in Russia.

FACT FILE With a Dutch mother and a Belgian father, fan Raymond Brul had a problem at Euro 2000. In the end, he showed his support for both nations by painting half his car in Dutch team colors and half in Belgian colors.

FANS AND THE MEDIA

Few stadiums hold more than 60,000 spectators, but the rise of television coverage has opened up the game to millions of new fans. Some fans, however, criticize TV for concentrating on the top teams and moving games to different days and new starting times. TV companies spend a fortune on buying the rights to show live games and highlights from the top leagues. Back in the studio, famous ex-players and coaches comment on the action, while reporters and

▲ *Pelé's 1970 World Cup shirt was auctioned in 2002 for about $225,000, beating the sum paid for Geoff Hurst's 1966 World Cup shirt by about $90,000.*

statisticians provide interviews and highly detailed analyses of games.

Coverage of soccer in other media has boomed, too. Fans manage their own teams in computer simulations or fantasy soccer leagues, while results, news, and video clips are sent to their smartphones and tablets. They can read about their team in books, magazines, fanzines, and blogs. The rise of radio phone-ins and social media has allowed fans to voice their opinions on games, players, coaches, and referees.

MORE THAN A GAME

Fans look forward to certain games in particular—a clash between two teams at the top of the league standings, for example. A game between a small club and a top team allows fans to dream of a famous giant-killing victory. In 2008, Luxembourg fans (who had seen 59 defeats in the last 60 competitive games), were delirious when their team beat Switzerland. Sometimes, even results in exhibition games can surprise, such as Cape Verde beating Portugal 2–0 in an April 2015 game.

FACT FILE In 1998 Newcastle United fans draped the giant Angel of the North statue with a 30-ft. (9-m) high Alan Shearer soccer shirt that cost about $1,700 to be specially made.

▶ *Fans of Turkish club Galatasaray drum up a fearsomely loud atmosphere before the 2000 UEFA Cup final against Arsenal.*

The most anticipated and passionate of all games tend to be derby games between two neighboring teams. Most clubs have some form of derby, but certain rivalries have passed into soccer folklore. Among them are the Milan derby between Internazionale and AC Milan and, in Greece, the battle between Olympiakos and Panathinaikos. One of the most intense derbies in South America is between the two great Argentinian teams, Boca Juniors and River Plate. For some fans, beating their rivals in a derby can be even more important than league or cup success.

Some of the biggest derbies are not between neighboring teams, but between the top clubs in the country. Spain's *Superclassico*, for example, is contested by two teams that are 300 mi. (500km) apart—Real Madrid in the heart of the country and Barcelona on the east coast.

WHEN FANS TURN BAD

Sometimes the passion of fans at a game can turn violent. Fighting between fans has occurred since soccer's early days, but it became known as the "English disease" in the 1960s and 1970s as "hooliganism" flared up around the country. At the 1998 World Cup and Euro 2000, England fans fought running battles with other nationalities. More recently, fan problems at English clubs have declined dramatically thanks to CCTV cameras, undercover police operations, all-seater stadiums, and police forces working with clubs to identify, ban, and even jail troublemakers. Fan violence, though, continues to remain a problem in different parts of the world. England and Russian fans clashed violently in Marseille, France, during Euro 2016, for example, whilst large numbers of Turkish and Ukrainian soccer fans brawled after a 2016 Europa League game between Dynamo Kiev and Besiktas. In 2012, a terrible pitched battle between Al-Ahly and Al-Masry supporters in Port Said, Egypt, left more than 70 people dead and 1,000 injured. This tragic and unpleasant series of events should not mask the fact that the vast majority of soccer fans are peaceful and never cause trouble.

◀ *AC Milan goalie Dida is struck by a flare thrown by Internazionale fans during a Champions League quarterfinal in 2005. Referee Markus Merk abandoned the game and AC Milan were awarded a 3–0 win.*

THE FOOTBALL INDUSTRY

Soccer is extremely big business with club teams valued in their hundreds of millions of dollars. In 2017–2018, the 20 richest teams generated a staggering $9.2 billion of income. But the pressure to succeed has caused many clubs fall deeply into debt, some facing the threat of going entirely out of business.

BIG BUSINESS

In 2009 Manchester City's new owners, members of the Abu Dhabi royal family, made an audacious bid of almost $160 million to lure Kaka to the club. Money is no guarantee of success, however. Liverpool's last league title was in 1990, while the last European trophy of one of the richest clubs, Manchester City, was in 1970. Less wealthy clubs can still succeed in soccer. In 1997 Spain's Villareal were bottom of the second division, with only three staff members and a stadium that held 3,500 fans. The team, based in a small town with only 40,000 people, has since reached the Spanish first division and the semifinals of the 2004 UEFA Cup and 2006 Champions League. Porto does not figure in the list of the world's top 20 richest teams, but in 2004 they won the biggest club prize in Europe, the Champions League. More recently, in 2011, it added the UEFA Europa League crown to its achievements.

FACT FILE
In 1991 Manchester United were valued at $32 million. In 2005, to buy control of the club, American businessman Malcolm Glazer had to spend $1.4 billion.

FACT FILE In 1999 Romanian club Nitramonia Fagaras were so cash-strapped that it could not pay its gas bill. It had to transfer two players, Gabor Balazs and Ioan Fatu, to Gazmetan Medias (the gas company's soccer team) as payment.

▲ From his 2005 move to Corinthians in Brazil until being signed by Manchester City in 2009, Argentinian attacker Carlos Tevez was, unusually, "owned" by two companies, MSI and Just Sport Limited.

MONEY MATTERS

In the past, soccer teams received almost all of their money from selling programmes, tickets, food, and drink. Today these items often contribute less than one third of all the money a team generates in a year. Sales of merchandise and deals with advertisers may make up around a third of a team's income (sometimes more for the biggest teams). The largest part of a team's income comes from the sale of broadcasting rights, to television in particular, but also to radio and the Internet. In 2017–2018, Real Madrid earned $168 million from La Liga TV rights—a huge sum.

Some teams have succeeded through the backing of a wealthy company or individual who spends many millions on the team. Since 2003, it is estimated that Roman Abramovich has spent over $1.6 billion on Chelsea, while the Agnelli family—owners of car makers Fiat—has spent almost as much on Juventus. Some teams soll shares in the company that runs them, with mixed success. When Borussia Dortmund were knocked out of the Champions League

TRANSFER MILESTONES

YEAR	FEE	PLAYER
1905	$4,865	Alf Common (Sunderland to Middlesbrough)
1961	$397,600	Luis Suarez (Barcelona to Internazionale)
1968	$1.2m	Pietro Anastasi (Varses to Juventus)
1975	$2.63m	Giuseppe Savoldi (Bologna to Napoli)
1985	$6.74m	Diego Maradona (Barcelona to Napoli)
1992	$19.1m	Jean-Pierre Papin (Marseille to AC Milan)
1998	$35m	Denilson (São Paolo to Real Betis)
2001	$64.8m	Zinedine Zidane (Juventus to Real Madrid)
2009	$124m	Cristiano Ronaldo (Manchester United to Real Madrid)
2013	$132m	Gareth Bale (Tottenham to Real Madrid)
2017	$262m	Neymar (Barcelona to Paris Saint-Germain)

▲ Fans survey the wide range of merchandise for sale at the Nihondaira Stadium, one of the two homes of Japanese J-League side Shimizu S-Pulse.

FACT FILE
Lionel Messi can leave Barcelona if another team bids more than $765 million for him!

◄ Cristiano Ronaldo plays in his first game for Real Madrid after his $124 million signing in 2009. Between 2013 and 2015, Real spent more than $380 million on new players.

in 2003–2004, for example, the value of the team fell by over 15 percent.

Many teams have huge debts through excessive transfer fees and wages, the collapse of TV deals, or poor management. In Italy, the debt of Inter Milan alone is believed to be more than $355 million. Many teams in all leagues have been forced to sell their best players to raise money. Others, such as Glasgow Rangers, have been forcibly relegated to a lower division by their soccer authority (in this case the Scottish FA) because of financial problems, or they have officially gone bankrupt.

PLAYER POWER

Players have always moved from team to team, and for a century the best players have often cost some sort of transfer fee. During the 2012–2013 season, Chelsea could field a side including Juan Mata, Oscar, Eden Hazard, and Fernando Torres, which cost more than $400 million in transfer fees alone. Fees spiraled from the mid-1980s,

with peaks including the 2001 transfer of Zinedine Zidane ($65 million), Cristiano Ronaldo ($124 million) in 2009, and in 2017, Neymar's $262 million transfer to Paris Saint-Germain. In summer 2016 alone, English Premier League clubs spent over $1.5 billion. For many other teams, growing debts mean that they are less able to splurge on such big-money signings. Partly, these debts are due to spiraling player salaries. In 1995 a ruling by the European Court of Justice—the Bosman ruling—made it easier for players to move from team to team at the end of their contracts through a free transfer. Teams were forced to offer higher salaries to lure or to keep star players. In 2018, Lionel Messi signed a new contract with Barcelona, believed to pay him over $61 million a year.

RICH REWARDS?

More of a soccer team's money is spent on buying and paying players than on any other expenditure. In 2017–2018, Barcelona spent $539 million on wages, more than any other European team, while Paris Saint-Germain paid its players an average of over $7.9 million each per year. The rewards for top players are similar in the world's richest leagues, which are all in Europe. Players employ agents to handle transfer moves, from which they may receive five percent or more of the overall fee plus a sign-on bonus. Advertising and endorsing products, sponsorship deals, and writing books and newspaper columns can greatly boost the income of a player. In 2017, Forbes magazine reported that Cristiano Ronaldo earned $86.7 million, some from businesses and endorsements. But in the lower divisions of the top leagues and in smaller leagues around the world the rewards are much smaller and job security for players can be weak.

◄ Walter Strutz, chairman of Mainz, despairs as his team misses out on promotion to the German Bundesliga. For teams everywhere, playing in the top division—where the financial rewards are greatest—is a major goal.

SOCCER NIGHTMARES

Soccer has a dark side. With passions running high on and off the field and with so much at stake in big games, the sport has sometimes lurched into a nightmare world of cheating, abuse, violence, and even death.

CUT OFF IN THEIR PRIME

A number of players have died suddenly through on-field collisions or because of a medical problem. In 1973 Pedro Berruezo died of heart failure while playing for Sevilla. Thirty years later, during a Confederations Cup game against Colombia, Cameroon's 28-year-old midfielder Marc-Vivien Foe collapsed and died shortly afterward.

In 2019, Cardiff City's Argentinian striker, Emiliano Sala, died in a light airplane crash before he had played a game for the Welsh club. Other plane crashes have wiped out entire teams, including Bolivia's most popular team, The Strongest, in 1969, 18 members of the Zambian national squad in 1993, and

▲ Fans pay tribute to Colombian defender Andrés Escobar. The scorer of an own goal in a 2–1 loss to the United States at the 1994 World Cup, Escobar was murdered in his home country ten days later, shot 12 times by an unknown gunman.

Brazilian club Chapecoense in November 2016. Airplane crashes have also devastated club sides, such as the 1958 Munich disaster that killed eight Manchester United players and 11 officials and journalists.

▲ In the 1940s, Torino won four league titles in a row. When their aircraft crashed in 1949, 18 players died, comprising most of the Italian national side.

GAME-FIXING AND CHEATING

In 1909 George Parsonage was banned for life after asking for a $240 sign-on fee when he joined Chesterfield (the maximum allowed was $48). This looks tiny compared to today's examples of corruption, bribery, and game-fixing. In 1999 the former head coach of Romania's Dynamo Bucharest, Vasile Ianul, was sentenced to 12 years in jail for

FACT FILE
In 1999 the owner of Doncaster Rovers, Ken Richardson, was sent to prison for four years for conspiring to burn down the team's main stand.

stealing more than $2.5 million from the team. German soccer was rocked in 2004 when referee Robert Hoyzer owned up to fixing games. He was sentenced to more than two years in jail. In 2006, after a game-rigging scandal, Juventus were relegated to Serie B while AC Milan, Lazio, Fiorentina, and Reggina Calcio were fined, removed from European competitions and had league points deducted. An attempt to fix a game on the field occurred when Chile was being outplayed by Brazil in a 1989 World Cup qualifier. Goalkeeper Roberto Rojas cut himself with a razor blade hidden in his glove and pretended to have been injured by an object thrown from the crowd. The game was abandoned, but video footage proved Rojas' cheating. He was banned, and Chile were prevented from qualifying for the 1994 World Cup. In 2013 Europol, the European Union's police, announced an investigation into more than 300 soccer games in Europe.

STADIUM DISASTERS

Crumbling stadiums, overcrowding, poor safety rules, and weak crowd control have caused many stadium disasters. The worst soccer tragedy ever occurred in Lima, Peru, in 1964 when more than 300 fans were killed and more than 500 injured in panic stampedes and riots. In a 1982 European Cup match in Moscow 340 people died,

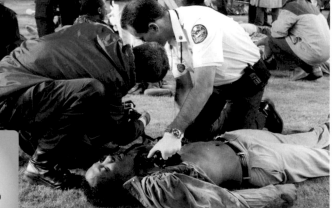

▲ Emergency workers tend to a victim of a tragedy at South Africa's Ellis Park in 2001. Four major stadium disasters occurred in Africa in that year. Altogether, they took the lives of more than 200 people.

Newcastle United players and Aston Villa's Gareth Barry try to separate brawling teammates Kieron Dyer and Lee Bowyer in April 2005. Both players had fallen foul of the authorities before and been criticized as poor role models for youngsters.

FACT FILE In November 2004 the mother of Brazilian star Robinho was kidnapped and only released 41 days later. The mothers of two more Brazilian star players were kidnapped shortly afterward.

most by crushing, when police tried to force fans out of a crowded section of the stadium and down an icy staircase. Two major disasters occurred in 1985—a wooden stand at Bradford City's ground caught fire, killing 56 people, while the European Cup final also ended in tragedy. A wall collapsed at the Heysel Stadium in Belgium and a riot flared when some Liverpool fans charged at Juventus supporters. One Belgian and 38 Italian spectators died as a result.

POOR ROLE MODELS?

Soccer players are highly esteemed as role models to young people, but some have abused their positions and been convicted of crimes. In 2013 Manchester City's Courtney Meppen-Walter was jailed for 16 months for causing death by dangerous driving. Other players have behaved violently on and off the field. In November 2005, a huge brawl begun by Turkish players in a World Cup qualifier against Switzerland led to the country having to play its next six

▲ *At Liverpool's Anfield ground, fans lay tributes to the 96 people who died during the 1989 FA Cup semifinal at Hillsborough Stadium.*

home games in other countries. Players have also fought with fans. Manchester United's Eric Cantona, for example, kicked a Crystal Palace supporter in 1995.

Like athletes in other sports, soccer players are tested for illegal drug use. In 2018 Samir Nasri received a backdated 18-month ban for a doping incident in 2016 and did not play soccer again until he joined West Ham United at the start of 2019. Diego Maradona remains soccer's most notorious drugs cheat. He was sent

home from the 1994 World Cup after testing positive for the stimulant ephedrine; in recent years, Maradona has fought an addiction to cocaine. Many other soccer players have battled against alcohol addiction, from former England captain Tony Adams to Brazilian legend Garrincha.

RACISM AND INTIMIDATION

Some fans, players, and coaches have been found guilty of racially insulting or abusing opponents. Racism in soccer was thought to be on the wane, with nonwhite players making up a fifth or more of the total number of players in many European leagues. Antiracism campaign work has been carried out by many clubs, governments, and groups such as FARE (Football Against Racism in Europe). However, incidents of racist chanting still occur. In January 2013 AC Milan's Kevin-Prince Boateng walked off the field, followed by the rest of both teams, after he and other black players were targets of racial abuse from some fans. Violence and intimidation can occur on and off the field; sometimes, referees are the target. In 2005 referee Luiz Carlos Silva was drawn into a fist fight after being attacked on the field by a fan during the Brazilian derby between America MG and Atlético Mineiro. In 2012 a Dutch referee's assistant was attacked by teenagers from Nieuw Sloten B1, one of the teams taking part in the game. He died the next day.

▲ *Referee Anders Frisk was hit by an object thrown by Roma fans during a 2004 Champions League game against Dynamo Kiev. Frisk abandoned the game at halftime and UEFA awarded Kiev a 3–0 victory. In 2005 Frisk retired from refereeing after he and his family received death threats.*

SPAIN WIN AT LAST

A fourth-place World Cup finish and a single European Championship in 1964 was a poor return for a team of Spain's incredible caliber. Spain entered Euro 2008 with a skilled team, packed with talents such as Xavi Hernández, Andrés Iniesta, goalkeeper Iker Casillas, and predatory striker Fernando Torres. Spain purred through their group, mauling Russia 4–1 and beating Sweden and reigning champions Greece. The team endured a tense battle against world champions Italy, going through 4–3 on penalties, before brushing aside Russia again in the semifinal. Spain met Germany in the final, with Torres striking the game's only goal in the 33rd minute. At last Spain's attacking flair and intricate passing play had turned them into worthy tournament winners. The team built on this European success to become the world's most dominant team, winning the 2010 World Cup and Euro 2012.

Iker Casillas, Spain's goalkeeper and captain, punches the ball to safety during the final of Euro 2008. Casillas had earlier been the hero of Spain's quarterfinal win against Italy, saving two penalties in a shoot-out.

THE WORLD CUP

Exhibition or charity games are entertaining, but for a soccer game to have meaning it has to be part of a wider competition. Soccer has spawned hundreds of different competitions, but none can compete in global interest and prestige with the World Cup. From small beginnings with 13 competing countries, it has grown to the point where 203 nations attempted to qualify for the 2018 competition.

▲ Sepp Blatter announces the hosts of the 2018 and 2022 World Cups on TV.

HOPING TO HOST

Six nations expressed an interest in hosting the first World Cup, held in 1930, and ever since, countries have prepared their bid many years in advance to try and secure the World Cup within their borders. The tournament was first held in Africa in 2010 and will be hosted in the Middle East for the first time in 2022. Only one tournament has been cohosted (Japan/South Korea in 2002), but the 2026 World Cup will feature three hosts—Canada, the United States, and Mexico—with an expanded format containing 48 teams.

▲ Argentina's goalkeeper, Juan Botasso, makes a despairing dive but fails to stop Hector Castro scoring Uruguay's fourth goal in the 1930 final.

URUGUAY 1930

Final
Uruguay 4 • Argentina 2
Semifinals
Uruguay 6 • Yugoslavia 1
Argentina 6 • USA 1
Games 18 **Goals** 70
Goals per game 3.89

It took 19 minutes for France's Lucien Laurent to write his name in the record books as the scorer of the first World Cup goal. France beat Mexico 4–1, but it was their only victory and, like Belgium and Romania, they went out at the group stage. Four European sides made the long trip to South America by boat, but only Yugoslavia reached the semifinals. It and the United States were thrashed in the semis by Uruguay and Argentina respectively. Argentina boasted the best forward of the competition, Guillermo Stabile, but Uruguay—on home ground and as reigning Olympic champions—were firm favorites. In the final, the team came back strongly after Argentina had taken a 2–1 lead, to become the first World Cup winners.

ITALY 1934

Final
Italy 2 • Czechoslovakia 1
Semifinals
Italy 1 • Austria 0
Czechoslovakia 3 • Germany 1
Games 17 **Goals** 70
Goals per game 4.12

In 1934, the South American teams had not forgotten the lack of European entrants for the first World Cup. As a result, world champions Uruguay chose not to defend their title, while Brazil and Argentina sent understrength teams to Italy. Yet 32 nations, mostly European, were keen to enter the competition. With 16 places available, qualification games began in June 1933. Italy's 4–0 win over Greece marked the first and only time that a World Cup host has had to play a qualifier to get into the finals. Egypt was the first nation outside of the Americas or Europe to qualify, but following one round of knockout games, the eight remaining teams were all European. After a 7–1 thrashing of the United States, Italy's goals dried up, and they only just sneaked past Spain and Austria on their way to the final. In that game, Italy's Luisito Monti (formerly of Argentina) became the only player to have appeared in a World Cup final for different countries. Against a battling Czech team, a goal five minutes into extra time from Italy's Angelo Schiavio secured the Jules Rimet trophy for the hosts.

▼ Coach Vittorio Pozzo is carried by triumphant Italian players after masterminding their 1934 World Cup campaign.

FRANCE 1938

Final

Italy 4 • Hungary 2

Semifinals

Italy 2 • Brazil 1

Hungary 5 • Sweden 1

Games 18 **Goals** 84

Goals per game 4.67

With the threat of war looming over Europe, Spain and Austria were forced to pull out of the tournament. But the 1938 World Cup did feature the first team from Asia, the Dutch East Indies (now Indonesia), as well as a Cuban side that sprang a major shock by beating Romania in a replay. Sweden thrashed Cuba 8–0, but were then on the receiving end of a 5–1 semifinal mauling by the first great Hungarian side. The other semifinal saw one of the great managerial blunders when the Brazil coach, Adhemar Pimenta, either because of arrogance or through injury fears, rested his star player, Léonidas da Silva. Léonidas had lit up the tournament, most notably in an epic 6–5 thriller against Poland in which he became the first player to score four goals in a World Cup final game, only for Poland's Ernest Wilimowski to do the same five minutes later. Without the tournament's top scorer, Brazil crashed to defeat against Italy, who went on to become champions for the second time.

▶ Léonidas da Silva twists and turns at the 1938 World Cup. An amazingly skilled attacker, the Brazilian was one of the first players to master the overhead kick.

FACT FILE Dr. Ottorino Barassi, the vice president of the Italian FA, smuggled the World Cup out of a bank in Rome and hid it to prevent the Nazis from stealing the trophy. For much of World War II, soccer's greatest prize lay in a shoebox under Barassi's bed.

▲ Brazilian keeper Moacir Barbosa gathers the ball during a 1950 group game against Yugoslavia. The match, watched by more than 142,000 spectators in the Maracanã, ended in a 2–0 victory to Brazil.

BRAZIL 1950

Final pool

Uruguay 5 pts • Brazil 4 pts

Sweden 2 pts • Spain 1 pt

Games 22 **Goals** 88

Goals per game 4.00

The only World Cup to feature a final pool of four instead of a final, the 1950 tournament started poorly. Scotland and Turkey withdrew, only 13 nations attended and the mighty Maracanã Stadium was not ready to host the first match. But the competition built in excitement and drama as the goals flowed, often from the cleats of the hosts who, after topping their group, ran rampant in the final pool stages, scoring seven against Sweden and six against Spain. Before that point, there had been several notable shocks, including the United State's 1–0 defeat of a highly qualified England team. The final pool format could have been a letdown, but the outcome went down to the very last game, with Uruguay and Brazil separated by one point and playing in front of around 199,850 fans. Despite falling a goal behind to the favorites, Uruguay won the game 2–1 to lift the World Cup once again.

FACT FILE At the 1930 World Cup, not one of the 18 games was tied. Neither was there a play-off game to decide third place.

WORLD CUP "GOLDEN BOOT" WINNERS (GOALS)

1930	Guillermo Stabile, Argentina (8)
1934	Oldrich Nejedly, Czech. (5)
1938	Léonidas da Silva, Brazil (8)
1950	Ademir Menezes, Brazil (9)
1954	Sandor Kocsis, Hungary (11)
1958	Just Fontaine, France (13)
1962	Garrincha, Brazil; Vava, Brazil; Valentin Ivanov, USSR; Leonel Sanchez, Chile; Florian Albert, Hungary; Drazan Jerkovic, Yugoslavia (4)
1966	Eusebio, Portugal (9)
1970	Gerd Müller, West Germany (10)
1974	Gregorz Lato, Poland (7)
1978	Mario Kempes, Argentina (6)
1982	Paolo Rossi, Italy (6)
1986	Gary Lineker, England (6)
1990	Salvatore Schillaci, Italy (6)
1994	Hristo Stoichkov, Bulgaria; Oleg Salenko, Russia (6)
1998	Davor Suker, Croatia (6)
2002	Ronaldo, Brazil (8)
2006	Miroslav Klose, Germany (5)
2010	Thomas Müller, Germany; Wesley Sneijder, Netherlands; Diego Forlán, Uruguay; David Villa, Spain (5)
2014	James Rodriguez, Colombia (6)
2018	Harry Kane, England (6)

SWITZERLAND 1954

Final

West Germany 3 • Hungary 2

Semifinals

West Germany 6 • Austria 1

Hungary 4 • Uruguay 2

Games 26 **Goals** 140

Goals per game 5.38

As the home to the headquarters of FIFA, which was celebrating its 50th birthday, Switzerland was an obvious host for the 1954 tournament. It featured newcomers such as Turkey, South Korea, and the western half of a divided Germany (which had been barred from the 1950 competition). The fans saw plenty of drama and goals, none more than in Austria's 7–5 defeat of Switzerland (the highest-scoring game in the history of the World Cup finals). Hungary, boasting the incredible talents of Ferenc Puskas, Sandor Kocsis, and Nandor Hidegkuti, was the most menacing team, scoring an incredible 27 goals in only five games. At its third World Cup, Uruguay thrashed Scotland 7–0 and beat England 4–2 to reach the semifinals. It was the only team never to have been beaten in the World Cup until they came up against Hungary, who won 4–2 and went into the final as favorite. West Germany, however, overturned the odds to record a highly emotional victory.

◄ Pelé chases the ball during Brazil's exciting semifinal against France. The score was poised at 2–1 to Brazil before Pelé scored three goals in 21 minutes.

FACT FILE Vava's goal in the 1962 final (to add to his pair of goals in the 1958 final) made him the only player to have scored in the finals of successive World Cups.

SWEDEN 1958

Final

Brazil 5 • Sweden 2

Semifinals

Brazil 5 • France 2

Sweden 3 • West Germany 1

Games 35 **Goals** 126

Goals per game 3.60

Fifty-five countries entered the 1958 qualifying tournament, and some big names, including Italy, the Netherlands, Spain, and Uruguay, failed to qualify. All four U.K. home nations (Scotland, England, Northern Ireland, and Wales) reached the finals—the only time this has ever happened. England had lost key players in the Munich airplane crash (see page 79), but was the only team to hold a rampant Brazilian team to a tie and to stop Brazil scoring. It was the

World Cup's first 0–0 tie. Yet it was the two smaller British nations, Wales and Northern Ireland, who qualified for the quarterfinals, with the Irish sensationally beating a strong Czechoslovakian team. Free-scoring France and Brazil quickly emerged as the favorites, and their semifinal clash was an epic in which the 17-year-old Pelé blasted a hat trick toward Brazil's victory. France had to be content with a 6–3 mauling of West Germany to secure third place. Just Fontaine's four goals in that game propelled him to the "Golden Boot" with 13 goals in total, a record to this day. The hosts, Sweden, had quietly and efficiently seen off some very strong teams—including Hungary, the Soviet Union, and West Germany—to reach the final, but they were no match for Brazil. In a rematch of the pair's third-place play-off at the 1938 World Cup, Brazil triumphed 5–2 to win the tournament for the first time.

◄ Hungary's Zoltan Czibor outjumps Ottmar Walter of West Germany in the 1954 final. Czibor scored to put Hungary 2–0 up but found himself on the losing team after a heroic comeback by the Germans.

▲ Argentina's Jorge Albrecht (left) and Uwe Seeler of West Germany struggle for the ball in 1966. Seeler played in each of the four World Cups sandwiched between West Germany's victories in 1954 and 1974.

CHILE 1962

Final

Brazil 3 • Czechoslovakia 1

Semifinals

Brazil 4 • Chile 2

Czechoslovakia 3 • Yugoslavia 1

Games 32 **Goals** 89

Goals per game 2.78

Chile was a controversial choice to host the World Cup, with its small population and its infrastructure damaged by an earthquake in 1960. As it turned out, most of the problems happened on the field. A series of bad-tempered games occurred in the first round, including the infamous "Battle of Santiago," during which armed police invaded the field three times in order to split up warring Chilean and Italian players. Chile made it through to a semifinal against Brazil by beating the Soviet Union, while two strong Eastern European teams, Yugoslavia and Czechoslovakia, battled it out in the other semifinal. The Brazilians lost Pelé to injury after only two games, but in Garrincha and Vava they had two of the best players of the tournament. Brazil efficiently won the final with a team featuring eight World Cup winners from the 1958 tournament.

ENGLAND 1966

Final

England 4 • West Germany 2

Semifinals

England 2 • Portugal 1

West Germany 2 • Soviet Union 1

Games 32 **Goals** 89

Goals per game 2.78

The 1966 World Cup was a well-organized tournament and the first to feature a mascot (World Cup Willie). West Germany and Portugal were the most free-scoring teams in a competition characterized by defensive play. Two huge shocks occurred early on—Brazil was eliminated by Portugal and newcomer North Korea knocked out Italy with a stunning 1–0 victory. The North Koreans won the support of many neutral fans, and the team's quarterfinal meeting with Portugal was a classic. North Korea was 3–0 up within 20 minutes before Portugal, inspired by the tournament's eventual top scorer, Eusebio,

▲ *Portugal's star striker, Eusebio, walks off in tears after his team is eliminated from the 1966 World Cup following a 2–1 defeat by England.*

hit back to win 5–3. In the semifinal, Eusebio's 82nd-minute strike could not stop England going through to meet West Germany in what proved to be an epic final. The Germans went ahead, then England scored twice to lead until a surprise last-minute German goal took the game into extra time. Geoff Hurst scored two more goals to secure a dramatic victory for the host nation (see pages 68–69).

FACT FILE Two pairs of brothers have played on winning teams in a World Cup final—Fritz and Ottmar Walter of West Germany (1954) and England's Jack and Bobby Charlton (1966).

MEXICO 1970

Final

Brazil 4 • Italy 1

Semifinals

Brazil 3 • Uruguay 1

Italy 4 • West Germany 3

Games 32 **Goals** 95

Goals per game 2.97

For many seasoned soccer observers, the 1970 World Cup remains the best. Most of the brutal, physical play seen in the 1962 and 1966 tournaments was absent. In its place were fascinating tactical and skillful contests between the world's greatest teams. Although the tournament was the first to feature red and yellow cards, no player was sent off, and some of the games have passed into soccer legend. These include a chesslike battle between Brazil and England that the South Americans narrowly won 1–0; Italy's 4–1 defeat of Mexico; and the Italians amazing 4–3 victory against West Germany in the semifinal. But the final tops the list. Brazil had powered through the rounds, with star players such as Jairzinho (who set a record by scoring in all six of Brazil's games), Pelé, and Rivelino exhibiting great attacking flair. In the final Brazil was unstoppable, recording their third World Cup win and claiming the Jules Rimet trophy in recognition of the team's unique feat.

▼ *Brazilian striker Tostao holds off Italy's Roberto Rosato during the 1970 World Cup final. Tostao suffered a freak eye injury before the tournament, and only last-minute surgery enabled him to play.*

WEST GERMANY 1974

Final

West Germany 2 • Netherlands 1

Third-place play-off Poland 1 • Brazil 0

Games 38 **Goals** 97

Goals per game 2.55

Ninety-nine nations attempted to qualify for the 1974 tournament, which would see the winners lift a new trophy—the FIFA World Cup. Spain, France, and England all failed to reach the tournament, while Zaire, Haiti, East Germany, and Australia made their debuts. Changes to the competition format meant that there would be no semifinal games. Instead, the winners of the two second-round groups would contest the final and the group runners-up would play off for third place. The Netherlands, exhibiting its brand of "total soccer," swept aside Bulgaria (4–1), Uruguay (2–0), Brazil (2–0), and Argentina (4–0) to top Group A and reach the final. Poland were the surprise team of the tournament. Propelled in part by the goals of striker Gregorz Lato, it finished second in Group B after narrowly losing 1–0 to West Germany. The West Germans had taken time to reach full speed, but with Franz Beckenbauer pulling the strings and the prolific Gerd Müller in fine form, the team made the final. There, it overcame the setback of a first-minute Dutch goal from a penalty to win the World Cup for a second time.

> **FACT FILE** On June 14, 1974, Carlos Caszely of Chile became the first player to receive a red card in a World Cup tournament.

▼ Peru's Teofilo Cubillas (center) runs at Argentina's defense during his team's controversial 6–0 defeat. Cubillas scored five goals at the 1978 World Cup, matching his total at the 1970 competition.

ARGENTINA 1978

Final

Argentina 3 • Netherlands 1

Third-place play-off Brazil 2 • Italy 1

Games 38 **Goals** 102

Goals per game 2.68

A colorful and at times controversial tournament, the 1978 World Cup may have lacked some stand-out stars, but it was rarely short of soccer drama. The host found themselves in the toughest of groups with France, Hungary, and a young Italian team that beat it, but Argentina made it through to the second group stage. Tunisia caused a shock by tying with holder West Germany and beating Mexico 3–1 to become the first African team to win a World Cup finals game. Austria, with its star striker Hans Krankl, played strongly in the early stages, beating Spain, Sweden, and West Germany. But it was crushed 5–1 by a Dutch team that lacked Johan Cruyff, who had pulled out of the tournament for family reasons. Scotland's campaign held promise but went askew when it failed to beat Iran and lost to Peru. Then the team roused itself, however, to beat the Netherlands 3–2. In the second group stage, Italy, Argentina, Brazil, and the Netherlands emerged as the frontrunners. Much controversy centerd around the Argentina-Peru game. The last game in Group B, it would determine whether Argentina or Brazil reached the final. Peru had played well in the early stages of the tournament, winning its group ahead of the Netherlands. The team's 6–0 loss to Argentina was suspicious and meant that Brazil was knocked out without having suffered a defeat, while Argentina progressed to the final, in which it beat the Netherlands.

◄ Germany's defense, marshalled by legendary goalkeeper Sepp Maier and the incomparable Franz Beckenbauer (far right), holds firm against a Dutch attack in the 1974 World Cup final.

SPAIN 1982

Final

Italy 3 • West Germany 1

Semifinals

Italy 2 • Poland 0

West Germany 3 • France 3 (5–4 penalties)

Games 52 **Goals** 146

Goals per game 2.81

In 1982 the format of the tournament changed again so that 24 countries would appear at the finals. Teams played in six groups of four, with the top 12 teams playing in four groups of three to determine the semifinalists. Belgium surprised the holder, Argentina, beating it and El Salvador to win its group, while England topped its group ahead of France. The two surprise teams were Northern Ireland, who beat Spain to reach the second round, and Algeria, who had stunned fans by winning its game against West Germany. Poland made the semifinals, but the hosts went out after winning only one game. The toughest second-round group, containing Brazil, Argentina, and Italy, saw the Italians go through, beating Brazil in a 3–2 thriller. At the semifinal stage West Germany beat France in an equally exciting encounter but could not stop the Italians from winning their third World Cup.

▶ *In 1982 an Algerian fan waves banknotes in protest as West Germany and Austria conspire to achieve a result which took both European teams through at the expense of Algeria. All final group games are now played simultaneously to give teams an equal chance.*

MEXICO 1986

Final

Argentina 3 • West Germany 2

Semifinals

Argentina 2 • Belgium 0

West Germany 2 • France 0

Games 52 **Goals** 132

Goals per game 2.54

Colombia had been due to host the 1986 World Cup, but troubles in that country meant that it had to withdraw. When Mexico stepped in, it became the first nation to host the tournament twice. More than 120 nations battled for the 24 places in the finals, in which Canada and Iraq both made their debuts. Morocco became the first African nation to reach the second round when it won a group that

contained Portugal, Poland, and England. Denmark looked promising until it was thrashed 5–1 by Spain, while Belgium squeezed past the Soviet Union 4–3 in one of the best games of the tournament. The quarterfinals were extremely close games. Three went to penalty shoot-outs, while the fourth game saw England face Argentina. Maradona arrived at the World Cup as the world's most expensive player and a heavily marked man. His incredible dribbling and scoring skills made him the best player of the tournament. In the quarterfinal, his two goals (one a deliberate handball, the other a magnificent solo effort—see pages 56–57) sank England, and he repeated the feat against Belgium in the semifinal. In the final, West Germany went 2–0 down, rallied to 2–2, but was beaten by an 88th-minute goal from Argentinian midfielder Burruchaga.

▲ *Marco Tardelli (left) charges away after scoring Italy's second goal in the 1982 World Cup final against West Germany. Teammates Claudio Gentile and Gabriele Oriali are just as jubilant.*

◀ *Argentina's Diego Maradona celebrates as his team triumphs over West Germany in the 1986 final.*

ITALY 1990

Final

West Germany 1 • Argentina 0

Semifinals

West Germany 1 • England 1 (4–3 penalties)

Argentina 1 • Italy 1 (4–3 penalties)

Games 52 **Goals** 115

Goals per game 2.21

This well-organized and attended World Cup is remembered for moments of great drama, from veteran Cameroon striker Roger Milla's dance at the corner flag to Costa Rica's joy at defeating both Scotland and Sweden to qualify for the second round. Sadly, the tournament also saw a lot of negative soccer and a record number of bookings (164), as well as 16 send-offs. Every previous winner of the World Cup made it through the group stages, with Cameroon the talk of the tournament after its defeats of Romania and Colombia set up a quarterfinal against England. Cameroon went 2–0 up, but two Gary Lineker penalties and a third England goal in extra time saw every neutral's favorite team go out. The Netherlands arrived as European Champion but failed to win a game, while Brazil and the Soviet Union had similarly disappointing tournaments. Both semifinals were tense games that went to penalty shoot-outs, but the final was deeply forgettable. West Germany beat Argentina courtesy of an 85th-minute penalty, while Pedro Monzon was the first of two send-offs for Argentina and the first player to be red carded in a World Cup final.

▼ Italian goalkeeper Walter Zenga concedes a headed goal to Argentina's Claudio Caniggia in the 1990 semifinal.

UNITED STATES 1994

Final

Brazil 0 • Italy 0 (3–2 penalties)

Semifinals

Brazil 1 • Sweden 0

Italy 2 • Bulgaria 1

Games 52 **Goals** 141

Goals per game 2.71

Some feared the crowds at the 1994 World Cup would be small in a country where male soccer is not a dominant sport. But they were proven wrong by a tournament attended by an average of 70,000 fans per game. Attacking play was encouraged by the adoption of both the back-pass rule (see page 24) and three instead of two points for a win during the group-stage games. Despite losing many players since the breakup of the Soviet Union, Russia recorded the biggest win, 6–1 against Cameroon, with Oleg Salenko scoring five goals—the most by one player in a single World Cup game. Maradona left the tournament when he failed a drugs test, but plenty of other stars were there. The Republic of Ireland caused the biggest shock of the group stages by beating Italy 1–0, but Saudi Arabia's win against

◄ Bulgaria's Iordan Letchkov (left) beats Germany's Thomas Hassler to score a spectacular diving header at the 1994 World Cup.

Belgium and Bulgaria's defeat of Argentina came close. Bulgaria had a great tournament, knocking out Germany and finishing fourth. European teams dominated the quarterfinals, taking seven out of the eight spots, but Brazil beat the Netherlands, Sweden, and Italy, and took the trophy for a record fourth time.

FRANCE 1998

Final

France 3 • Brazil 0

Semifinals

France 2 • Croatia 1

Brazil 1 • Netherlands 1 (4–2 penalties)

Games 64 **Goals** 171

Goals per game 2.67

With places at this tournament increased to 32, newcomers included Jamaica, Japan, and South Africa. Iran caused a shock in its first World Cup for 20 years by beating the United States. Nigeria upset the odds with a 3–2 defeat of Spain that effectively knocked out the European team. Despite 22 red cards, the competition was enthralling, with Croatia, Denmark, Brazil, France, and the Netherlands playing attacking soccer. England narrowly went out, losing on penalties to Argentina in one of the best games of the tournament. Croatia progressed and won against Germany 3–0 in the quarterfinal. For the second World Cup in a row, Italy was knocked out on penalties, this time to France at the quarterfinal stage. A France-Brazil final was an exciting prospect, but Ronaldo was sick before the game and was extremely subdued. France won with relative ease, aided by two goals from Zinedine Zidane.

SOUTH KOREA AND JAPAN 2002

Final
Brazil 2 • Germany 0
Semifinals
Brazil 1 • Turkey 0
Germany 1 • South Korea 0
Games 64 **Goals** 161
Goals per game 2.52

An amazing 193 nations attempted to qualify for the first World Cup held in Asia. Surprise failures included Holland, Uruguay, and Colombia. A shock came in the opening game in which Senegal beat the World Cup holders, France, 1–0. France then lost to Denmark and exited the tournament, as did Russia, Poland, and Portugal. Cheered on by passionate crowds, the South Koreans were headline news, knocking out Italy, Spain, and Portugal to reach the semifinals, along with Turkey who eventually finished third. The final saw Brazilian striker Ronaldo turn back the years to score two goals that defeated Germany.

GERMANY 2006

Final
Italy 1 • France 1 (5–3 penalties)
Semifinals
Italy 2 • Germany 0 (after extra time)
France 1 • Portugal 0
Games 62 **Goals** 147
Goals per game 2.3

▲ Turkey's Hakan Sukur (right) tangles with South Korea's Lee Min-Sung during the 2002 third-place play-off.

Despite a thrilling opening match (Germany 4–2 Costa Rica), this tournament saw defences on top and a record card count (345 yellow and 28 red). Italy's miserly defence, led by Fabio Cannavaro, let in just one goal on the way to the first all-European final since 1982. Elsewhere, only one (Ghana) of the five African nations present progressed from their group whilst Australia, Oceania's first team at a World Cup since 1982, surprisingly qualified from a group featuring Brazil, Japan, and Croatia. In the final, Zinedine Zidane—playing his last competitive match—scored a penalty only for Italian defender Marco Materazzi to equalize. During extra time, Zidane was sent off for head-butting Materazzi in the chest. With the game ending in a stalemate, Italy won a tense penalty shootout to secure the World Cup for a fourth time.

SOUTH AFRICA 2010

Final
Spain 1 • Netherlands 0 (after extra time)
Semi-finals
Netherlands 3 • Uruguay 2
Spain 1 • Germany 0
Games 64 **Goals** 145
Goals per game 2.27

The first tournament to be held in Africa will be remembered as a noisy, colorful affair with some 3.18 million spectators attending matches in ten stadiums. Serbia and Slovakia made their tournament debuts but failed to progress from their group, a fate which also befell Cameroon, Denmark, Italy, and France.

The Germans would score the most goals (16) in the tournament, but they finished in third place after being knocked out in the semifinals. The Netherlands were also on a roll, taking their World Cup and World Cup qualifying winning run to 13 games when they knocked out Brazil in the quarterfinals. Spain lost their very first game, 1–0 against Switzerland, but they won each one of their four knockout games 1–0, including a tense final against the Netherlands, to claim their first ever World Cup.

▼ Senegal beat France 1–0 in the opening game of the 2002 World Cup, the first in a series of surprise results. Here, French midfielder Patrick Vieira (left) fights for the ball with Senegalese defender Papa Bouba Diop.

BRAZIL 2014

Final
Germany 1 • Argentina 0 (a.e.t.)
Semi-finals
Germany 7 • Brazil 1
Argentina 0 • Netherland 0 (4-2 penalties)
Games 64 **Goals** 171
Goals per game 2.67

The first World Cup in Brazil for 64 years saw the debut of Bosnia & Herzegovina, goal-line technology, and vanishing foam used by referees to mark out distances for free kicks. Defending champions, Spain, crashed out at the group stage after being thrashed 5–1 by the Netherlands and losing 2–0 to an impressive Chile. In Group D, Uruguay and Costa Rica progressed, knocking out England and Italy, while Algeria qualified for the first time in their history. The host's hopes were crushed in an extraordinary semi-final where Germany scored five times in just 20 first-half minutes to end up 7–1 winners. They met Argentina in the final where a Mario Götze goal made Germany the first European team to win a World Cup held in the Americas. Colombia's James Rodriguez won the Golden Boot for top scorer with six goals, while Lionel Messi was awarded the Golden Ball as the tournament's best player.

RUSSIA 2018

Final
France 4 • Croatia 2
Semi-finals
France 1 • Belgium 0
Croatia 2 • England 0
Games 64 **Goals** 169
Goals per game 2.64

A celebration of football and fandom, Russia proved welcoming hosts. The football often dazzled and entertained with only one of the 64 games, France against Denmark, ending in a goalless draw. With a population of less than 340,000, Iceland became the smallest country to play in a World Cup. They failed to qualify out of their group, as did all the African nations and the defending champions, Germany. Losing to both Mexico and South Korea, it was the first time Germany had failed to qualify from their group since 1938. The hosts, however, fared better, progressing from their group then beating Spain in a penalty shootout that gripped spectators around the world. Exciting young stars like Kevin De Bruyne and Kylian Mbappé helped propel Belgium and France to the semi-finals, whilst England recorded their biggest ever World Cup win, overpowering Panama 6-1. England's Harry Kane would win the Golden Boot as top scorer whilst Luka Modric won

▲ *Xabi Alonso of Spain lifts the World Cup after a tense 1–0 win over the Netherlands in the 2010 final.*

the Golden Ball as the tournament's best player, but the glory and a second World Cup win went to France.

THE WOMEN'S WORLD CUP

CHINA 1991

Final U.S. 2 • Norway 1
The first Women's World Cup was a great success and proved that women's soccer had a major global audience. China, Denmark, Chinese Taipei, and Italy were all knocked out in the quarterfinals, leaving the United States, Norway, Sweden, and Germany in the semifinals. About 65,000 spectators watched the final, in which the United States beat Norway with a goal from Michelle Akers just three minutes from full time.

SWEDEN 1995

Final Norway 2 • Germany 0
The tournament's 26 games saw many goals. Brazil were thrashed 6–1 by Germany, who then lost a 3–2 thriller to Sweden. The United States and China tied in an epic 3–3 encounter, and Norway powered through its group, putting 17 goals past Canada, England, and Nigeria, before knocking out the United States at the semifinal stage. Sweden's Ingrid Jonsson became the first woman to referee a FIFA final—Norway scored two first-half goals to secure the world crown.

UNITED STATES 1999

Final U.S. 0 • China 0 (5–4 penalties)
Expanded to 16 teams, the tournament was a huge success and saw Nigeria become the first African team to reach the quarterfinals. The United States, with Mia Hamm, Brandi Chastain, and Tiffeny Milbrett all playing superbly, had to come from behind against a strong German team, before overcoming Brazil in the semifinals. In contrast, China cruised to the final, mauling cup-holder Norway 5–0. The final, played in front of more than 90,000 fans at the Rose Bowl in Pasadena, California, was a very tense affair. The game went to penalties, with Briana Scurry saving Ying Liu's spot kick to see the United States win the shoot-out 5–4.

UNITED STATES 2003

Final Germany 2 • Sweden 1
An epidemic of the SARS virus prevented China from hosting the World Cup, and the tournament was moved to the United States at the last minute. The 2003 World Cup was predicted to be a successful swan song for many U.S. veteran players. However, a vibrant, attacking German side—headed by the tournament's leading scorer, Birgit Prinz—

► *Mesut Özil of Germany kicks the ball away from Lucas Biglia of Argentina during the 2014 World Cup final game.*

▼ Brazil's Marta was the top scorer, with seven goals, at the 2007 Women's World Cup, held in China.

knocked them out at the semifinal stage. In a memorable final a "golden goal" by subsitute Nia Kuenzer secured Germany their first Women's World Cup.

CHINA 2007

Final Germany 2 • Brazil 0

The tournament got off to a record start with Germany thrashing Argentina 11–0 in Group A while Brazil, led by top scorer Marta, mauled New Zealand 5–0 and China 4–0 in Group D. These two teams, along with Norway and the United States, made it out of their groups and into the semifinals, where Brazil handed a surprise 4–0 defeat to the United States to join Germany in the final. Two second-half goals from Birgit Prinz and Simone Ladehr propelled Germany to its second World Cup final victory in a row.

GERMANY 2011

Final Japan 2 • U.S. 2 (3–1 penalties)

A successful, exciting, well-staged tournament saw almost a million spectators watch games between the 16 teams, which included both Colombia and Equatorial

Guinea for the first time. Two of the quarterfinals went to penalty shoot-outs, with France prevailing over England after a 1–1 tie and Brazil losing to the U.S. team after an epic game in Dresden. The U.S. went down to ten players after a red card in the 65th minute, but managed to take the game into extra time and equalized in the 122nd minute. The U.S. went through to the final where they came up against the newest force of women's soccer. Japan, led by the tournament's best player, Homare Sawa, became the first team from Asia to win a World Cup.

CANADA 2015

Final U.S. 5 • Japan 2

Canada hosted the tournament, which was expanded to include 24 teams (16 participated in 2011). The six stadiums all featured artificial turf instead of grass, which caused controversy and complaints from some players, but otherwise the tournament was considered a success and showcased elite women's soccer with some compelling games and stunning displays. Switzerland defeated Ecuador 10–1 in a game where Ecuador's Angie Ponce scored two own goals, while Germany thrashed the Ivory Coast 10–0. Many other games though were close, tense affairs with eight of the 12 round of 16 and quarterfinal games being decided by 1–0 or 2–1 scorelines. England knocked out the hosts at the quarterfinal stage while Australia defeated a highly-rated Brazilian team at the same stage, lost narrowly to Japan but beat Germany in the playoff game to finish third overall. Former champions United States met current holder Japan in the final where a spectacular hat trick from U.S. midfielder Carli Lloyd included an incredible shot from the halfway line. Lloyd was awarded the "Golden Ball" as player of the tournament— she scored six goals and tied with Germany's Célia Šašic as the top scorer.

FRANCE 2019

Final U.S. 2 • Netherlands 0

The 2019 competition was the biggest Women's World Cup ever, with more than one million spectators in France and global television audiences passing one billion. There were goals galore as host nation France kicked off with an emphatic 4–0 win over South Korea, the first of 52 matches and 146 goals in total. The U.S. entered the competition as defending champions and firm favorites. They did not disappoint, hammering Thailand with a record-breaking scoreline of 13–0 in their opening match and a record-breaking five goals in one game for striker Alex Morgan. The U.S. knocked out Spain, France, and England on their way to the final where they beat the Netherlands 2–0 in their fourth World Cup win. U.S. co-captain Megan Rapinoe stole the headlines, bagging the Golden Ball for best player and the Golden Boot for six goals. More history was made when Brazilian legend Marta scored against Italy, bringing her World Cup record to 17 goals, more than any player, male or female, to date. This tournament saw a welcome boost in investment, sponsorship, and publicity for female football. Plans are already underway for the 2023 World Cup with 32 teams set to take part and a doubling of the prize money.

▲ Homare Sawa, captain of the Japanese team, lifts the trophy awarded to the winners of the 2011 Women's World Cup. Sawa was the tournament's leading goalscorer, with five goals.

THE EUROPEAN CHAMPIONSHIPS

The European Championships started life in 1958 as the UEFA European Nations Cup but struggled to find enough nations to compete. Today, however, the competition is the largest international soccer competition behind the World Cup. Like that tournament, it is held every four years.

A DEVELOPING COMPETITION

Early tournaments consisted of qualifying rounds with just four teams progressing to a mini tournament of semifinals and a final. France v Yugoslavia picked the game of the first competition with the Yugoslavs coming back from 4-2 down to win 5-4, only to lose in the final to the Soviet Union. Strong teams from Eastern Europe dominated early tournaments, reaching the first five finals, including in 1976 when Czechoslovakia defeated then world champions, West Germany, four days after knocking out France to win the tournament. By Italy 1980, the format was expanded to allow eight teams to contest the finals. That number doubled in 1996 when England hosted the competition for the first time. In between, gifted and skilful

French and Dutch teams swept rivals aside in 1984 and 1988 respectively, but many favored teams missed out on the finals during the period before expansion, such as England and the Soviet Union in 1984, Spain in 1992, and Italy in 1984 and 1992.

EURO 1992

The 1992 tournament saw perhaps the biggest surprise win in the competition's history. Denmark had failed to qualify, most of its players were on vacation, and the team's coach was decorating his kitchen when news emerged of Yugoslavia's disqualification and Denmark's invitation to join. In a dramatic semifinal against the Netherlands, a heroic penalty save by Peter Schmeichel saw them through to the final, where they beat Germany to win the most unlikely of European Championship crowns.

EURO '96 AND 2000

Euro '96 got off to a strong start, with England's Paul Gascoigne scoring the goal of the tournament against Scotland, the Czech Republic stunning Italy with a 2–1 win, and Croatia effectively knocking the holder, Denmark, out of the competition. In the final, Germany defeated the Czech Republic with a "golden goal," the first to decide a major soccer competition.

Euro 2000 was cohosted (for the first time) by the Netherlands and Belgium. The Dutch team scored the highest number of goals in a finals game, thrashing Yugoslavia 6–1.The Spanish impressed, but fell to the eventual winner, France, in the semifinal.

> **FACT FILE** Midfielder Michel Platini holds the record for the most goals scored in a European Championships. He scored nine of France's 14 goals in the 1984 competition.

HOSTS AND WINNERS

YEAR	HOST	FINAL
1964	Spain	Spain 2-1 U.S.S.R.
1968	Italy	Italy 2-0 Yugoslavia (after replay)
1972	Belgium	West Germany 3-0 U.S.S.R.
1976	Yugoslavia	Czechoslovakia 2-2 W. Germany (5-3 pen)
1980	Italy	West Germany 2-1 Belgium
1984	France	France 2-0 Spain
1988	West Germany	The Netherlands 2-0 U.S.S.R.
1992	Sweden	Denmark 2-0 Germany
1996	England	Germany 2-1 Czech Republic
2000	Belgium / Holland	France 2-1 Italy
2004	Portugal	Greece 1-0 Portugal
2008	Austria / Switz.	Spain 1-0 Germany
2012	Poland / Ukraine	Spain 4-0 Italy
2016	France	Portugal 1-0 France

▶ *Spain's Gaizka Mendieta (left) and Yugoslavia's Goran Djorovic compete for a header during the European Championships 2000. Spain secured a 4–3 victory in injury time after they had been 3–2 down with just moments to play.*

EURO 2004

Euro 2004 began with 50 nations taking part in the qualifying competition. The first round produced a series of surprises as Spain and Italy were knocked out; the same fate overcame Germany, who tied with Latvia in their group. In Group A, Russia beat Greece, thanks to a Dmitri Kirichenko goal scored after only 67 seconds—the fastest in the history of the European Championships. The Czech Republic and France topped their groups unbeaten, but both were knocked out by a hardworking, well-organized Greek team, as was Spain. The Greeks also beat Portugal twice (in the first and last games of the competition) to win the trophy.

EURO 2008

Held jointly in Austria and Switzerland, the tournament was packed with nonstop soccer-action, particularly from the eventual winners, Spain, who beat Russia twice—they also beat Greece, Sweden, Italy, and, in the final, Germany. Russia, who supplied two players to the team of the tournament in Arshavin and Zhirkov, had seemed fighting-fit beforehand, knocking the Netherlands out 3–1, while Turkey impressed with their never-say-die spirit but were beaten 3–2 by Germany in a thrilling semifinal. A total of 1.14 million fans watched the 31 games played.

EURO 2012

The third tournament to be jointly held, this time in Poland and Ukraine, Euro 2012 set an attendance record with more than 1.4 million spectators (46,481 per game). Shocks included the Netherlands failing to win a game and Russia losing out to Greece in qualifying for the quarterfinals. Only Germany qualified from the groups with a perfect three wins from three games. Two of the other group winners, the Czech Republic and England, went out at the quarterfinal stage—England losing on penalties to Italy. The Italians, propelled by two goals from Mario Balotelli, beat Germany to reach the final, but had no answer to a Spanish

▲ Portugal's forward, Cristiano Ronaldo, holds up the winners' trophy after beating France 1-0 at the Euro 2016 final.

FACT FILE Spanish leader General Franco, a critic of communism, refused the Soviet team entry into Spain to play their qualifying game for the 1960 competition. The Soviets were awarded a win.

team fully intent on attack. With player of the tournament Andrés Iniesta pulling the strings, Spain won 4–0, a record margin of victory in a European Championships final.

EURO 2016

The tournament returned to France for the third time in 2016 when it became the first to be contested by 24 teams, with five teams making their competition debuts. Two of these sides, Wales and Iceland, provided some of the most memorable moments. Wales topped their group and knocked out Northern Ireland and Belgium to reach the semifinals, whilst Iceland, with

▶ Spanish striker Fernando Torres is on the attack during the Euro 2012 final against Italy. Torres scored Spain's third goal of four after coming on as a 75th-minute substitute. The game was watched by 63,170 spectators at the Gdansk Arena in Poland.

▲ Antoine Griezmann of France tries to get the ball away from Portugal's Adrien Silva and William Carvalho during the Euro 2016 final. Griezmann won the Golden Boot as the tournament's top scorer, with six goals and two assists in seven games.

a population of just 330,000, the smallest nation ever to take part in the finals, defeated Austria and England. Iceland, themselves, were knocked out by France, for whom Antoine Griezmann would become the player of the tournament, and its top scorer with six goals.

In the final, the hosts, buoyant after a narrow win over world champions, Germany, met a Portuguese side that, apart from Cristiano Ronaldo, were largely unheralded. Portugal, though, defended resolutely and Eder's thunderous shot in the 109th minute of the game sealed Portugal's first ever major international tournament victory.

THE OLYMPICS

Until the emergence of the World Cup, the Olympics provided soccer's leading world competition. Soccer appeared in the 1896 games as an exhibition event and became a full Olympic sport 12 years later. With the exception of the 1932 Los Angeles Games, it has featured at every Olympics since. The competition was boosted in the 1990s by the admittance of professional stars and the emergence of African soccer, which produced two Olympic gold medalists in Nigeria and Cameroon.

AMATEURS ONLY

For most of its history, Olympic soccer was played by amateurs only. The rise of professional soccer in the 1920s meant that many of the world's best professionals were unable to appear at the Games. State-run teams from Eastern Europe dominated the Olympics after World War II—from 1952 to 1988, every Olympic winner came from Eastern Europe with the exception of the 1984 French team, while Hungary remains the only team to have won soccer gold three times. But as the Olympics began to accept professional athletes in other sports, so it changed

the rules for soccer. Professionals who were part of their national under-23 teams appeared at the 1992 games. In 1996 the rule was relaxed to allow each team to field three professional players over the age of 23. At Sydney 2000, Chile, led by 33-year-old striker Ivan Zamorano, won bronze. Zamorano's six goals made him top scorer at the Games.

EMERGING PLAYERS

Great professional players have emerged from the Olympics. For example, French midfielder Michel Platini and Mexican legend Hugo Sanchez burst onto the international scene at the 1976 Montreal games. The 1996 Brazil team included Rivaldo and Ronaldo. The 1952 Olympics in Helsinki, Finland, saw the arrival of a stunningly good Hungarian team. Featuring players such as Ferenc Puskas, Nandor Hidegkuti, and Sandor Kocsis, the Hungarians conceded two goals but scored 20 on their way to the gold medal. These players went on to form the core of the Hungarian team that lit up international soccer through the 1950s (see page 70).

▲ *Celestine Babayaro of Nigeria in action during the gripping 1996 Olympic semifinal against Brazil. Nigeria won 4–3 and went on to beat Argentina 3–2 in the final to become the first African team to win a major international tournament.*

> **FACT FILE** The 1952 Olympics produced three amazing games. Egypt caused a shock by beating Chile 5–4. Luxembourg eclipsed that with a 5–3 win over England. Yugoslavia led the Soviet Union 5–2 with only 14 minutes to go, but the game ended as a thrilling 5–5 tie.

> **FACT FILE** The first official Olympic tournament, in 1908, saw an average of eight goals per game. This tally was helped by Denmark's 17–1 thrashing of France. Sophus Nielsen scored ten times including three goals within the first six minutes of the game!

◄ *Mexico's Oribe Peralta is mobbed after scoring the winner at the 2012 Olympic final against Brazil.*

OLYMPIC WOMEN

Women's soccer finally became part of the Olympics at the 1996 Atlanta Games, after many years of lobbying for inclusion. With no time for a qualifying competition, the top eight nations at the 1995 Women's World Cup were invited to take part, with the exception of England, who was ineligible to compete. The final saw China beaten 2–1 by the United States in front of 76,481 spectators, a world record for a women's sporting event at that time. Five nations—the U.S., China, Germany, Norway, and Brazil—shared all of the medals until 2012, when powerful Canadian and Japanese teams emerged. But the qualification system now in place will ensure that Asia, Africa, and Oceania are all represented at future Olympics.

▲ The U.S. team celebrates winning a gold medal at the 2004 Olympics. Mia Hamm (front row, second from right), the most famous player in women's soccer, announced her retirement shortly after receiving the gold medal.

► Paraguay's Edgar Barreto (left) shields the ball from Cristian Gonzalez during the 2004 Olympic final. Argentina's win secured their first Olympic gold medal in any event for more than 50 years.

OLYMPIC GOLD MEDALISTS

MEN

1908	Great Britain
1912	Great Britain
1920	Belgium
1924	Uruguay
1928	Uruguay
1936	Italy
1948	Sweden
1952	Hungary
1956	Soviet Union
1960	Yugoslavia
1964	Hungary
1968	Hungary
1972	Poland
1976	East Germany
1980	Czechoslovakia
1984	France
1988	Soviet Union
1992	Spain
1996	Nigeria
2000	Cameroon
2004	Argentina
2008	Argentina
2012	Mexico
2016	Brazil

WOMEN

1996	United States
2000	Norway
2004	United States
2008	United States
2012	United States
2016	Germany

2012 AND 2016 GAMES

The 2012 tournament saw Great Britain appear for the first time since 1960 and Honduras deliver a blindside, beating Spain 1–0. Mexico and Brazil despatched Asian opponents (Japan and South Korea) to meet in the final, which Mexico won. In the women's game, Japan beat Brazil and France to meet reigning champions, the U.S. in the final, where two goals from Carli Lloyd saw the U.S. women win gold again. The 2016 men's tournament saw Honduras build on their previous efforts, defeating South Korea, drawing with Argentina, and advancing to the semifinals, where they were defeated by the eventual winners, Brazil, who beat Germany on a penalty shoot-out in the final. Germany fared better in the women's tournament, defeating Sweden in the final to win their first Olympic gold soccer medal.

THE COPA AMERICA

The oldest continental cup competition, the Copa America has been played under a bewildering array of names and formats ever since the first tournament, a three-way affair between Argentina, Uruguay, and Chile in 1910. One thing has remained constant—its status as a major soccer prize for the nations of South America.

▲ *The Brazilian team celebrates with the Copa America trophy after beating Argentina in a penalty shoot-out in 2004.*

CUP DOMINATION

The Copa America has had to contend with clubs reluctant to release players and the increasing popularity of international club competitions. Yet it still maintains a strong appeal. There have been 47 Copa America competitions, eight of which have been unofficial but are counted for the records. The tournament has been dominated by the "big three" South American nations of Argentina, Brazil, and Uruguay. Fifteen Copas passed until another country, Peru, won it. Since then, Argentina and Uruguay (both with 15 titles) have maintained a strong grip. Brazil has won eight times; Paraguay and Peru twice; and Bolivia, Chile, and Colombia have each won once.

FACT FILE Two players have scored 17 Copa goals—Norberto Mendez (Argentina) and Zizinho (Brazil).

INVITED GUESTS

In 1993 the Copa was expanded to 12 teams. Teams are invited to participate from outside of South America, including Mexico (twice runner-up), United States, Costa Rica, and Honduras—who caused a sensation in 2001 by beating Brazil 2–0 in the quarterfinals. Mexico appeared for the sixth time at the 2015 Copa, tying 3–3 with hosts Chile, who progressed to the final. Chile beat Uruguay and Peru in the quarterfinal and semifinal and, in the final, defeated Argentina 4–1 on penalties to win their first-ever Copa. Chile won the tournament again the next year.

◀ *Uruguay's Egido Arevaldo (right) battles for the ball during the 2011 Copa America final against Paraguay. Uruguay knocked out Argentina in the quarterfinals, and Peru in the semifinals.*

COPA AMERICA WINNERS

Year	Winner	Year	Winner
1910*	Argentina	1956*	Uruguay
1916*	Uruguay	1957	Argentina
1917	Uruguay	1959*	Argentina
1919	Brazil	1959	Uruguay
1920	Uruguay	1963	Bolivia
1921	Argentina	1967	Uruguay
1922	Brazil	1975	Peru
1923	Uruguay	1979	Paraguay
1924	Uruguay	1983	Uruguay
1925	Argentina	1987	Uruguay
1926	Uruguay	1989	Brazil
1927	Argentina	1991	Argentina
1929	Argentina	1993	Argentina
1935*	Uruguay	1995	Uruguay
1937	Argentina	1997	Brazil
1939	Peru	1999	Brazil
1941*	Argentina	2001	Colombia
1942	Uruguay	2004	Brazil
1945*	Argentina	2007	Brazil
1946*	Argentina	2011	Uruguay
1947	Argentina	2015	Chile
1949	Brazil	2016	Chile
1953	Paraguay	2019	Brazil
1955	Argentina	*unofficial tournament	

THE AFRICA CUP OF NATIONS

Now the Africa Cup of Nations, the first African Nations Cup, held in 1957, was played by only three of Africa's nine independent nations at the time—Sudan, Ethiopia, and the eventual winner, Egypt. Since then the number of independent African countries has risen sharply. For the 2019 tournament, the first to be held in summer, more than 50 teams battled to qualify for the 24 places at the finals.

AFRICAN NATIONS CUP WINNERS

Year	Winner	Year	Winner
1957	Egypt	1990	Algeria
1959	Egypt	1992	Ivory Coast
1962	Ethiopia	1994	Nigeria
1963	Ghana	1996	South Africa
1965	Ghana	1998	Egypt
1968	Congo-Kinshasa	2000	Cameroon
1970	Sudan	2002	Cameroon
1972	Congo-Brazzaville	2004	Tunisia
1974	Zaire	2006	Egypt
1976	Morocco	2008	Egypt
1978	Ghana	2010	Egypt
1980	Nigeria	2012	Zambia
1982	Ghana	2013	Nigeria
1984	Cameroon	2015	Ivory Coast
1986	Egypt	2017	Cameroon
1988	Cameroon	2019	Algeria

◀ *Samuel Eto'o and Hosny Abd Rabou battle for possession during the 2008 African Nations Cup final.*

FACT FILE In 1998 Egyptian coach Mahmoud al-Gohari became the first person to have won the African Nations Cup as both a player (in 1959) and as a coach.

WINNERS AND LOSERS

A qualifying stage for the African Nations Cup was introduced in 1968, with eight places up for grabs. This was increased to 12 in 1992 and 16 for the 1998 competition. Champions have come from around the continent—from Africa's northernmost country, Morocco (the winner in 1976), to its southernmost nation, South Africa, who returned from the international wilderness to win an emotional competition in 1996. Eight tournament finals have ended in penalty shoot-outs, including the 2015 tournament, when the Ivory Coast defeated Ghana 9–8 despite missing their first two penalties. One of the most unlucky nations has to be Zambia, who lost an entire team in a 1993 airplane crash (see page 104), yet still reached the final in 1994. Zambia finally triumphed in 2012, after a period of dominance by Egypt—three wins in a row—which took them to the top of the winners' table. The 2017 final was contested by the cup's most successful sides, Egypt (7 titles) and Cameroon (5 titles), while Algeria won their second title in 2019.

UPS AND DOWNS

The African Nations Cup has had to endure its ups and downs, with poor playing facilities in some countries, hostilities between nations, and major controversies. These continue into the modern era. Nigeria, one of Africa's top teams, was expelled from the 1998 tournament after it had refused to travel to the 1996 competition. Since the early 1990s the best teams in the competition have relied on calling back as many of their foreign-based stars as possible. In 2006, for example, not one player in the Ivory Coast and Cameroon teams was based in his home country. Four years later, Cameroon striker Samuel Eto'o notched his 18th goal, making him the tournament's all-time leading goalscorer.

▶ *Ambroise Oyongo Bitolo (right) of Cameroon during the 2017 African Nations Cup semifinal between Cameroon and Ghana.*

THE ASIAN GAMES AND ASIAN CUP

Asia is the one continent that has two major soccer competitions for its nations—the Asian Games and the Asian Cup. Both tournaments are held every four years, but in cycles that keep them two years apart.

THE ASIAN GAMES

The Asian Games is a multisport competition in which soccer is only one of a number of events. In the first tournament soccer featured alongside weight lifting, cycling, and basketball, and was played in games lasting 80, not 90, minutes. India, Burma (now Myanmar), and Taiwan dominated the early competitions. The South Koreans have shared the title twice, after the final was tied. Penalty shoot-outs were later introduced to decide the winner and Iran beat North Korea 4–1 on penalties to capture the 1990 title. After a self-imposed exile from the Asian Games in the mid-1990s, Iran powered to victories

▲ Iran's Yahya Golmohammadi (left) and goalie Ebrahim Mirzapour run a victory lap after a shock defeat of Japan to win the 2002 Asian Games.

in 1998 and 2002. By the 2002 competition, the tournament had been altered to become an under-23 competition, with teams allowed to field up to three overage players. The 2018 competition saw South Korea win again, beating Japan in the final, with the United Arab Emirates third.

THE ASIAN CUP

First held in Hong Kong with only four teams, the Asian Cup has grown in importance. Qualification for the 12-team tournament held in Lebanon in 2000 attracted 42 countries. The soccer-playing gap between rich and poor Asian nations was highlighted when Kuwait recorded the highest-ever victory in qualifying, beating Bhutan 20–0. However, the

gradual emergence of higher-quality teams from the former Soviet Republics, smaller Gulf states such as Bahrain and Qatar, and countries in Southeast Asia promises to make future tournaments more competitive. Iran, Japan, and Saudi Arabia are the competition's most successful teams, winning the cup three times each, while Israel was a major force in the early years. It competed in the final of the first four Asian Cups, winning in 1964. In 1975, however, Israel were expelled from the Asian Football Confederation, and joined UEFA in 1992. China became hosts for the first time in 2004, when the tournament was expanded to include 16 teams. The Japan-China final attracted great interest. The game was broadcast live to 60 nations; in China alone, the TV audience was more than 250 million viewers.

Australia entered the fray from 2007 onwards, finishing runners-up in 2011 but triumphing in 2015, defeating South Korea 2-1 in the final. They joined other recent first-time champions including Iraq in 2007 and, sensationally, Qatar in 2019. The Qataris went through the entire tournament unbeaten and, propelled by nine goals from Almoez Ali, reached the final where they defeated Japan 3-1.

◄ Zheng Zhi (left) of China and Japan's Takayuki Suzuki jump for a header during the 2004 Asian Cup final, held in Beijing. Japan took the trophy with a 3–1 victory.

ASIAN GAMES AND ASIAN CUP WINNERS

GAMES WINNERS		CUP WINNERS	
1951	India	1956	South Korea
1954	Taiwan	1960	South Korea
1958	Taiwan	1964	Israel
1962	India	1968	Iran
1966	Burma	1972	Iran
1970	Burma and South Korea	1976	Iran
1974	Iran	1980	Kuwait
1978	North Korea and South Korea	1984	Saudi Arabia
		1988	Saudi Arabia
1982	Iraq	1992	Japan
1986	South Korea	1996	Saudi Arabia
1990	Iran	2000	Japan
1994	Uzbekistan	2004	Japan
1998	Iran	2007	Iraq
2002	Iran	2011	Japan
2006	Qatar	2015	Australia
2010	Japan	2019	Qatar
2014	South Korea		
2018	South Korea		

THE CONCACAF CHAMPIONSHIP

Of all the soccer-playing regions of the world, North America, Central America, and the Caribbean islands have had the most complex history of competitions. Five different tournaments have been played there, starting with the CCCF Championship in 1941.

THE GOLD CUP

For a number of years, competition in the CONCACAF zone was used as a direct way of qualifying for the World Cup. In 1991 the tournament was renamed the Gold Cup, which today features 12 teams at the finals. Every Gold Cup has been hosted by the United States, either alone or jointly with Mexico. Teams from outside CONCACAF have often been invited to play. In 1996 the Brazilian under-23 side lost to Mexico in the final. South Korea was a guest in 2000, but it lost out on a quarterfinal place to Canada on a coin toss. Canada went on to beat another guest, Colombia, in the final. The U.S. team won the 2002 competition for the first time since 1991 and matched Mexico win for win over the next nine tournaments. In recent years, the two sides' dominance has been threatened by an enterprising Jamaican team that knocked the U.S. out of the 2015 tournament, Mexico out of the 2017 competition, and reached the semifinals in 2019.

▲ Manley Junior Tabe of Vanuatu releases the ball ahead of New Zealand's Aaron Lines in the 2002 Oceanian Nations Cup.

THE OFC NATIONS CUP

Oceania's competition is the smallest of the continental championships. It has been held nine times since 1973, and was later decided that the competition should be held every four years. The 2004 tournament saw a major surprise as the Solomon Islands defeated New Zealand to make the final, losing that game to Australia. The 2012 tournament saw further surprises, with New Caledonia knocking out New Zealand and Tahiti emerging as the champions. New Zealand triumphed in 2018, defeating Papua New Guinea on penalties in the final.

GOLD CUP WINNERS

Canada	2000
U.S.	1991, 2002, 2005, 2007, 2013, 2017
Mexico	1993, 1996, 1998, 2003, 2009, 2011, 2015, 2019

▲ Wilmer Lopez (left) of Costa Rica kicks the ball between the legs of Cobi Jones of the United States during the first half of the 2002 Gold Cup final, which the U.S. won 2-0.

▲ Mexican captain Pavel Pardo celebrates with the CONCACAF Gold Cup in 2003 after his team's 1–0 victory over Brazil in the final.

SOCCER LEAGUES

Clubs compete in leagues that are made up of several divisions. Rules, numbers of teams, and the length of a league season vary around the world. Many top leagues—in Spain, Italy, France, and Germany, for example—have 18 or 20 teams.

NUMBERS AND BREAKS

The top divisions of Sweden and Russia each contain 16 teams, while Australia has 10, and Latvia feature just eight teams. In most leagues the teams play each other twice, home and away, during a season. In Denmark, the 14 teams play each other three times. Scotland's top division has an unusual format—there are 12 teams, but the season lasts for 38 games. Teams play each other three times, before the league turns into two groups of six for a further round of games. Some leagues—in Argentina and Mexico, for example—are split into two short seasons every year. League teams in Spain, France, Bulgaria, Hungary, and some other countries take a midwinter break, while in northern European nations, such as Norway and Finland, the league season begins in the spring.

▼ Toluca (in yellow) battle with Tigres in the Mexican league. Toluca won the 2002–03 Clausura, or winter, championship—their fourth league title since 1998.

PROMOTION AND RELEGATION

While leagues in Australia and the United States guarantee each team a place for the following season, most leagues have a system of promotion and relegation, with top and bottom teams switching places for the new season. In Uruguay, relegation and promotion are determined by the performance of teams over two seasons. In Austria and Scotland, one team is promoted and one relegated each season. In Hungary, the Czech Republic, and the Ukraine, two

▲ PSV Eindhoven's Philip Cocu fights for the ball with Feyenoord's Shinji Ono (right) during a Dutch premier league game in 2004.

▲ South Korean Ahn Jung-Hwan, playing for Japanese team Yokohama F Marinos, celebrates his winning goal in a J-League encounter against the Kashima Antlers.

▶ *Shinji Ono (left) of the Western Sydney Wanderers in action in the A-League Grand Final in 2013, a game won 2–0 by their opponents— the Central Coast Mariners.*

teams go up and down, while in Germany, France, Spain, and Portugal it is three.

In Germany, the third-place team in the second division contests a two-game play-off with the team finishing 16th in the Bundesliga, to determine who will play in the top division the following season. Other nations, such as Italy and England, hold a play-off series featuring semifinals and a final to determine which of four teams will be promoted along with others that won automatic promotion above them. In Italy, play-offs are also used to determine which team joins three other relegated teams from Serie A. Play-off systems are criticized for turning a whole season into a lottery over one, two, or three games, but many people think they maintain interest and generate drama.

FAST RISERS

Some leagues have been dominated by a small number of teams throughout their history. For 43 seasons from 1932, the Uruguayan league title was won by either Peñarol or Nacional (Defensor was the champion in 1976). Scotland's Glasgow Rangers holds the world record for the most league championships, with a staggering 54 titles, four more than their arch rivals, Celtic. In some leagues small teams have

risen dramatically from humble beginnings to become champions or contenders. In Europe, the now mighty Bayern Munich was not considered successful enough to join the Bundesliga in the early 1960s, but since then the team has become one of the pillars of German soccer.

FACT FILE
The Isles of Scilly, off the coast of southwestern England, are home to the Scillonian League, the world's smallest. Woolpack Wanderers and Garrison Gunners are the only two teams to play in the league, as well as two cup competitions.

▶ *River Plate's Paraguayan striker Nelson Cuevas is challenged by defender German Re of Newell's Old Boys during an Argentinian first division game in Buenos Aires.*

HARD FALLERS

Just as clubs can rise, so can they fall. In the 2018–2019 season, 12 former champions of the English league (with 33 titles between them) played outside the top division. A slide down the division can either be gradual or sudden. Napoli was one of Italian soccer's aristocrats and the home of Diego Maradona, winning the Italian league in 1987 and 1990 and finishing runner-up in the two intervening years. Yet, by the early 2000s it was bankrupt and playing in Serie C, two divisions down from the top of the class.

Rarely, however, has a downturn been more dramatic than that experienced by Manchester City or Tasmania 1900 Berlin. In 1937 Manchester City was the English league champion. In the following season, the team scored 80 league goals, more than any other side, but was relegated. Tasmania 1900 Berlin was joint first in the early stages of the 1965–1966 Bundesliga season. By the end, it was bottom and the holder of a series of unenviable records for one season, including: fewest wins (two), most losses (28), most goals against (108), and lowest points total (eight).

SERIE A

For decades, Serie A was considered the ultimate test for the world's top players. South American stars have played for its clubs for many years; they were joined in the 1990s by great talents from Africa and Asia. Some clubs are now struggling financially as a result of their lavish spending on players. Winning Serie A is sometimes referred to as the *scudetto* ("small shield"), as the champions' shirt the following season bears a small coat of arms in Italian colors. Sometimes the quality of Serie A has meant that a team which is successful overseas has struggled at domestically. Internazionale, for example, won the UEFA Cup in 1994, but could only manage 13th place in the league. Juventus is the most successful Serie A club, with 35 titles, followed by AC Milan and Internazionale (both 18), and Genoa (nine). In 2004 Serie A was expanded from 18 to 20 teams, but was rocked two years later by a game-fixing scandal. Juventus was stripped of its 2005 and 2006 titles, leading to Inter being awarded the 2006 *scudetto*.

LA LIGA

The Spanish league banned foreign players between 1963 and 1973, but since then it has been the home of some of the world's greatest soccer players, from Johan Cruyff and Diego Maradona to current stars Luis Suárez, Lionel Messi, and Antoine Griezmann. The league can be highly competitive but is mostly dominated by Real Madrid and Barcelona.

La Liga has two professional divisions and a series of amateur divisons. Unlike other national leagues, the reserve teams of the major clubs play in the lower divisions, not in a separate reserves' league. Real Madrid and Barcelona remain La Liga's wealthiest and most successful clubs, with nearly 60 league titles between them.

▼ *Simone Perrotta of Roma (in red) clashes with Fabio Firmani of Lazio during a Serie A derby game in 2005. Lazio won 3–0.*

▼ *Barcelona's Argentinian striker Lionel Messi (right) is one of the stars of La Liga.*

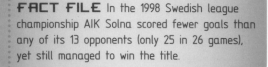
THE BUNDESLIGA

After the division of Germany into East and West following World War II, the West German Bundesliga was first contested in 1965. In 1991, after reunification, two teams from the former East Germany were admitted into the top division. Since then eastern teams have struggled to maintain a regular presence in the Bundesliga. Bayern Munich is by far the most successful Bundesliga team, with 29 titles, followed by Borussia Mönchengladbach and Borussia Dortmund (five each), Werder Bremen (four), and Hamburg and VfB Stuttgart (three).

▲ *Werder Bremen displays the German Bundesliga trophy after winning the 2003–2004 title. The team secured a league and cup double two weeks later.*

The Bundesliga was one of the last major leagues to adopt a system of three points for a win (in 1995), and Bayern Munich gained a record 91 points in 2012–2013. In 2008–2009 the Bundesliga took a fascinating twist when VfL Wolfsburg, which had never won a major German competition, scooped the league, propelled by 54 goals from strikers Grafite and Edin Dzeko. Grafite's tally of 28 goals was the highest since the early 1980s but still short of the record 40 goals Gerd Müller scored for Bayern in 1971–1972. Müller's total of 365 Bundesliga goals is unlikely to be beaten for many years.

◀ *Leicester City's Shinji Okazaki turns past Chelsea's N'Golo Kante in this 2017 meeting of the 2015–2016 and 2016–2017 English Premier League champions. Kante won the league with both teams.*

THE ENGLISH PREMIER LEAGUE

In the early 1990s England's first division clubs broke away from league control to form the Premier League. Money has flooded into the top clubs' bank accounts, and a wide gap has opened up between established teams and newly promoted teams, who find it very hard to stay on top. Manchester United won 13 of the first 21 titles. Their battle for supremacy was mainly fought with Arsenal and Chelsea in the 2000s, whilst Manchester City—bolstered by stars like David Silva and Sergio Aguero—has taken four recent titles, including 2018–19. Games are often very exciting and attract massive worldwide TV audiences, making it the most watched domestic league on the planet.

LIGUE 1

Despite having produced some of the world's greatest players, the French league has traditionally not been as well funded as others in Europe. Its homegrown stars, such as Yohan Cabaye and Franck Ribéry, usually move overseas. Despite this, French teams appear to be on the rise, reaching the final of both the Champions League and the UEFA Cup in 2004. The French league is highly competitive. Between 1983 and 2003, only three teams—Auxerre, Monaco, and Paris Saint-Germain—played in the top division

▼ *WUSA, the first fully professional women's league in the world, ran for just three seasons in the U.S. until 2009. It was replaced by the WPS and then the NWSL.*

every season. AS Saint-Étienne and Marseille have each won the league ten times, but more recently Lyon (Olympique Lyonnais) and Paris Saint-Germain have won. PSG have won six out of the last seven titles.

ASIAN LEAGUES

The first professional league in Asia was South Korea's K-League, which began with only five teams in 1983 and now features 22 teams split over two divisions. The league's most successful team is Seongnam Ilhwa Chunma, with seven titles. Japan's J-League kicked off in 1993 and now has two divisions. In 2004 Yokohama F Marinos became the first club to win three J-leagues in a row, while Kashima Antlers are the most successful side, with eight titles. The Chinese Super League has been won by Guangzhou Evergrande seven times since it began in 2004.

MAJOR LEAGUE SOCCER (MLS)

Early attempts at setting up a professional league in the United States included the heavily financed North American Soccer League (NASL), which ran from 1968 to 1984 and featured global superstars such as Pelé, albeit near the end of their careers. The MLS celebrated the start of its 20th season in 2015 and mixes homegrown players with international stars such as Thierry Henry and Bradley Wright-Phillips. In 2017, the league grew to 22 with teams from Atlanta and Minnesota joining. Teams play in two divisions, Eastern and Western. Unlike most leagues, there is no relegation and promotion. The LA Galaxy with five championships and D.C. United with four are the most successful teams in MLS history.

CLUB CUP COMPETITIONS

In 1872 the Wanderers beat Royal Engineers by one goal to zero to win the first FA Cup—the oldest surviving major cup competition. Since that time hundreds of cup competitions have been introduced all over the world. Some, such as the Asian Supercup and the African Supercup, are contested between the winners of other cup competitions.

▲ Boca Juniors celebrates its penalty shoot-out victory over AC Milan in the 2003 World Club Cup. Argentinian clubs have won the competition nine times, more than any other country.

CONTINENTAL CUP COMPETITIONS

Every continent has one or more cup competitions for its best clubs. The two most famous are the Copa Libertadores and the UEFA Champions League (see pages 132–133). The winners of these two competitions used to play each other in the Intercontinental Cup (later, the World Club Cup) but in 2000, a new competition, the FIFA Club World Cup, ran and eventually took over. It features the winners of each continent's leading club competition. The 2018 competition held in UAE featured seven teams and was won by Real Madrid who beat Al-Ain 4-1 in the final.

In Africa, the African Cup-Winners' Cup and the CAF Cup are exceeded in prestige only by the African Champions League, which was first played for in 1964. Egyptian side Al-Ahly has won the competition eight times, while Tunisian team, ES Tunis won in 2018, its first triumph since 1988. The Asian Cup-Winners' Cup ran from 1991 to 2002 and was won by Saudi Arabian teams six times. In contrast, the AFC Champions League has seen winners from nine countries. South Korean clubs, such as 2012 winners Ulsan Hyundai, have triumphed in the competition 11 times; Japanese clubs—such as 2018 champions Kashima Antlers—have won the title seven times.

◄ Action from a 2005 AFC Champions League game between Al-Ain of the United Arab Emirates and Saudi Arabian team Al-Ittihad. The Saudi team won the title in both 2004 and 2005.

COPA LIBERTADORES

South America's first international club competition was staged by Chilean club Colo Colo in 1948 and won by Brazilian team Vasco da Gama. However it was not until 1960 that a regular competition, the Copa Libertadores, was set up. Uruguayan team Peñarol won the first two competitions, but was defeated in the final of the third by Santos, thanks to two goals from Pelé. Today the Copa Libertadores begins with nine groups of four teams and culminates in a second round, quarterfinals, semifinals, and a pair of games—at home and away—between the finalists. It is open to the top teams of each South American country, but Mexican teams were also invited to compete from 1999 to 2001. The Copa Libertadores has continually outshone the national team competition—the Copa

America—and other South American cups in popularity and passion. This intensity has led to flare-ups on the field and in the stands. In the 1971 Copa game between Boca Juniors and Sporting Cristal, a fight ended in the arrest of most of the players, while Colombia's Atletico Nacional was banned from the 1990 competition after a referee received death threats.

The Copa Libertadores has mainly been won by teams from Brazil, Argentina, and Uruguay. Independiente hold the record of seven victories; the only teams to have reached the final more often are Peñarol and Boca Juniors (both ten times). Uruguay's Nacional has won three Copas. Colombia's clubs lost seven out of eight finals before 2004. In that year, Once Caldas beat Brazilian favorites Santos and São Paulo to become unexpected champions, a feat matched by Ecuador's LDU Quito in 2008, Atlético Mineiro in 2013, and Colombia's Atlético Nacional in 2016.

◀ *São Paulo's Ricardo Oliveira (left) fights for the ball with Internacional's Fabiano Eller during the final of the 2006 Copa Libertadores. Internacional won the trophy and went on to stun Barcelona four months later, beating them 1–0 in the World Club Cup.*

▶ *Rubin Kazan's Salomon Rondon (right) tries to shield the ball from Levante defender Sergio Ballesteros during their 2013 Europa League encounter. Former Russian league champions, Rubin Kazan beat Inter Milan in the group stages and then knocked out Spanish teams Levante and Atlético Madrid, before falling to Chelsea at the quarterfinal stage.*

CUPS IN EUROPE

Most leagues in Europe have one or more cup competitions for their teams to contest. Among the best-known domestic cup competitions are the English FA Cup; the Scottish Cup, which started in 1874; the Spanish Cup, which began in 1902; and the French Cup, which was first played for in 1918. From 1960 until 1999, the winners of national cup competitions in Europe played in the Cup-Winners' Cup. The first and last Cup-Winners' Cups were won by Italian teams (Fiorentina and Lazio), but the most successful team was Barcelona, who lifted the trophy four times. It suffered a surprising loss in the 1969 final to Slovan Bratislava (now in Slovakia), who became the first Eastern European club to win a major continental cup. Since the Cup-Winners' Cup was abandoned, cup winners in Europe's strongest nations have competed for the UEFA Cup/Europa League Trophy.

The UEFA Cup's forerunner began in 1955 as the Inter-Cities Fairs Cup, a competition that took two years to complete. By 1960, the Fairs Cup was played over the course of a year and, for the 1971–1972 season, a new trophy and new name—the UEFA Cup—were introduced. In 1972 the European Supercup arrived, and was contested between the winners of the European Champions Cup and the Cup-

◀ *CSKA Moscow's Venaumin Mandrikin celebrates with the 2005 UEFA Cup as his team becomes the first Russian club to win a major European trophy, beating Sporting Lisbon 3–1 in the final.*

Winners' Cup. UEFA Cup winners have so far come from 11 nations, with Spanish clubs taking the title on 11 occasions, Italian and English sides winning nine times, and German teams six times. More than 100 teams now enter the first stages of the competition, and places are granted through winning a national cup, a high league finish, or being knocked out of the Champions League group stage. In 2009 the UEFA Cup was renamed as the Europa League, with a group stage containing 12 mini-leagues of four clubs each.

EUROPEAN CHAMPIONS

European club competitions date back to 1927, when the Mitropa Cup was first contested by the leading clubs of central Europe. Sparta Prague was its first winner. The last Mitropa Cup was won by Yugoslav side Borac Banja Luka in 1992, but by then the glamour of the Mitropa had long been eclipsed by the mighty European Cup, a competition that is now known as the European Champions League.

◄ *Real Madrid keeper Rogelio Dominguez claims the ball during the 1959 European Cup final against French club Stade de Reims. The game ended 2–0 to Real, who lifted their fourth European Cup in a row.*

▶ *Julius Aghahowa of Shakhtar Donetsk is challenged by Barcelona's Fernando Navarro in a 2004–2005 Champions League game. Aghahowa's two goals gave the Ukrainian team a surprise victory.*

EARLY DAYS

The European Champion Clubs' Cup, usually known as the European Cup, developed out of a meeting set up by Frenchman Gabriel Hanot. Italian, Spanish, French, and Portuguese club teams were eager to take part, as were teams from many other countries. The first European Cup, held in 1955–1956, featured major names such as Real Madrid, Sporting Lisbon, Anderlecht, and AC Milan. Clubs that are less well known today also entered—Århus GF and FC Saarbrucken, for example. English league champion Chelsea, however, was forbidden from entering, but Scottish club Hibernian reached the semifinal. The first winners of the trophy were Real Madrid.

CHANGING CHAMPIONS

Real won the first five European Cups, before the tournament hit a golden age of competition in the 1960s, with Benfica, Internazionale, and AC Milan all winning the trophy. The 1970s saw both Ajax and Bayern Munich crowned champions three years in a row. English clubs won six European Cups in succession

from 1977, but were banned from European competition for five years after the 1985 Heysel Stadium disaster (see page 105). There have been 18 Spanish winners, 13 English, and 12 Italian champions.

As the European Cup grew in intensity, it became harder to successfully defend the title. No team managed to retain its crown between AC Milan's win in 1990 and Real Madrid's in 2017. The first year that the final went into extra time was 1958, while the first penalty shoot-out in the final was in 1984. The two finals won by Eastern European teams, Steaua Bucharest (1986) and Red Star Belgrade (1991), both went to nail-biting penalty shoot-outs.

EXPANSION AND DOMINATION

The format of the European Cup remained almost unchanged for its first 35 years. Teams competed in knockout rounds, playing one game at home and one away. If the scores were tied after the two games, the team with more away goals would go through. For many years the competition was open only to the league champions of each country. Today, as many as four

▲ *Nottingham Forest celebrates winning its second European Cup title in a row after winger John Robertson's single goal was enough to defeat German team Hamburg in the 1980 final.*

EUROPEAN CUP/CHAMPIONS LEAGUE WINNERS

1956	Real Madrid	1978	Liverpool	2000	Real Madrid
1957	Real Madrid	1979	Nottingham Forest	2001	Bayern Munich
1958	Real Madrid	1980	Nottingham Forest	2002	Real Madrid
1959	Real Madrid	1981	Liverpool	2003	AC Milan
1960	Real Madrid	1982	Aston Villa	2004	Porto
1961	Benfica	1983	Hamburg	2005	Liverpool
1962	Benfica	1984	Liverpool	2006	Barcelona
1963	AC Milan	1985	Juventus	2007	AC Milan
1964	Internazionale	1986	Steaua Bucharest	2008	Manchester United
1965	Internazionale	1987	Porto	2009	Barcelona
1966	Real Madrid	1988	PSV Eindhoven	2010	Internazionale
1967	Celtic	1989	AC Milan	2011	Barcelona
1968	Manchester United	1990	AC Milan	2012	Chelsea
1969	AC Milan	1991	Red Star Belgrade	2013	Bayern Munich
1970	Feyenoord	1992	Barcelona	2014	Real Madrid
1971	Ajax	1993	Marseille (see p83)	2015	Barcelona
1972	Ajax	1994	AC Milan	2016	Real Madrid
1973	Ajax	1995	Ajax	2017	Real Madrid
1974	Bayern Munich	1996	Juventus	2018	Real Madrid
1975	Bayern Munich	1997	Borussia Dortmund	2019	Liverpool
1976	Bayern Munich	1998	Real Madrid		
1977	Liverpool	1999	Manchester United		

▲ Liverpool's Andrew Robertson and Jordan Henderson take on Real Madrid's Isco in the 2018 Champions League final. The game ended in a 3–1 win to Real Madrid, the 13th title and third in a row for the Spanish team.

▼ Robert Lewandowski scores Borussia Dortmund's first goal in their 2013 Champions League semifinal first-leg game against Real Madrid. In an extraordinary game, Lewandowski became the first player to ever score four goals in a semifinal. Dortmund won 4–1 in that game and went on to reach an all-German Champions League final against Bayern Munich.

FACT FILE
Cristiano Ronaldo started 2019 as the all-time leading goalscorer in the Champions League with 121 goals, 15 ahead of Lionel Messi.

teams from each top league take part.

The competition was revamped as the Champions League in 1992. Group stages were introduced, guaranteeing more games and vast sums of television money for competing clubs. With close to two billion euros of prize money as well to be shared out amongst the 32 group stage teams, Champions League success is now essential for the financial health of Europe's top teams. In 2017–2018, Liverpool's run to the final of the competition earned them $88.6 million—more than a fifth of the club's entire income that year. For a big side reliant on Champions League revenues, failure to qualify can be a financial disaster. Criticism of too many games saw the group stages reduced to one from two for the 2003–2004 season onwards, but the competition continues to flourish and pits more of the world's elite players against each other than any other.

FACT FILE
Swedish striker Zlatan Ibrahimovic is the only player to have scored in Champions League games for six different teams: Ajax, Juventus, Internazionale, Barcelona, AC Milan, and Paris Saint-Germain.

SNAPSHOT
BRAZIL 2014

Brazil is a country that plays first-rate soccer. More than 500 Brazilians play for teams in the top leagues of Europe while the country has won the World Cup five times—more than any other country. Brazil welcomed the FIFA World Cup tournament back to their country in 201—for the first time since 1950. Twelve stadiums, either new or refurbished, hosted the 32 teams, as hundreds of millions of soccer fans from all over the world tuned in to watch an exciting tournament. For Brazil's incredibly passionate fans, there was drama as the country powered through their group beating Croatia 3–1 and Cameroon 4–1 but they had to endure a tense penalty shoot-out to overcome a skilled and hard-working Chilean team. There was also heartbreak in the semifinals when their team came up against the Germans whose teamwork, passing, and attacking play destroyed a Brazilian team lacking their key defensive player, Thiago Silva. The result was a 7–1 thrashing, the biggest semifinal scoreline in World Cup history. The final, held at the atmospheric Estádio Jornalista Mário Filho, better known as the Maracanã, saw Germany defeat Argentina with a single goal in added time by Mario Götze. Germany became the first European team in World Cup history to be crowned champion in both North and South America.

▲ Thomas Müller of Germany celebrates with the trophy after winning the 2014 World Cup final game against Argentina.

Brazilian fans watch the first official international game (an exhibition match) at the newly refurbished Maracanã Stadium in Rio de Janeiro—a lively 2–2 tie between Brazil and England.

U.S. SOCCER

Soccer in the United States has a long history, with its first club team, Oneida in Boston, Massachusetts, having a roster of players as early as 1862. The country's first major cup competition, the American Cup, began in 1885, the same year that an unofficial national team played its first game, against Canada. The United States joined FIFA in 1914, and a year earlier its governing body, the United States Soccer Federation, was founded. In addition to sanctioning the majority of U.S. domestic leagues and competitions, it also awards the Soccer Athlete of the Year, the country's most illustrious soccer award.

PROFESSIONAL LEAGUES

Numerous attempts at establishing national leagues have come and gone, but Major League Soccer (MLS) is thriving, with increasing crowds, media interest, and team numbers in recent seasons. The league has expanded to 24 teams with a flurry of new arrivals including New York City FC (2015), Atlanta United (2017), and FC Cincinnati (2019). Further teams from Miami, Nashville, and Austin are expected in the near future. Below the MLS is the National American Soccer League (NASL) and below that, the United Soccer League (USL). USL teams in the past have performed well in the U.S. Open Cup, with three USL teams reaching the quarterfinal stages or further in 2017 and 2018. Launching in 2009 with seven teams, Women's Professional Soccer took over from the defunct WUSA as the highest tier of women's club soccer in North America, but sadly only survived three seasons. In 2013 the National Women's Soccer League (NWSL) kicked off. It contains nine teams after the Houston Dash joined in 2014 and the Utah Royals replaced FC Kansas City in 2018, and consists of 24 regular season games with the top four sides contesting play-offs for the championship.

INTERNATIONAL OUTLOOK

Currently world ranked by FIFA at 25, above Japan and Russia but eight places behind Mexico, the U.S. men's team looks to rally after a tumultuous recent period that saw the departures of two head coaches, Jurgen Klinsmann in 2015 and Bruce Arena in 2017, as well as retirements of key players including Clint Dempsey, Landon Donovan, and DaMarcus Beasley. Sandwiched in between was a creditable top four finish in the Copa America and, in 2017, unbeaten wins through the entire CONCACAF Gold Cup tournament to secure a sixth Gold Cup for the United States. Fans remain optimistic as young players gain experience in the MLS or overseas, with Christian Pulisic's $73 million move from Borussia Dortmund to Chelsea in 2019 being far and away the highest fee paid for a U.S. player.

In 2019, the women's U.S. team began its fifth straight year at the top of the world rankings. A disappointing fifth place finish at the 2016 Olympics was offset by World Cup glory in 2015 and consecutive CONCACAF Gold Cup titles in 2014 and 2018. A surprise loss in a 2019 friendly to France ended the team's spectacular 28-game unbeaten streak but that disappointment was soon forgotten after the U.S. claimed the 2019 Women's World Cup for a record fourth time.

BOOKS AND MAGAZINES

100 Years of Soccer in America: The Official Book of the U.S. Soccer Federation (Rizzoli, 2014)
A thorough and detailed guide to the history of football in the United States.

The U.S. Women's Soccer Team: An American Success Story (Scarecrow Press, 2013)
Short, poetic pieces about the passions and emotions involved in watching and playing soccer.

Inverting the Pyramid: A History of Football Tactics (Jonathan Wilson, Orion, 2009)
A detailed guide to how tactics and formations have developed in soccer over time.

Soccer America magazine (Soccer America Publishing)
Long-running U.S. magazine packed with news, features, and photographs.

Soccer Smarts: 75 Skills, Tactics & Mental Exercises to Improve Your Game (Rockridge Press, 2018) A great guide to tips, training, and tactics to help young soccer players improve their game.

Soccer IQ: Things That Smart Players Do, Vol. 1 (CreateSpace, 2012)
Interesting and useful soccer coaching guide for players written by a leading USSF coach.

FACTS AND FIGURES

U.S. SOCCER ATHLETE OF THE YEAR

Men

1984 Rick Davis
1985 Perry van der Beck
1986 Paul Caligiuri
1987 Brent Goulet
1988 Peter Vermes
1989 Mike Windischmann
1990 Tab Ramos
1991 Hugo Perez
1992 Marcelo Balboa
1993 Thomas Dooley
1994 Marcelo Balboa
1995 Alexi Lalas
1996 Eric Wynalda
1997 Kasey Keller
1998 Cobi Jones
1999 Kasey Keller
2000 Chris Armas
2001 Earnie Stewart
2002 Brad Friedel
2003 Landon Donovan
2004 Landon Donovan
2005 Kasey Keller
2006 Oguchi Onyewu
2007 Clint Dempsey
2008 Tim Howard
2009 Landon Donovan
2010 Landon Donovan
2011 Clint Dempsey
2012 Clint Dempsey
2013 Jozy Altidore
2014 Tim Howard
2015 Michael Bradley
2016 Jozy Altidore
2017 Christian Pulisic
2018 Zack Steffen

Women

1985 Sharon Remer
1986 April Heinrichs
1987 Carin Jennings-Gabarra
1988 Joy Biefield
1989 April Heinrichs
1990 Michelle Akers
1991 Michelle Akers
1992 Carin Jennings-Gabarra
1993 Kristine Lilly
1994 Mia Hamm
1995 Mia Hamm
1996 Mia Hamm
1997 Mia Hamm
1998 Mia Hamm
1999 Michelle Akers
2000 Tiffeny Milbrett
2001 Tiffeny Milbrett
2002 Shannon MacMillan
2003 Abby Wambach
2004 Abby Wambach
2005 Kristine Lilly
2006 Kristine Lilly
2007 Abby Wambach
2008 Carli Lloyd
2009 Hope Solo
2010 Abby Wambach
2011 Abby Wambach
2012 Alex Morgan
2013 Abby Wambach
2014 Lauren Holiday
2015 Carli Lloyd
2016 Tobin Heath
2017 Julie Ertz
2018 Alex Morgan

NATIONAL ASSOCIATION FOOTBALL LEAGUE (NAFL)

Following a failed attempt by baseball team owners to fill their stadiums in the off-season with a league in 1894, the NAFL started the following year. It struggled at first but received a boost when the U.S. won gold in soccer at the 1904 Olympics.

1895 Bayonne Centerville
1898 Paterson True Blues
1907 West Hudson
1908 Paterson Rangers
1909 Clark A. A.
1910 West Hudson
1911 Jersey A. C.
1912 West Hudson
1913 West Hudson
1914 Brooklyn F. C.
1915 West Hudson
1916 Alley Boys
1917 Jersey A. C.
1918 Paterson F. C.
1919 Bethlehem Steel
1920 Bethlehem Steel
1921 Bethlehem Steel

AMERICAN SOCCER LEAGUE (ASL) I AND II

Featuring teams mostly based in and around the East Coast, the ASL was the first U.S. league with major financial support, enough to attract players from Europe. In the mid-1920s the league boasted large attendances, but difficulties saw it fold in 1933. However, a successor, ASL II, formed the following year.

ASL I

1922 Philadelphia F. C.
1923 J. & P. Coats
1924 Fall River Marksmen
1925 Fall River Marksmen
1926 Fall River Marksmen
1927 Bethlehem Steel
1928 Boston Wonder Workers
1929 Fall River Marksmen
1930 Fall River Marksmen
1931 New York Giants
1932 New Bedford Whalers
1933 Fall River F. C.

ASL II

1934 Kearney Irish-Americans
1935 German-Americans
1936 New York Americans
1937 Scots-Americans
1938 Scots-Americans
1939 Newark Scots
1940 Newark Scots
1941 Newark Scots
1942 Philadelphia Americans
1943 Brooklyn Hispano
1944 Philadelphia Americans
1945 Brookhattan
1946 Baltimore Americans
1947 Philadelphia Americans
1948 Philadelphia Americans
1949 Philadelphia Nationals
1950 Philadelphia Nationals
1951 Philadelphia Nationals
1952 Philadelphia Americans
1953 Philadelphia Nationals
1954 New York Americans
1955 Uhrik Truckers (Philadelphia)
1956 Uhrik Truckers (Philadelphia)
1957 New York Hakoah
1958 New York Hakoah
1959 New York Hakoah
1960 Colombo
1961 Ukrainian Nationals (Philadelphia)
1962 Ukrainian Nationals (Philadelphia)
1963 Ukrainian Nationals (Philadelphia)
1964 Ukrainian Nationals (Philadelphia)
1965 Hartford Football Club
1966 Roma Soccer Club
1967 Baltimore St. Gerards
1968 Washington Darts
1969 Washington Darts
1970 Ukrainian Nationals (Philadelphia)
1971 New York Greeks
1972 Cincinnati Comets
1973 New York Apollo
1974 Rhode Island Oceaneers
1975 New York Apollo
1976 Los Angeles Skyhawks
1977 New Jersey Americans
1978 New York Apollo
1979 Sacramento Gold
1980 Pennsylvania Stoners
1981 Carolina Lightnin'
1982 Detroit Express
1983 Jacksonville Tea Men

NORTH AMERICAN SOCCER LEAGUE (NASL)

Two competing organizations were formed in the 1960s—the National American Soccer League (NASL) changed its name to the United Soccer Association (USA) to avoid a name clash with its rival, the National Professional Soccer League (NPSL). They merged in 1968 to form the North American Soccer League (NASL). The NASL peaked in the mid- to late 1970s, importing some of the big names in world soccer, including Pelé and George Best. Overexpansion, rising costs, and the lack of a TV deal saw the league fold in 1984.

1967 Oakland Clippers (NPSL Champions)
1968 Atlanta Chiefs
1969 Kansas City Spurs
1970 Rochester Lancers
1971 Dallas Tornado
1972 New York Cosmos
1973 Philadelphia Atoms
1974 Los Angeles Aztecs
1975 Tampa Bay Rowdies
1976 Toronto Metros-Croatia
1977 New York Cosmos
1978 New York Cosmos
1979 Vancouver Whitecaps
1980 New York Cosmos
1981 Chicago Sting
1982 New York Cosmos
1983 Tulsa Roughnecks
1984 Chicago Sting

NATIONAL PROFESSIONAL SOCCER LEAGUE

Starting as the American Indoor Soccer Association in 1984, this professional indoor league changed its name in 1990.

1992 Detroit Rockers
1993 Kansas City Attack
1994 Cleveland Crunch
1995 St. Louis Ambush
1996 Cleveland Crunch
1997 Kansas City Attack
1998 Milwaukee Wave
1999 Cleveland Crunch
2000 Milwaukee Wave
2001 Milwaukee Wave

MAJOR LEAGUE SOCCER (MLS)

After the great interest spawned by the U.S. hosting the 1994 World Cup, the MLS kicked off in 1996 with ten teams. Today the league is made up of 24 teams.

1996 D. C. United (OT)
1997 D. C. United
1998 Chicago Fire
1999 D. C. United
2000 Kansas City Wizards
2001 San Jose Earthquakes (OT)
2002 Los Angeles Galaxy (OT)
2003 San Jose Earthquakes
2004 D. C. United
2005 Los Angeles Galaxy
2006 Houston Dynamo
2007 Houston Dynamo
2008 Columbus Crew
2009 Real Salt Lake
2010 Colorado Rapids
2011 Los Angeles Galaxy
2012 Los Angeles Galaxy
2013 Sporting Kansas City
2014 Los Angeles Galaxy
2015 Portland Timbers
2016 Seattle Sounders
2017 Toronto FC
2018 Atlanta United FC

WOMEN'S SOCCER LEAGUES

The W-League was the first of three semiprofessional or professional leagues that arose in the U.S. in the 1990s. For a while it was divided into an upper and lower division (W-1 and W-2). It was joined by the WPSL and then the WUSA, which only lasted for three seasons. Women's Professional Soccer (WPS) began in 2009, with seven teams recruiting many of the world's leading female soccer players. The National Women's Soccer League began in 2013 with eight teams, four of which originally played in WPS.

W-League
1995 Long Island Lady Riders
1996 Maryland Pride
1997 L. I. Lady Riders
1998 Raleigh Wings
1999 Raleigh Wings
2000 Chicago Cobras
2001 Boston Renegades
2002 Boston Renegades
2003 Hampton Roads Piranhas
2004 Vancouver Whitecaps
2005 New Jersey Wildcats
2006 Vancouver Whitecaps
2007 Vancouver Whitecaps

Women's Premier Soccer League (WPSL)
1998 Silicon Valley Red Devils
1999 California Storm
2000 San Diego WFC
2001 Ajax Southern California
2002 California Storm
2003 Utah Spiders
2004 California Storm
2005 F. C. Indiana
2006 Long Island Fury
2007 F. C. Indiana

National Women's Soccer League
2013 Portland Thorns F. C.
2014 F. C. Kansas City
2015 F. C. Kansas City
2016 Western New York Flash
2017 Portland Thorns F.C.
2018 North Carolina Courage

U.S. OPEN CUP CHAMPIONSHIP

One of the oldest soccer cup competitions in the Americas, the U.S. Open Cup dates back to 1914. Only one team, Greek-American of New York, has won the cup three times in a row (1967–1969). Since 1996, a Women's Open Cup competition has also been played.

1914 Brooklyn Field Club
1915 Bethlehem Steel
1916 Bethlehem Steel
1917 Fall River Rovers
1918 Bethlehem Steel
1919 Bethlehem Steel
1920 St. Louis Ben Millers
1921 Brooklyn Robins Dry Dock
1922 St. Louis Scullins Steel
1923 Paterson F. C./St. Louis Scullin Steel (cochampions)
1924 Fall River Marksmen
1925 Shawsheen (MA) Indians
1926 Bethlehem Steel
1927 Fall River Marksmen
1928 New York Nationals
1929 New York Hakoah
1930 Fall River Marksmen
1931 Fall River F. C.
1932 New Bedford Whalers
1933 St. Louis Stix, Baer & Fuller
1934 St. Louis Stix, Baer & Fuller
1935 St. Louis Central Breweries
1936 Philadelphia German-American
1937 New York Americans
1938 Chicago Sparta
1939 Brooklyn St. Mary's Celtic
1940 Baltimore S. C./Chicago Sparta A & BA (cochampions)
1941 Pawtucket F. C.
1942 Pittsburgh Gallatin
1943 Brooklyn Hispano
1944 Brooklyn Hispano
1945 New York Brookhattan
1946 Chicago Vikings
1947 Fall River Ponta Delgada
1948 St. Louis Simpkins-Ford
1949 Pittsburgh Morgan S. C.
1950 St. Louis Simpkins-Ford
1951 New York German-Hungarians
1952 Pittsburgh Hamarville
1953 Chicago Falcons
1954 New York Americans
1955 S. C. Eintracht
1956 Pittsburgh Hamarville
1957 St. Louis Kutis
1958 Los Angeles Kickers
1959 San Pedro McIlvane Canvasbacks
1960 Philadelphia Ukrainian Nationals
1961 Philadelphia Ukrainian Nationals
1962 New York Hungarians
1963 Philadelphia Ukrainian Nationals
1964 Los Angeles Kickers
1965 New York Ukrainians
1966 Philadelphia Ukrainian Nationals
1967 New York Greek-American
1968 New York Greek-American
1969 New York Greek-American
1970 S. C. Elizabeth
1971 New York Hota
1972 S. C. Elizabeth
1973 Los Angeles Maccabee
1974 New York Greek-American
1975 Los Angeles Maccabee
1976 San Francisco A. C.
1977 Los Angeles Maccabee
1978 Los Angeles Maccabee
1979 Brooklyn Dodgers
1980 New York Pancyprian Freedoms
1981 Los Angeles Maccabee
1982 New York Pancyprian Freedoms
1983 New York Pancyprian Freedoms
1984 New York A. O. Krete
1985 San Francisco Greek-Americans
1986 St. Louis Kutis
1987 Washington Club España
1988 St. Louis Busch Seniors
1989 St. Petersburg Kickers
1990 Chicago A. A. C. Eagles
1991 Brooklyn Italians
1992 San Jose Oaks
1993 San Francisco C. D. Mexico
1994 San Francisco Greek-Americans
1995 Richmond Kickers
1996 D. C. United
1997 Dallas Burn
1998 Chicago Fire
1999 Rochester Ragin' Rhinos
2000 Chicago Fire
2001 Los Angeles Galaxy
2002 Columbus Crew
2003 Chicago Fire
2004 Kansas City Wizards
2005 Los Angeles Galaxy
2006 Chicago Fire
2007 New England Revolution
2008 D. C. United
2009 Seattle Sounders F. C.
2010 Seattle Sounders F. C.
2011 Seattle Sounders F. C.
2012 Sporting Kansas City
2013 D. C. United
2014 Seattle Sounders F. C.
2015 Sporting Kansas City
2016 F. C. Dallas
2017 Sporting Kansas City
2018 Houston Dynamo
2019 Atlanta United F. C.

INDIVIDUAL AND TEAM RECORDS

Top league goalscorers

1975	Steve David	23
1976	Derek Smethurst	20
1977	Steve David	26
1978	Giorgio Chinaglia	34
1979	Giorgio Chinaglia	26
1980	Giorgio Chinaglia	32
1981	Giorgio Chinaglia	29
1982	Ricardo Alonso	21
1983	Roberto Cabanas	25
1984	Steven Zyngul	20
1985	Josue Partillo	8
1986	Brent Goulet	9
1987	Joe Mihaljevic	7
1988	Jorge Acosta	14
1989	Ricardo Alonso, Mirko Castilo	10
1990	Chance Fry	17
1991	Jean Harbour	17

1992 Jean Harbour	13
1993 Paulinho	15
1994 Paul Wright	12
1995 Peter Hattrup	11
1996 Roy Lassiter	27
1997 Jaime Moreno	16
1998 Stern John	26
1999 Stern John, Roy Lassiter, Jason Kreis	18
2000 Mamadou Diallo	26
2001 Alex Pineda	19
2002 Carlos Ruiz	23
2003 Carlos Ruiz, Taylor Twellman	15
2004 Amado Guevara	10
2005 Taylor Zwellman	17
2006 Jeff Cunningham	16
2007 Luciano Emilio	20
2008 Landon Donovan	20
2009 Jeff Cunningham	17
2010 Chris Wondolowski	18
2011 Dwayne De Rosario	16
2012 Chris Wondolowski	27
2013 Camilo Sanvezzo	22
2014 Bradley Wright-Phillips	27
2015 Sebastian Gicovinco	22
2016 Bradley Wright-Phillips	24
2017 Nemanja Nikolic	24
2018 Josef Martinez	31

MLS Most Valuable Player

1997 Preki, Kansas City Wizards
1998 Marco Etcheverry, D. C. United
1999 Jason Kreis, F. C. Dallas
2000 Tony Meola, Kansas City Wizards
2001 Alex Pineda Chacón, Miami Fusion
2002 Carlos Ruiz, LA Galaxy
2003 Preki, Kansas City Wizards
2004 Amado Guevara, MetroStars (New Jersey)
2005 Taylor Twellman, New England Revolution
2006 Christian Gomez, D. C. United
2007 Luciano Emilio, D. C. United
2008 Guillermo Barros Schelotto, Columbus Crew
2009 Landon Donovan, LA Galaxy
2010 David Ferreira, F. C. Dallas
2011 Dwayne De Rosario, D. C. United
2012 Chris Wondolowski, San Jose Earthquakes
2013 Mike Magee, Chicago Fire
2014 Robbie Keane, Los Angeles Galaxy
2015 Sebastian Giovinco, Toronto F.C.

2016 David Villa, New York City F.C.
2017 Diego Valeri, Portland Timbers
2018 Josef Martinez, Atlanta United F.C.

All-time MLS goalscorers (1996–2017)

Landon Donovan	145
Chris Wondolowski	144
Jeff Cunningham	134
Jaime Moreno	133
Kei Kamara	114
Ante Razov	114
Jason Kreis	108
Dwayne De Rosario	104
Bradley Wright-Philips	104
Taylor Twellman	101
Edson Buddle	100
Carlos Ruiz	89

Leading international appearances (men)

Cobi Jones	164
Landon Donovan	157
Michael Bradley	143
Clint Dempsey	141
Jeff Agoos	134
Clint Dempsey	132
Marcelo Balboa	128
DaMarcus Beasley	126

Leading international goalscorers (men)

Clint Dempsey	57
Landon Donovan	57
Jozy Alitdore	41
Eric Wynalda	34
Brian McBride	30

Leading international appearances (women)

Kristine Lilly	354
Christie Rampone	311
Mia Hamm	276
Julie Foudy	274
Carli Lloyd	266

Leading international goalscorers (women)

Abby Wambach	184
Mia Hamm	158
Kristine Lilly	130
Michelle Akers	107
Carli Lloyd	105
Tiffeny Milbrett	100

HIT THE NET

www.ussoccer.com
The official home of U.S. soccer in its many forms. It includes news and results from the U.S. leagues and also of U.S. players overseas.

www.futsal.com
Home page of the U.S. Futsal Federation, complete with rules, tips, and news.

http://uslsoccer.com
The official website of the United Soccer Leagues, complete with standings, tables, and news on the USL first and second divisions, the W-League, the Super-20 League, and the Super Y-League.

www.usyouthsoccer.org
The site of the U.S. Youth Soccer Association, featuring news about young players and their coaches, as well as a list of upcoming competitions and a calendar of events.

www.wpslsoccer.com
The official website of the Women's Premier Soccer League.

www.mlssoccer.com
The official website of MLS is a huge collection of history, team data, statistics, news, and opinions. Also included are the rules of the game and coaching advice.

www.nwslsoccer.com
The website of the National Women's Soccer League gives all the facts, stats, news, and results from the competition, along with full game details.

www.fifa.com/womens-football/index.html
FIFA's official webpages on women's international soccer are full of games, results, and features.

http://sbisoccer.com
Solid soccer news website focusing on North American teams, players, and competitions, including international sections.

www.canadiansoccernews.com
Comprehensive guide to all the news and opinion on Canadian soccer players and teams.

http://americansoccernow.com
This interactive online soccer magazine carries news and ranks and profiles of the 100 best U.S. male players

www.espnfc.us
ESPN's soccer website is full of information about the world's major cups, leagues, and international competitions.

GLOSSARY

Advantage rule A rule that allows the referee to let play continue after a foul if it is to the advantage of the team that has been fouled against.

AFC The Asian Football Confederation, responsible for running football in Asia.

Agent A person who represents footballers and negotiates contracts and transfer moves.

Anchor A midfielder positioned just in front of, and who protects, the defenSe. An anchor player may allow other midfielders to push farther forward.

Assist A pass that releases a player to score a goal. An assist can be a pass on the ground, a flick, or a cross from which a headed goal is scored.

Away goals rule A rule used in some cup competitions. If the scores are equal over two legs, the team that has scored more goals away from home wins.

Back-pass rule A law stating that a deliberate pass backward by a player to his or her goalkeeper cannot be handled by the goalie.

CAF The *Confédération Africaine de Football*, which runs football in Africa.

Cap Recognition given to a player for each appearance in an international game for his or her country.

Catenaccio A defensive tactical system in which a sweeper plays behind a solid defense.

Caution Another word for a yellow card (a warning from the referee to a player for a foul or infringement). A player who receives two yellow cards in one game is automatically shown a red card and sent off the field.

Central defender The defender who plays in the middle of the last line of defense.

Chip A pass lofted into the air from a player to a teammate or as a shot on goal.

CONCACAF The Confederation of North, Central American, and Caribbean Association Football, which runs soccer in North and Central America.

CONMEBOL The *Confederación Sudamericana de Fútbol*, which runs football in South America.

Counterattack A quick attack by a team after it regains possession of the ball.

Cross To send the ball from a wide position towards the center of the pitch, often into the opposition penalty area.

Cushioning Using a part of the body to slow down a ball in order to bring it under control.

Derby A match between two rival teams, often located in the same town or city.

Direct free kick A kick awarded to a team because of a serious foul committed by an opponent. A goal may be scored directly from the kick.

Dissent When a player uses words or actions to disagree with the referee's decision.

Distribution The way the ball is released by a goalkeeper or is moved around the field by a team.

Dribbling Moving the ball under close control with a series of short kicks or taps.

Drop ball A way of restarting play in which the referee releases the ball to a player of the team that last touched the ball. All other players must be at least 13 ft. (4 m) away.

Extra time A way of deciding a tied game. It involves two periods of additional play, usually lasting 15 minutes each.

FA (Football Association) The national soccer federation of England.

Feinting Using fake moves of the head, shoulders, and legs to deceive an opponent and put him or her off balance.

FIFA *The Fédération Internationale de Football Association*, the international governing body of soccer.

Formation The way in which a team lines up on the pitch in terms of the numbers of defenders, midfielders, and forwards.

Foul An action committed intentionally by a defender to stop an opponent who has a clear run on goal.

Fourth official An additional match official responsible for displaying added-on time, checking substitutions, and aiding the referee and his or her two assistants.

Futsal A type of five-on-five soccer, supported and promoted by FIFA.

Golden Boot An award given to the player who scores the most goals at a World Cup. It is also an annual award given to the top goalscorer in European club football.

Golden goal A system used to decide a tied knockout game in extra time. The first goal scored wins the game.

Handball The illegal use of the hand or arm by a player.

Hat trick Three goals scored by a player in a single match.

Indirect free kick A kick awarded to a team because of a minor foul committed by an opponent. A goal cannot be scored from the kick unless the ball is first touched by a player other than the kicker.

Instep The part of a player's foot where his or her shoelaces lie.

Interception When a player gains possession of the ball by latching onto a pass made by the opposition.

Jockeying A defensive technique of delaying an attacker who has the ball.

Laws of the game The 17 main rules of football, established and updated by FIFA.

Libero "Free man." *See also* sweeper.

Man-to-man marking A system of marking in which a defender stays close to and goalside of a single opposition player.

Marking Guarding a player to prevent him or her from advancing the ball toward the goal, making an easy pass or receiving the ball from a teammate.

MLS Major League Soccer, the U.S. professional male league.

Narrowing the angle A technique in which a goalkeeper moves toward an attacker who has the ball in order to cut down the amount of goal the attacker can aim a shot at.

Obstruction When a player, instead of trying to win the ball, uses his or her body to prevent an opponent from playing it.

OFC The Oceania Football Confederation, which runs soccer in Oceania.

Offside A player is offside if he or she is closer to the other team's goal than both the ball and the second-to-last opponent at the moment that the ball is played forward.

Offside trap A defensive tactic used to trick opposition attackers by leaving them offside. Defenders who play the offside trap usually move upfield together, in a straight line, when the ball is played toward their goal.

Overlap To run outside and beyond a teammate down the side of the pitch in order to create space and a possible passing opportunity.

Overload When an attacking team has more players in the opposition's half or penalty area than the defending side. An overload often leads to a scoring chance.

Penalty shoot-out A method of deciding a drawn match by a series of penalties, all taken at one end of the field.

Playmaker A skilled midfielder or deep-lying attacker who coordinates the attacking movement of a team.

Play-off A match, pair, or series of matches used to decide a final placing. In the World Cup the two losing semifinalists contest a single play-off game for third place. In many leagues play-off matches are used to decide relegation and promotion issues.

Referee's assistant An official who assists the referee during the game by signaling for fouls, infringements, and offsides.

Reserve team A team made up of players who are not in the first team at a club or national side.

Scout A person employed by a soccer team who attends games and training sessions to look for up-and-coming players.

Set piece A planned play or move that a team uses when a game is restarted with a free kick, penalty kick, corner kick, goal kick, throw-in, or kickoff.

Shielding A technique used by the player with the ball to protect it from a defender who is closely marking him or her. The player in possession keeps his or her body between the ball and the defender.

Simulation Pretending to be fouled or feigning injury in order to fool the referee. A player found guilty of simulation by the referee receives a yellow card.

Stoppage time Time added to the end of any period of a game to make up for time lost during a major halt in play. Also known as added time or injury time.

Substitution Changing the team lineup on the pitch by replacing one player with another from the substitutes' bench.

Sweeper A defender who can play closest to his or her goal, behind the rest of the defenders, or in a more attacking role with responsibility for bringing the ball forward.

Tactics Methods of play used in an attempt to outwit and beat an opposition team.

Target man A tall striker, usually the player furthest upfield, at whom teammates aim their forward passes.

Through ball or pass A pass to a teammate that puts him or her beyond the opposition's defense and through on goal.

Total football A style of soccer in which players switch positions all over the field. It was made famous by the Dutch national side and Dutch teams such as Ajax.

UEFA The Union of European Football Associations, which organizes soccer in Europe.

VAR Short for video assistant referee, this official can be instructed by a referee to review a major incident, such as a penalty or direct red card, on video screens to ensure the right decision is made.

Volley Any ball kicked by a player when it is off the ground.

Wall pass A quick, short pair of passes between two players that sends the ball past a defender. Also known as a one-two pass.

Wingback A defender on the sides of the pitch who, when the opportunity occurs, makes wide runs forward in attack.

WUSA The world's first professional soccer league for women, based in the United States.

Zonal marking A defensive system in which defenders mark opponents who enter their area of the field.

INDEX

Note: references to main entries are in **bold**.

A

Abbondanzieri, Roberto 12
Abramovich, Roman 102
AC Milan 30, 40, **82**, 101, 102, 104, 128, 133
Adriano 22
advantage rule 20, **140**
AFC (Asian Football Confederation) **13**, 140
Africa 12, 13, 116, 130
African Champions League 78, 88, **130**
African Cup-Winners' Cup 78, **130**
Africa Cup of Nations 77, **123**
Aghahowa, Julius 132
Ahn Jung-Hwan 72, 126
Ajax 75, **89**, 94, 99
Al-Ahly **78**, 101
Al-Ain 130
Al-Ittihad 130
Al-Masry 101
Aliyu, Musa 88
Alberto, Carlos 76, 77
Albrecht, Jorge 110
Aldridge, John 37
Algeria 113, 123
Alonso, Xabi 116
Anderlecht 44, **87**
Appiah, Stephen 26
Arevaldo, Egido 122
Argentina 11, 12, 48, 58, 77, 108, 112, 113, 114, 116, 121, 122, 131
Arsenal **84**, 95, 96, 129, 133, 137, 138
Asia 12, 13, 109, 117, **129**, 130
Asian Cup **124**
Asian Games 34, **124**
Aston, Ken 8
Aston Villa 34, 88, 105, 137, 138
Atlético Madrid 55, 86, 91
Atsuto, Uchida 17
attacking **26–7**
Australia 12, 13, 59, 115, 125
Austria 65, 108, 110, 113, 126
Ayala, Roberto 48

B

Babayaro, Celestine 29, 120
backpass rule 6, 24, 114
Baggio, Roberto 32, 33, **49**, 85
Bale, Gareth 44, 91, 102
Balotelli, Mario 20, 119
ball control **16**, 24, **25**
Ballesteros, Sergio 131
Banks, Gordon **35**, 74
Barbosa, Moacir 109
Barcelona 44, **78**, 99, 100, 101, 102, 133
Baresi, Franco 32, **40**, 61, 82
Barreto, Edgar 121
Barry, Gareth 105
Barthez, Fabien 34, 72, 98
Batistuta, Gabriel 28, **55**
Battaglia, Sebastian 90
Bayern Munich 66, 71, **86**, 100, 127, 128
beach soccer 95
Bebeto 29, 40
Beckenbauer, Franz **39**, 61, 71, 86, 112

Beckham, David 16, 23, **42**, 87, 96, 97, 98, 139
Belgium 11, 105, 113, 118, 121
Belodedici, Miodrag 83, 85
Benfica 23, 46, 52, 66, 79, **86**, 133
Bergkamp, Dennis 48, 84, 89, 94
Best, George 38, **47**, 55, 79
Blatter, Sepp 108
Boateng, Jerome 86
Boca Juniors 23, **81**, 90, 101, 130, 131
Bolivia 104, 122
Bonhof, Rainer 71
Boniek, Zbigniew 45
Borussia Dortmund 38, 100, 102, 128
Borussia Mönchengladbach 46, 71, 28
Bosman ruling 103
Botafogo 43, 45, 46, 79, 84
Botasso, Juan 108
Bouhaddi, Sarah 25
Boulahrouz, Khalid 26
Bowyer, Lee 105
Brazil 2, 7, 12, 13, 19, 32, 35, 54, 60, **76**, 77, 109, 110, 111, 112, 114, 115, 116, 120, 122, 125, 130, 131, **134–5**
women's team 117, 121
Bronze, Lucy **37**
Buffon, Gianluigi 24, 30, 34
Bugaev, Alexei 22
Bundesliga 66, 86, 103, 127, **128**
Busby, Matt 79

C

CAF (Confédération Africaine de Football) **13**, 130, 140
Camara, Henri 62
Cameroon 9, **77**, 114, 123
Canada 39, 113, 125
Caniggia, Claudio 114
Cantona, Eric 95, 105
Caribbean 12
Carle, Nick 17
Carling Cup 138
Carragher, Jamie 88
Carrick, Michael 7
Casillas, Iker 25, **34**, 107
Castro, Hector 108
catenaccio **60–1**, 67, 80, 140
cautions **21**, 140
Cech, Petr 24,
Celtic 23, 53, 66, **90**, 100, 127, 137, 138
Ceni, Rogério 25
Champions League see European Cup
Chapman, Herbert 60, **66**, 84
Charisteas, Angelos 106
Charles, John **40**
Charlton, Bobby **50**, 55, 74, 79, 111, 139
Chastain, Brandi 117
cheating 8, **104**, 105
Chelsea 23, 62, 64, 103, 129, 132, 137, 138
Chile 77, 104, 111, 120, 122
China 10, 13, 65, 94, 115, 124, 129
women's team 40, 117, 121
chip 17, **140**
Choi Jin-Cheul 72
Chrysostomos, Michael 80
Cissé, Djibril 62
Clodoaldo 76, 77
club teams 11, **78–91**, 130–1
coaches 20, 21, 60, 61, 62, 63, **66–7**, 87, 89, 90, 109, 136
role 58, 59, **64–5**
Cocu, Philip 126

Cohen, George 68
Colo Colo 37, **90**, 130
Colombia 50, 77, 104, 122, 125, 131
women's team 117
Coluna, Mario **46**, 86
CONCACAF (Confederation of North, Central American and Caribbean Association Football) **12**, 75, 116, **125**, 140
confederations **12–13**
CONMEBOL (Confederacíon Sudamericana de Fútbol) **12**, 140
Copa America **122**, 130
Copa Libertadores **130–1**
Corinthians 11, 45, 79, 102
Costa Rica 12, 114, 115, 122, 125
counterattacking 62, **63**
crosses 17, **140**
Croatia 119
Cruyff, Johan 42, 47, **47**, 67, 75, 78, 89, 94, 112, 128
Cruyff turn 27, 47
CSKA Moscow 131
Cubillas, Teofilio 37, 112
Cuevas, Nelson 82, 127
cushioning **16**, 140
Czech Republic / Czechoslovakia 76, 80, 108, 111, 118, 119, 121, 126
Czibor, Zoltan 70, 110

D

da Silva, Eduardo 97
da Silva, Marta Vieira **53**
da Silva, Ze Carlos 79
Dalglish, Kenny **51**, 89, 139
Danso, Mavis 46
de Boer, Ronald 89
deaths 79, 104–5
decoy runs 18, 26
defenders 28, **37–40**, 61
defending **22–3**
del Bosque, Vicente 65
del Piero, Alessandro 85
Dembele, Ousmane 27
Dempsey, Clint 62
Denmark 11, 62, 118, 119, 120, 126
derby games **101**, 105, 140
Desailly, Marcel **37**, 72
Deschamps, Didier 92
Dhorasoo, Vikash 83
Di Stefano, Alfredo 14, 15, **51**, 82, 91
Dick, Kerr Ladies 11, **81**
Dida 101
Diou, Salif 62
Diouf, El Hadji 62
distribution 25, 140
Djorovic, Goran 118
Dominguez, Rogelio 132
Donovan, Landon 41, 87, 94
dribbling 17, 27, 43, **140**
drug use 51, **105**
dummy movements 18, 27
Dyer, Kieron 105
Dynamo Kiev 50, 67, **91**, 105
Dzajic, Dragan 43

E

Egypt 55, 78, 108, 123
Eintracht Frankfurt 14–15
Elizondo, Horacio 21
England 2, 10, 18, 35, 60, **74**, 111, 114, 117, 119
league 127, **129**, **136**, **137**, 138
Eriksson, Sven-Goran 58
Escobar, Andres 104

Esperance Sportive Tunis 23, **88**
Espindola, Fabian 28
Eto'o, Samuel 9, 77, 96, 123
Europe 12, 13, 118, 131
European Championships 11, 12, 72, 106–7, **118–19**
European Cup / Champions League 12, 14–15, 79, 91, 131, **132–3**
European Cup-Winners' Cup 78, **131**
European Supercup 131
Eusebio **52**, 109, 111
Everton 8, 137, 138

F

FA (Football Association) 9, **10**, 11, 81, 140
FA Cup 10, 51, 59, 98, 130, 131, 136, **137–8**
Fabregas, Cesc 94
Falcao, Radamel 64
fans 6, 28, 85, **100–1**, 105, 117
Ferguson, Alex 34, 59, 65, **67**, 79
Fernandez, Gaston 82
Ferreira, Edmilson 28
field 8, 66, 99
FIFA (Fédération Internationale de Football Association) 7, 9, 11, 12, 19, 134, 140
FIFA U-17 World Championship 94
FIFA U-20 World Cup 94
Figo, Luis 45, 94,
Figueroa, Elias 37
Fiorentina 49, 104, 131
Firmani, Fabio 128
five-on-five soccer **19**
Flamengo 49, **79**, 84
Fluminense 54, **84**
Fontaine, Just **49**, 72, 109, 110
footballs 9, 95
formations **60–1**, 62, 140
fouls 21, **24**, 28, 141
fourth official **20**, 140
France 11, **72**, 92–3, 109, 110, 113, 114, 116, 117, 118, 121
league 127, 131
women's team 16
free kicks 17, 19, 24, **30**, 42, 140
Frisk, Anders 105
futsal **19**, 140

G

Galatasaray 45, **85**
Gallego, Americo 75
game-fixing 83, 85, **104**, 128
Gao Hong **34**
Garrincha 27, **43**, 105, 109, 111
Gentile, Claudio 113
George, Finidi 89
Germany 28, 31, 37, 38, 52, 99, 108, 115, 116, 117, 118, 119, 134
women's team 74, 117, 121
see also West Germany
Ghana 25, 27, 115, 123
Gibbs, Kieran 129
Giggs, Ryan 67, 79
Giresse, Alain 41, 43
Giske, Anneli 54
Giuly, Ludovic 26
Given, Shay 24
Glazer, Malcolm 102
goal area 8
goal celebrations 28, 29
goalkeepers 25, **34–6**
goalkeeping 23, **24–5**, 30, 31
goalscoring 8, 25, **28–9**, 40, 43, 46, 55

Golden Boot 55, **109**, 119
Golmohammadi, Yahya 124
Gomes, Nuno 22
Gonzalez, Cristian 121
Greece 10, 100, 118, 119, 120
Griezmann, Antoine 92, 119
Grobbelaar, Bruce 58
Grosics, Gyula 70
Grosso, Fabio 115
Guardiola, Josep 'Pep' 32, 60, 136
Gullit, Ruud **51**, 82
Guttman, Bela **66**, 86

H

Hagl, Gheorghe **45**, 85
Haiti 112, 125
Hamburg 39, 100, 128, 132
Hamm, Mia **53**, 71, 117, 121
Hansen, Alan 58, 89
Hassan, Hossam and Ibrahim 78
Helguera, Ivan 23
Helmer, Thomas 6
Henry, Thierry 72, 84
Herberger, Josef 'Sepp' 58
Hernandez, Javier 75
Hernandez, Luis 75
Hernández, Xavi **42**, 63, 73, 107
Herrera, Helenio 60, **67**, 80
Hiddink, Guus 59, 72
Higuita, Jose 77
Hirase, Tomoyuki 78
history 8, 9, 10, 136
Holiday, Lauren 11
Holland 11, 31, 48, **75**, 112, 115, 118, 119
Honda, Yasuto 78
Hong Myung-Bo **40**, 72
hooliganism 101
Hungary **70**, 109, 110, 120, 121, 126
Hurst, Geoff 69, 74, 101, 111
Hwang Sun-Hong 72

IJ

Ibra Kebe, Baye Ali 88
Ibrahimovic, Zlatan 27, 133
India 9, 124
Iniesta, Andrés 18, **42**, 107, 119
injuries 39, 40, 47, 49, 53, 54, 59, **96–7**, 111
Inter-Cities Fairs Cup 66, 67, 87, **131**
Inter Milan *see* Internazionale
Internazionale 60, **80**, 95, 101, 102, 128
Italy 10, 11, 32, 61, **73**, 76, 77, 108, 109, 111, 112, 113, 114, 116, 118, 119, 121, 131
Iwabuchi, Mana 11
J-League 78, 103, 126, 129
Jairzinho 35, **46**, 76, 77
Jamaica 114, 125
James, Alex 9, 66, 84
Jancker, Carsten 6
Japan 8, 10, 12, 13, 103, 114, 117, 124, 129
Jennings, Pat **36**, 139
Jesus, Gabriel 94
Johnstone, Jimmy 90
Jones, Cobi 87, 125
Joma, Issam 88
Juninho 87
Juventus 30, 40, 66, **85**, 102, 103, 104, 105, 128

K

Kahn, Oliver 34, 40
Kaizer Chiefs **83**

Kaka 82, 102
Kaladze, Kakhaber 28
Kameni, Idriss Carlos 77
Kane, Harry 95, 109
Kanu, Nwankwo 89
Kashima Antlers 49, 53, **78**, 126, 129
Keegan, Kevin 51, 89, 94
kemari 10
Kempes, Mario 58, 82, 109
Kennedy, Alan 58
Kennedy, Ray 89
kit 8, 9, 11 *see also* strips
Klinsmann, Jürgen **52**, 65
Klopp, Jurgen 65
Klose, Miroslav 28, 109
Kocsis, Sandor 55, 70, 109, 110
Koeman, Ronald 61, 78
Kolarov, Aleksandar 24
Kopunek, Kamil 59
Kovac, Radoslav 80
Krol, Ruud **39**, 75, 89

L

La Liga 78, 91, 127, **128**
La Maquina 51, 82
Lahm, Philipp 60
Lannoy, Stephane 20
Larsson, Henrik **53**
Lato, Gregorz 109, 112
Latvia 23, 119, 126
Laudrup, Brian 45, 119
Laudrup, Michael **45**, 78
Law, Denis 31, **55**, 79, 139
laws *see* rules
Lazio 36, 45, 60, 102, 128, 131
leagues 10, 83, **126–9**, 131
Lee, Sammy 58
Lee Chun-Soo 72
Lee Min-Sung 115
Leeds United 40, 66, 101, 137, 138
Leonardo 29
Léonidas da Silva 79, 109
Letchkov, Iordan 114
Lewandowski, Mariusz 26
Lilly, Kristine 71
Lineker, Gary 109, 114, 139
Lines, Aaron 125
linesmen *see* referee's assistants
Liverpool 28, 51, 58, 88, **89**, 96, 105, 133, 137, 138, 139
Lizarazu, Bixente 72
Lloris, Hugo 93
Lloyd, Carli **52**, 68, 69
Lobanovsky, Valery **67**, 91
Lopez, Wilmer 125
Los Angeles Galaxy **87**
Loy, Egon 14
Lukaku, Romely 96

M

Mabedi, Patrick 83
Maier, Sepp 71, 86, 112
Maldini, Cesare 38, 52
Maldini, Paolo **38**, 82
managers *see* coaches
Manchester City 102, 127, 129, 137, 138
Manchester United 31, 44, 50, 64, 65, 67, **79**, 100, 104, 129, 137, 138
Maradona, Diego 27, **51**, 56–7, 58, 102, 105, 113, 127
marking 23, 62, **141**
Marseille *see* Olympique Marseille
Marta 28, **53**
mascots 100, 111

Materazzi, Marco 21, 44, 115
Matthäus, Lothar **46**
Matthews, Stanley 27, **41**
Mazurkiewicz, Ladislao 54
Mba, Sunday 74
Mbappé, Kylian 92
Meazza, Giuseppe 73
Medalen, Linda **40**
media 7, 13, 21, 100–1, 102, 103, 124, 133
Mendes da Silva, David 27
Mendieta, Gaizka 118
Merk, Markus 101
Messi, Lionel 7, 16, 18, 27, 31, **48**, 97, 103, 128
Mexico 12, **75**, 98, 113, 99, 120, 121, 122, 125, 126, 130
Michels, Rinus 47, 58, 61, **67**, 75, 89
midfielders 28, 29, **41–6**
Miguel 18
Mihajlovic, Sinisa 60
Milla, Roger **50**, 77, 114
Milutinovic, Bora 65
Minda, Oswaldo 87
Mirzapour, Ebrahim 124
MLS (Major League Soccer) 40, 41, 87, 126, **129**, 141
Modric, Luka 17, **46**
Mokone, Steve 12
Monaco 52, 129
money 13, **102–3**, 133
see also transfers
Moon, W. R. 11
Moore, Bobby **38**, 74
Morace, Carolina **50**
Morgan, Willie 43
Morocco 113, 123
Mortensen, Stan 70
Mostroem, Malin 11
Mourinho, José 61, 62, 64, 136
Müller, Gerd 37, **49**, 55, 71, 86, 109, 128
Munoz, Miguel 51, 64

N

NAC Breda 27
Nacional 88, 127, 131
national sides **70–71**
Navarro, Fernando 132
Navas, Jesus 27
Nazarenko, Sergiy 17
Neeskens, Johan 75, 89
Netherlands 116
Neuer, Manuel 34, **36**
Neuville, Oliver 31
New Zealand 125
Newcastle United 99, 101, 105, 137
Neymar 81
Nigeria **74**, 77, 99, 120, 123
women's team 116
Nordby, Bente 24
Nordin, Krister 20
North Korea 111
Northern Ireland 113, 136
Norway 126
women's team 24, 54, 117, 121
Nottingham Forest 132, 133, 137, 138

O

obstruction 17, 22, 30, 141
Oceania **13**, **125**
officials **20–1**, 136
offside law 19, 30, 141
offside traps 23, **26**, **62**, 141
Olinga, Fabrice 96

Olympiakos 23, 70, 101
Olympics 73, 77, **120–1**
women's football 11, 34, **121**
Olympic Lyonnais Féminin 88
Olympique Marseille **83**, 102, 104, 129
O'Neill, Martin 20
Ono, Shinji 126, 127
Oriali, Gabriele 113
Oscar 94
Overath, Wolfgang 71
overloads **26**, 141
own goals 28
Oyongo Bitolo, Ambroise 123
Özil, Mesut 18, 116

PQ

Papin, Jean-Pierre 83, 102
Paraguay 20, 25, 121, 122
Paralympics 95
Park Ji-Sung 72
Passarella, Daniel **37**
passing **17**, 18, 26, 141
Pazzini, Giampaolo 31
Pelé 6, 29, 35, 38, **54**, 76, 77, 81, 98, 101, 110, 111, 130
penalty kicks 8, **30**
penalty shoot-outs 19, 25, **31**, 32–33, 72, 122, 132, 141
Peñarol 23, **88**, 122, 127, 130, 131
Pepe 91
Peralta, Oribe 120
Perrotta, Simone 128
Peru 104, 112, 122
Peters, Martin 68, 69, 74
Petignat, Nicole 20
Pirlo, Andrea 21
Platini, Michel **43**, 45, 72, 95, 118, 120
players 7, 13, **34–57**, **96–7**, 136
see also transfers
Poland 46, 77, 112, 113, 121
Porto 64, 102
Portugal 6, 45, 111, 118, 119, 127
Pozzo, Vittorio 60, 73, 108
Premier League *see* England league
Preud'homme, Michel 34
Prinz, Birgit **54**, 74, 117
Priskin, Tamas 23
professional fouls *see* fouls
Puskas, Ferenc 15, **47**, 51, 55, 70, 86, 91, 110
Puyol, Carles 78
Qatar 108, 124

R

racism **105**
Ramos, Sergio 17
Ramsey, Alf 74
Rangers 67, 136, 138, 139
Raúl **49**, 133
Real Madrid 14–15, 64, 65, 77, **91**, 100, 101, 102, 103, 128, 132
red cards 8, **21**, 22, 42, 111, 112, 114, 115
referees 20, 21, 101, 105, 116
role 8, 9, 19, **20**, 99
referee's assistants 8, **20**, 105, 141
Republic of Ireland 37, 114
Ribéry, Franck 26, 129
Ricardo 25
Rijkaard, Frank 82
Rio Championship 79, 84
Rivaldo 21, 120
Rivelino, Roberto 76, 77
River Plate **82**, 101, 103, 127
Roa, Carlos 48

Robben, Arjen 18, 22, 27
Robinho 105
Rodriguez, James 96, 109
role models 20, 40, 41, 52, **97**, **105**
Roma 128
Romario 40, 84
Ronaldo **53**, 92, 109, 115, 120
Ronaldo, Cristiano 16, 20, 27, **44**, 60, 63, 91, 103, 119, 128
Rondon, Salomon 131
Rooney, Wayne 30, 129, 139
Rosato, Roberto 111
Rossi, Paolo **47**, 109
Roth, Werner 86
rules 10, 19, 20, 24, 30–31, 140, 141
Russia 11, 101, 104–5, 108, 114, 126, 131

S

Sacchi, Arrigo 82
Sala, Emiliano 104
Sala, Mohamed 63
Salcedo, Jose Domingo 90
Salgado, Michel 7
Sammer, Matthias **38**
Sanchez, Hugo 29, **55**, 120
Santos 9, 54, **81**, 130, 131
Saudi Arabia 124, 130
Sawa, Homare 71, 75, 117
Schmeichel, Peter **34**, 67, 119
Schollen, Davy 9
Schwarzenbeck, Hans-Georg 71
Scifo, Enzo **44**, 87
Scolari, Luiz Felipe 65
Scotland 10, 25, 60, 136
  league 22, 126, 127, 136, **137**
Scottish Cup 131, 136, **138**
Seeler, Uwe 110
sendings-off 20, 21, 22, 37, 45, 114
Senegal 62, 115, 123
Serie A 127, **128**
set pieces **26**, 141
seven-on-seven soccer 19, 95
Shakhtar Donetsk 26, 91, 132
Shankly, Bill 16, 89
Shea, Brek 17

Shevchenko, Andriy **50**, 67
Shew-Atjon, Etienne 17
shielding **17**, 141
Shilton, Peter 57, 139
shutouts **23**, 24, 35
Silva, Mauro 29
Silva, Thiago **39**
simulation **21**, 141
six-second rule 24
skills **16–17**, 24, 25
Socrates **45**
Solo, Hope **36**
Solskjaer, Ole Gunnar 59
Souness, Graeme 89
South Africa 7, 12, 99, 104, 116, 123
South America 11, 12, 13, 19, 122
South Korea 12, 59, **72**, 115, 124, 125, 129
Soviet Union 67, 70, 77, 104, 111, 118, 119, 121
space, using **18–19**
Spain 11, 19, **73**, 106–107, 109, 116, 118, 119, 121, 131
Sparta Prague 80, 132
stadiums 8, **98–9**, 100, 102, 103, 109
  disasters 85, **104–5**, 132
Stam, Ronnie 27
Steaua Bucharest 23, 45, **85**, 132
Stein, Jock **66**, 67, 90
Stiles, Nobby 79
Stoichkov, Hristo **42**, 109
strikers 28, 29, 34, 42, **47–55**, 75
Strutz, Walter 103
Suarez, Luis 80, 94, 102, 128
substitutions 20, 58, **59**, 62, 141
Suker, Davor 109
Sükür, Hakan 85, 115
Sun Wen **46**
Suzuki, Takayuki 124
Sweden 11, 109, 110, 114, 117, 121, 126, 128
sweepers 39, 45, **60**, 61, 141
Switzerland 11, 105, **110**

T

tackling **22**, 30

tactics 60, **62–3**, 141
Tapie, Bernard 83
Tardelli, Marco 113
team selection **58**
team staff 64
Tevez, Carlos 102
Thailand 31, 55
throw-ins 6, 18, 24, 26
time wasting 24, 29, 30
Torino 104
Torres, Fernando 23, 29, 107, 119
Tostao 35, 76, 111
total football 39, 47, **61**, 67, 75, 141
training 9, 66, 96, 97
transfers 27, 40, 41, 42, **44**, 47, 48, 51, 52, 53, 55, 64, 67, **102**, **103**
Trapattoni, Giovanni **66**
trapping 16
Trezeguet, David 72, 115
Tunisia 88, 112
Turkey 21, 31, 58, 105, 115
Tymoshchuk, Anatoliy 26

UV

UEFA (Union of European Football Associations) **12**, 118
UEFA Cup 20, **131**
uniforms 9, 24, 85, 88, 101
Uruguay 12, 54, 76, 98, 108, 109, 110, 111, 116, 122, 131
  league 37, 126, 127
USA 11, 12, 65, 108, 122, 125, 129
  women's team **71**, 117, 121
Valderrama, Carlos **41**
Valorón, Juan Carlos 21
van Basten, Marco **55**, 82, 94
van Persie, Robin 26, 129
VAR (video assistant referee) 21
Vava 109, 110, 111
Vera, Nelson 20
Vienna School 65
Vieira de Souza, Givanildo 13
Vieira, Patrick 115
Vieri, Christian 85
Vogts, Berti 71, 136

W

wall, defensive 24, 30, 31
Walter, Ottmar 110, 111
Walters, Jon 28
Wambach, Abby 71
Weah, George **52**
Wenger, Arsène 52, **64**, 84, 136
West Germany 58, **71**, 110, 111, 112, 113, 114, 118
Wharton, Arthur 25
Whittaker, Tom 66
wingbacks 26, 60, **141**
wingers 26, 41–46, 60
women's football **11**, 16, 71, 68–9, 81, **116–17**, 121
World Club Cup **130**
World Cup 10, 32–3, 35, 48, 54, 56–7, 68–9, 74, 76, 77, 92–3, **108–17**, 134–5
  trophies 109, 111, 112
  Women's **11**, 69, 71, 74, **117**
Wright, Tommy 35

XYZ

Yashin, Lev **35**
yellow cards 8, **21**, 22, 37, 111
Young, George 41
young players 89, **94–5**, 96
Yugoslavia 32, 108, 111, 118, 119, 121
Zabaleta, Pablo 23
Zagalo, Mario 39, 76
Zaire 112, 123
Zenga, Walter 114
Zenit Saint Petersburg **87**, 88
Zico **49**, 65, 78, 79, 89
Zidane, Zinedine 16, 21, **44**, 72, 91, **92**, 102, 115
Zoff, Dino 23, **36**, 95
Zonneveld, Mike 27
Zubizarreta, Andoni 78

ACKNOWLEDGMENTS

The publisher would like to thank the following for permission to reproduce their material.

Top = t, bottom = b, center = c, left = l, right = r

Front cover: l Getty/Tim Clayton - Corbis; c Getty/Visionhaus; r Getty/Elsa/Staff; back cover l Alamy/Action Plus Sports Images; r Alamy/Cal sport media; Inside images supplied by PA/Empics with the exception of: pages 4-5 The FA via Getty; 6bl PA/DPA; 6-7c Getty/ Shaun Botteril; 7br Image Source; 7tr PA/AP/Hassan Ammar; 8tr Getty/Oli Scarff; 8l Getty/ AFP; 9t Getty/ J.A. Hampton; 11br Getty/ Reinhold Thiele; 11tl Getty/The Asahi Shimbun; 12c Getty/ Clive Mason; 13bl Getty/LatinContent; 14-15 PA/PA Archive; 16tr Corbis/Julien Hekimian/ Sygma; 16cl PA/ABACA Pess; 16cr Getty/Christof Koepsel; 17bl PA/AP/Andrew Brownhill; 17br Getty/R Yeatts; 18tr Shutterstock/efecreata mediagroup; 19br Getty/AFP/Patrick Lin; 20c Getty/Michael Reagan; 20bl PA/Anders Wiklund/TT News Agency; 21cl Getty/Patrick Hertzog/AFP; 21bl Getty/Stu Forster; 22tr PA/Paulo Duarte; 22bl Getty/Javier Soriano; 23tl Getty/Paul Ellis; 23cr Getty/Stuart Franklin; 23b Shutterstock/LazloSzirtesi; 24cl Getty/Glynn Kirk/AFP; 24cr Getty/AFP/Stan Honda; 24br Getty/Mike Hewitt; 25cl Getty/Phil Cole; 25cr PA/Christophe Ena/AP; 26cl Getty/Valery Hachie/AFP; 27bl Getty/Khaled Desouki/AFP; 27br Shutterstock/Maxisport; 28c Getty/John Peters; 28br Getty/Adnreas Rentz; 29t Corbis/Reuters/Kai Pfaffenbach; 29c Shutterstock/Photo Works; 29b Getty/AFP/Patrick Hertzog; 30bl Getty/Matthew Peters; 30br Getty/Corbis/Reuters; 30-31 Getty/AFP/Stringer; 31tr PA/AP/Antonio Calanni; 31br Getty/Alexander Hassenstein; 32-33 PA/DPA/Deutsche Press Agentur; 34bl Shutterstock/efecreata media group; 35t PA/PA Archive; 36bl PA/PA Archive; 36c Alamy/imageBROKER; 38tr PA/Witters; 41tl Shutterstock/Photo Works; 42cr Shutterstock/Natursports; 42b Corbis/Eddie Keogh/Reuters; 43cr PA/Topham Picturepoint; 44c Shutterstock/Jonathan Larsen; 46tr Getty/Stephen Dunn; 48t Shutterstock/Natursports; 49tr Getty/Ben Radford; 49b PA/DPA; 51b PA/Topham Picturepoint; 53t PA/ Digital Sports Archive; 53br Getty/ Junko Kimura; 54c Getty/Rolls Pess/Popperfoto; 54tr Getty/Lars Baron/Bongarts; 56-57 Getty/Bob Thomas Sports Photography; 57tr PA/Daniel Moltz; 58b PA/DPA; 59tr Getty/Emmanuel Dunand/AFP; 59cl Getty/Christophe Simon; 60t Shutterstock/Maxisport; 60cr Getty/Claudio Volla/Grazia Nero; 61tl Shutterstock/Photo Works; 62tr Shutterstock/Photo Works; 63cl Corbis/Reuters/Jose Manuel; 63br Getty/AFP/Franck Fife; 64cl Getty/Gonzalo Arroyo Moreno; 64br Shutterstock/Maxisport; 65tr Getty/ Javier Soriano; 65br Getty/Mike Lawrie; 66cr Getty/Ben Radford; 67bl Corbis/Reuters/Ian Hodgson; 68-69 PA/PA Archive; 71b Getty/Kevin C Cox; 72tl Getty/Ben Radford/Allsport; 72b Getty/AFP/Roberto Schmidt; 73tr Getty/VI-Images; 73b PA/DPA; 74tr Corbis/Srdjan Suki/epa; 74bl Shutterstock/Maxisport; 75b Getty/AFP/Boris Horvat; 77 Getty/AFP; 78t Corbis/Christian Liewig; 79tl Corbis/Reuters; 79b Shutterstock/Jaggat Rashidi; 80tr Corbis/ Reuters/Petr Josek; 80bl PA/Barnaby's Picture Library; 81tr Getty/Helio Suenaga/STR; 81bl PA/Topham Picturepoint; 82tr Getty Sports/Laurence Griffiths; 82bl Corbis/Reuters/Andres Stapff; 83tr Getty/AFP/Chi Jae-Ku; 84tl Corbis/Reuters/Bruno Domingos; 84br PA/Sean Dempsey; 85tl Corbis/Reuters/Bruno Domingos; 86cl Getty/Alexander Hassenstein; 87bl Getty/Victor Decolongon; 88tl Getty/AFP/Fethi Belaid; 88bl Getty/AFP/ Daniel Sosa; 90bl PA/AFP/Roberto Candia; 91tr Getty/AFP/Sergei Supinsky; 91c PA/Topham Picturepoint; 91br Getty/Angel Martinez; 92-93 Corbis/Sygma/Jacques Langevin; 94c Getty/Ian MacNicol; 94bl Getty/AFP/Oliver Lang; 94-95 Getty/Alfonso Cervantes; 95tr Getty/Tom Shaw; 95br Getty/Chris Lobina; 96bl Shutterstock/katatonia82; 96cr Getty/Christof Koepsel; 96br Getty/Gonzalo Arroyo Moreno/Stringer; 97tl PA/Marko Lukunic/Pixsell; 97tr PA/Nick Potts; 97br Getty/Alexander Hassenstein - FIFA; 98b Getty/Ross Kinnaird; 99br Getty/Christophe Simon; 100cl PA/Andrew Parsons; 101tl PA/Sean Dempsey; 101tr Getty/Lutz Bongarts; 101b Getty/Mike Hewitt; 102tr Getty/AFP/Goh Chai Hin; 103tr Getty/Laurence Griffiths; 103b PA/DPA; 104c PA/Studio Buzzi; 104br Getty/S.A.S.I.; 105tl Getty/Laurence Griffiths; 105c Getty/Pascal Rondeau; 105br Getty/AFP; 106-107 Getty/Shaun Botteril; 108cl Getty/Pierre-Philippe Marcou; 108br PA/Buzzi Press; 109t PA/DPA; 109b Getty/AFP; 110 PA/DPA; 112b PA/Wilfried Witters; 113c PA/DPA; 113cl Corbis/Bettmann; 113br PA/DPA; 114 Getty/AFP; 114b Getty/Simon Bruty 115tr Getty/Jimin Lai; 115br Getty/AFP; 116tc Getty/Bob Thomas Sports Photography; 116bl Shutterstock/Jefferson Bernardes; 117t Getty/Guang Niu; 117br FIFA via Getty Images; 118br Getty/Phil Cole; 119t Getty/Anadolu Agency; 119tr Getty/VI Images; 119b Shutterstock/YiAN Kourt; 120b Getty/Michael Regan; 122bl Getty/Heuler Andrey; 123l PA/Anesh Dbeiky/Sports Inc; 123br Getty/Ulrik Pedersen; 124tc Corbis/Reuters; 124bl Corbis/Reuters/Andrew Wong; 125tr Getty/stringer; 125bl Getty/Jeff Gross; 125br PA/Mario Castillo; 126cr Getty/AFP/Robert Vos; 126bl PA/Zuma Press;126br Getty/AFP/Jiji Press; 127tl Getty/Robert Cianflone; 127br Corbis/Reuters/Marcos Brindicci; 128tr Getty/New Press; 128r PA/DPA; 128b Getty/Stuart Franklin; 129tl Getty/Roland Harrison; 129b Corbis/Reuters; 130bl Getty/Hassan Ammar/AFP; 130-131 PA/Andre Penner; 131tr Getty/Jose Jorden/Stringer; 131c Getty/Jamie McDonald; 132tr Corbis/Reuters/Gleb Garanich; 132cl PA/Topham Picturepoint; 133tr Getty/Bob Thomas Sports Photography; 133b Getty/Angel Martinez; 134-135 Getty/AFP; 135 Shutterstock/A.Ricardo.